IB English A: Literature
Study and Revision Guide
For Standard and Higher Level

Elizabeth Stephan

About This Book:

This book is intended as a student Guide to the IB Language A Literature programme from the start of the course, as well as a Revision Guide. This is because 55% of the course is completed *before* the final exams; and because the programme is based on skills that need to be built from the outset. These are identified in Chapter One. The key to success in this programme is acquiring competence in these skills, thus a major focus of the book is demonstrating how to do this.

Chapters Two and Three address the two skills that students consistently identify as their biggest challenges: how to read literary texts appropriately; and how to write effectively about them. These skills underlie the entire programme, and reference to them is made throughout the book.

Chapters Four to Eight respectively explain in detail the five assessed components in the course and the challenges particular to each. They discuss and interpret the assessment criteria; give guidance on how to build the essential skills for success; and provide student exemplars with plans, comments, and evaluations.

Each chapter identifies the main areas of weakness that student work has shown on that component in the past, and advises on how to avoid these. Each chapter also demonstrates how skills developed for one component relate to those needed for other components, and cross-references the relevant sections. Throughout the chapters, "Reflection" and "Study and Revision Activity" boxes invite readers to apply what they have learned from each section to their own texts and needs.

Acknowledgements

I am greatly indebted to a number of people for their part in the inspiration and production of this book, notably:
Brent Whitted of TASIS (The American School in England) who graciously hosted a series of my visits to the school between 2012 - 2013 and generously facilitated my involvement with IB Literature teachers and classes
TASIS teachers Brent Whitted, Courtney Hawes, Anna Androulaki and their classes, who collaborated in the testing and production of material and methods
Students of TASIS who read and commented on sections of the book and contributed sample work: Ben Daley, Eleni Ingram, Adedunmola Shonekan, Jenny Johnson, Amanda Boutaud and Sanjana Jethvani
My former students at Hockerill Anglo-European College, and especially the class of 2011, whose work I drew on for examples and samples
Teachers Courtney Hawes of TASIS, Tina Shobbrook of The International School of Brussels, and Gareth Roberts of Hockerill for reading and commenting on drafts of chapters
Alex Rees Stephan for his dedication and expertise in formatting, graphic design, and assembling the final form of the book
Mary Robbins for proofreading
Andrew for his tolerance and support
Anna Androulaki for her generous and sustained commitment to reading and commenting on all stages of the writing, and for her indispensable judgment and encouragement

Two Hands taken from *Root and Branch* by *Jon Stallworthy,* published by *Chatto & Windus* is reprinted by permission of The Random House Group Limited

Non-exclusive permission is granted to reprint "The Black Lace Fan My Mother Gave Me" by Eavan Boland, from *Outside History*, 1990, published by Carcanet Press

For Joseph, Lizzie, Alexei and Theo

Contents

CHAPTER ONE

The Language A Literature Programme: Getting started

Chapter Overview

The literature programme has always had a central and valued place in the IB Diploma programme. It is a complex and challenging as well as exciting programme. It can also be hard for students to see how it all fits together. This chapter aims to address these issues by answering the following questions and providing a helpful perspective on the course as you embark on it.

- Why does the IB place so much importance on literature?
- What does the IB literature programme look like, and what do you have to do?
- What is the rationale for the way the programme is organised?
- What is the point and value of studying literature?
- What does 'studying' literature really mean?

1. The Four "Parts" of the programme: what they are

The Literature programme is arranged in four Parts. Each Part:

- Has a different *focus*
- Is assessed through a different *kind of task*
- Is assessed by different *criteria*
- Consists of texts chosen by the teacher from *lists of authors and works* prescribed by the IB for all Parts (except Part Four, where choice is free)

The texts that teachers choose across their syllabus as a whole must cover a *range* of periods and genres (kinds) of literature.

The number of texts and requirements vary a little between Standard and Higher Levels, and some criteria are different.

The Parts do not have to be taught in a particular order, nor do all the texts in any one Part have to be taught in one sequence. The teacher decides on the sequence of Parts and texts, but these decisions may not all have been taken by the beginning of your course. Apart from the choice of texts for each Part, this Guide aims to clarify for you:

- What is expected of you from each Part
- What assignment you have to accomplish for each task
- How this task is assessed and how much it is worth in the final grade
- When each task is due (so as to plan your time effectively)
- How you can build the appropriate skills for success in each task

Due dates are indicated on the sample programme below. Subsequent chapters deal with each Part and its requirements in detail.

Part One: Works in Translation

- **The focus** is on the appreciation of the perspectives and context of the cultures represented in the texts, as well as the literary value of the works.
- **The assessment task** is a formal literary essay ("Written Assignment") produced in your own time on one of the texts, and sent to an Examiner during the second year
- **A further assessed task** is a 300-400 word reflection on a class "Interactive Oral", focusing on your understanding of cultural aspects, sent with the Written Assignment
- **A specified process** is required for the teaching and study of Part One texts
- **Assessment value**: 25% of the total mark (22 marks for the essay; 3 for the Reflective Statement)

Part Two: Detailed Study

- **The focus** is on the close "detailed" reading and literary analysis of well-established works in English.
- **The assessment task** is a formal eight-minute individual oral commentary on a short passage or poem from one of the texts studied, followed by two minutes of questions. For H Level the text will be a poem.
- **A further assessment task** at Higher Level is a ten-minute Discussion on one of the two remaining texts, immediately after the oral commentary.
- **Assessment value**: 15% of the total mark. Both H and S candidates are marked /30.
- **Assessment details**: the teacher records and marks the oral ("Internal Assessment"). Samples of the assessed work are sent to an examiner for moderation to ensure the accuracy of the marking across both oral tasks (in Part Two and Four).

Part Three: Literary Genres

- **The focus:** is a comparative study of texts in one particular genre (of your teacher's choice) and their use of "conventions" of that genre.
- **The assessment task** is a *written* examination essay (Paper Two) at the end of your course comparing at least two of the texts in terms of an aspect of the genre.
- **Assessment value**: 25% of the total mark.

Part Four: Options/free choice

- **The focus** is on works freely chosen by your teacher (of good literary standard, studied in any appropriate way).
- **The assessment task** is a fifteen-minute individual Oral Presentation on a topic of your choice based on any of the texts. Presentational skills receive attention.
- **Assessment value**: 15% of the total mark.
- **Assessment details**: Like the oral in Part Two it is marked by your teacher but not recorded. The marks are combined with the Part Two oral, moderated by an examiner through samples as detailed in Part Two above.

An Additional Assessed Task: Exam " Paper One"

- **The focus** is close literary commentary and analysis of a previously unseen (unstudied) passage of prose or poetry. This skill is the outcome of all your work in the other Parts.
- **The assessment task:** a written essay examination in Literary Commentary (H Level) or Guided Literary Analysis (S Level).
- **Assessment value**: 20% of the total mark.

2. Why students (and teachers) like this programme

As you start out, it can be reassuring to know why the programme has been popular. A big part of the pleasure is the *variety* of text, task, and skills, and the different ways you are examined. Marks are distributed through a range of criteria for each task, so no one criterion can fail you.

Students particularly value the skills – oral and written – that they develop, and the confidence and empowerment this brings. They appreciate the skills of analysis and independent critical judgement that the programme especially fosters. The following list demonstrates the variety in the programme:

- Part of the assessment is oral (30%) and part is written (70%)
- Some tasks are prepared in your own time (40%); some are exams (60%)
- Part of the course is assessed externally (70%), and part is assessed internally (30%) (though externally moderated)
- Deadlines are spread through the course, not all at the end. You can focus on one task at a time
- Different tasks have different assessment criteria; each task has several criteria
- Some texts are written in English; others in translation
- Texts are drawn from a wide range of genres, periods and authors
- Texts are studied in different ways, with a different focus in each Part
- Some texts and authors are chosen from an IB list; others are chosen freely by the teacher
- For some tasks you choose your own topic; for others you answer questions set

The distribution of marks: oral and written work

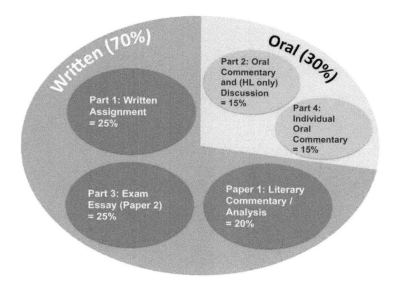

Reflection:

Which aspects of the programme particularly attract you, from the above sections?

---

3. What a (sample) Language A Literature programme looks like

Higher Level students study 13 texts. Standard Level students study 10 texts.

Part One: Works in Translation (H Level=3 works; S Level=2; any genre) 25% of final grade

Antigone: Sophocles (Drama; Greek; Greece)
I Will Marry When I Want: Ngugi wa Thiong'o (Drama; Gikuyu; Kenya)
Kitchen: Yoshimoto (Novella; Japanese; Japan)

Externally Assessed outcome: /25
A Reflective Statement (300-400 words) based on a class interactive Oral /3
A Written Assignment (1200-1500 words) /22
When Due: March of Year 2; (September for S Hemisphere)

Part Two: Detailed Study (H Level=3works; S=2; each a different genre) 15% of grade

15 poems of Seamus Heaney
Hamlet: Shakespeare
A Room of One's Own: Woolf (H Level only)

Internally Assessed (externally moderated) outcome: /30
10-minute oral (poetry for H Level; either text for S Level)
H Level only: Additional 10-minute Discussion on one of the other two works
When Due: April of Year 2 (S Hemisphere October)

Part Three: Literary Genres (H Level=4 works of same genre; S Level=3) 25% of grade

The Great Gatsby: Fitzgerald
Beloved: Morrison
Cat's Eye: Atwood
Pride and Prejudice: Austen

Externally Assessed outcome: /25
Examination Essay (2 hours-H Level; 1 ½ hours –S Level)
When Due: May of Year 2 (November S Hemisphere)

Part Four: "Options" (H and S Level=3 works) 15%

Maus: Spiegelman (Graphic Novel)
The Reluctant Fundamentalist: Hamid (with film)
An Anthology of Poetry: Various authors

Internally Assessed outcome: /30
10-15 minute Individual Oral Presentation
When due: Any time until April of Year 2 (October S Hemisphere)

Additional Task - Paper One: Literary Commentary (H) Guided Literary Analysis (S) 20%

Externally Assessed outcome: /20
Examination Essay (2 hours H Level; 1 1//2 hours S Level) on an "Unseen" passage
When due: *May of Year 2 (November S Hemisphere)*

4. The secret of success in the programme: twelve skills

A secret of this programme is that the assessment has more to do with the various *skills* you bring to studying and writing about literature, than just your knowledge and understanding of the *texts* you read.

Knowledge and understanding of texts (which is no mean feat) of course lie at the heart of your assessed tasks. However, if you look at the list of criteria for each task you will see that knowledge of texts constitutes only 20-33% of your grade (depending on the task). The remaining criteria assess, for example, your appreciation of style, the organisation, structure, and language of your writing or speech, and other skills specific to that task.

It is true that you have a substantial number of texts to cover, and this is a major part of what you do, but it is *how* you study, and the various skills that you are building while you study, that will really make the difference to your performance and success. This Guide focuses, chapter by chapter, on the skills you need for each Part and task, and how you can develop these.

Although different Parts of the Literature programme stress some of the following skills more than others, almost all of them play a part in each task. You will have had practice in some of these, but will need to develop others. As you go through the list, make a note of these. Don't be daunted by the list. Remember that all of these are valuable to your future life and are therefore a significant investment of your time.

(i) Knowledge of literary works
This refers to verifiable facts and information about texts:

*   Details of plot and character, setting, etc
*   The context in which the author wrote the text
*   Knowledge of the genre in which the work is written, and its conventions

You acquire 'knowledge' through careful reading of the text (several times), note-taking and background reading.

(ii) Understanding of literary works
Distinguish this from "knowledge". It refers to:

*   Grasping the focus and significance of the work
*   Interpreting the writer's intentions, and the thoughts and feelings involved
*   Inferring the rationale for the writer's choices of language, form, structure, etc.,
*   Determining how the context of writer and reader affect the interpretation

These skills you acquire through engaging with the text, developing sensitivity to the way language is being used, learning about ways to approach your reading (see Chapter Two), and listening to others' standpoints. Much of this Guide focuses on these skills.

(iii) Understanding of cultural values/ perspectives and the context of author and text
You need these specifically for Part One (Reflective Statement) and – at least by implication – for your Written Assignment, but they play a part in any text you read.

You learn these from the teaching, from reading strategies (Chapters Two and Six, for example) from secondary sources, and from class discussion.

(iv) Analysis/evaluation of literary techniques and their effects in texts
You need to recognise literary techniques as writers' choices, evaluate their effects, and appreciate the individuality of writers' styles.

You acquire the skill through the teaching, through reading instructional material dealing with literary analysis (see all following Chapters), through interest, and above all, practice.

(v) The ability to reflect on your learning process
You need this specifically for The Reflective Statement that accompanies The Written Assignment for Part One. It is also a skill that will serve you in all your work.

You can develop this on a daily or frequent basis in your notes, reflecting on how your understanding was developed; what processes helped you improve a skill; what you need to know or find out. The Class Notes grid in Chapter Two will help with this.

(vi) Independent literary criticism; negotiating different critical perspectives
You need the skill of reading between the lines of a text (interpreting); and of negotiating a personal point of view through considering the views of others (teacher, peers, critics, etc).

You acquire this through good reading habits as demonstrated in Chapter Two, by playing an active part in group discussion, and by reputable secondary sources and 'critical perspectives'.

(vii) The ability to answer questions relevantly and independently
The Higher Level Discussion (Part Two) and Paper Two require this skill and specifically reward it. It is the reverse of the skill of generating your own topic and thesis as in Parts One and Four. You need to understand what is being asked and focus on a relevant, thoughtful answer that shows you can think for yourself rather than simply repeating what you have learned.

You acquire this through active participation in class and attempting to answer questions thoughtfully. Negotiating others' points of view will help your independence of approach.

(viii) Comparing the way writers use a genre; seeing relationships between works
Paper Two specifically calls for this, but the frequent making of relationships between the works you study will enhance your understanding of the texts and your skill in analysis.

(ix) Clear organisation and presentation of material (written and oral). This includes:

- Clear focus; logical development of ideas and argument
- Substantiation of ideas through well integrated references and quotations
- Good understanding of the function of introductions, paragraphs, conclusions, etc

You acquire these from knowing what they mean (from teachers, Chapter Three and other texts), from seeing good samples that illustrate these qualities, and through practice.

(x) Language skills (written and oral), involving:
- Clear, accurate grammar (including sentences and punctuation)
- Varied and precise vocabulary
- Appropriate terminology for discussing literature

You can consciously develop your language skills through your reading, through study of grammar and good writing models, through glossaries of terminology, Chapter Four, etc.

(xi) Visual awareness

In some cases you will be reading graphic novels/works or viewing films that are based on a literary text, and will need to extend your reading skills and language to discuss these appropriately.

There are good critical sources on both film and graphic works, on the internet and in print, in addition to your teacher's guidance.

(xii) Time management and study skills

IB graduates always stress the importance of this. Although it is not an assessed skill, it makes all other skills and success in your tasks possible. Managing your time is also managing your frame of mind, which is essential for your sense of control over your study.

Chapter Two, 3.2 demonstrates this, and Chapter Five, 2.2.1 provides a time-management model.

The twelve skills for success

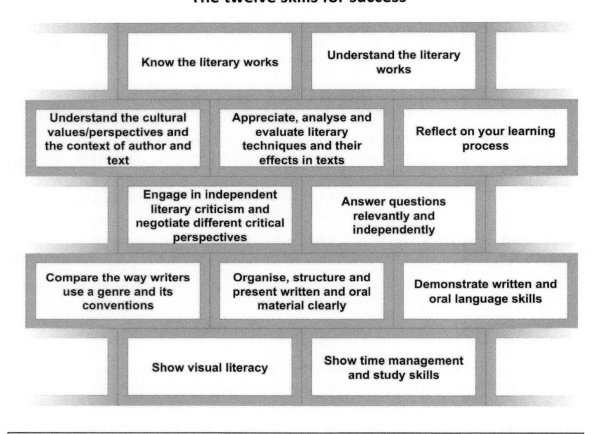

Know the literary works

Understand the literary works

Understand the cultural values/perspectives and the context of author and text

Appreciate, analyse and evaluate literary techniques and their effects in texts

Reflect on your learning process

Engage in independent literary criticism and negotiate different critical perspectives

Answer questions relevantly and independently

Compare the way writers use a genre and its conventions

Organise, structure and present written and oral material clearly

Demonstrate written and oral language skills

Show visual literacy

Show time management and study skills

Reflection:

Which of the above skills are going to take new efforts on your part?

Would you prioritise any of them?

Grid of overlapping skills and Part-specific skills

The following grid shows the way core skills overlap across all Parts and assessed tasks; and how each Part and task has a particular skill.

Skills:	Knowledge & understanding of texts	Appreciation of writer's choices	Organisation & structure of ideas	Part-specific skill		Language
Part 1: Written Assignment	How effectively has the student used topic and essay to show knowledge and understanding of the chosen text?	How well does student appreciate how writer's choices of language, structure, technique and style shape meaning?	How effectively are ideas organised and references to text integrated into development of ideas?	**Understand cultural and contextual elements in the text**	How much of this is shown in the student's Reflective Statement on the Interactive Oral?	
Part 2: Individual Oral Commentary	How well is knowledge and understanding shown in the interpretation of the poem/ passage? (HL: in the Discussion text?)	How well does student appreciate ways that language, structure, technique and style shape meaning?	How well does the student structure and sustain focus in the commentary?	**Present timed oral response to poem/ passage (SL and HL)** ---- **Respond to oral questions on a text (HL only)**	How effectively does student respond to Discussion questions?	
Part 3: Paper 2 Essay	How much knowledge and understanding of texts is shown in relation to question answered?	How well does student identify and appreciate the use of literary conventions in relation to texts, genre and question?	How coherently does the student organise, structure and develop ideas?	**Respond to exam questions relevantly/ compare two texts effectively/ show genre awareness**	How well has student understood and responded to specific demands of the question? How well have works been compared and contrasted?	How clear, varied and accurate is language? How appropriate is register and style (vocabulary tone, sentence structure, terminology)?
Part 4: Individual Oral Presentation	How much knowledge and understanding is shown of content and implications of the text presented?	(Is implied under Knowledge and Understanding)	(organisation/ structure is implied under 'Presentation' - see next box)	**Presentation** **Demonstrate presentational skills in timed oral**	How effective is the delivery of the Presentation? How purposeful are the strategies used to interest the audience?	
Paper 1: Guided Literary Analysis	How well does student's interpretation of passage show understanding of the thought and feeling in it? How well are ideas supported by textual reference?	How well does the analysis show appreciation of how writer's choices shape meaning?	How well-organised, structured and coherent is the development of ideas?	**Demonstrate literary analysis of 'unseen' passage**		

5. How readers value literature

The literature programme involves much time reading literary texts. Students sometimes feel that these texts are remote from their own experience and values, and have trouble seeing their 'relevance'. You will be more motivated and engaged if you understand how readers value literature, and why the IB has always made it central to the Diploma programme. If you approach your reading with this perspective, you will also have a better understanding of the purpose and effect, as well as the relevance of your texts. The following list reflects what students, teachers and other readers have said about their experience with literature.

- Literature opens our eyes to new worlds, new experiences and people, and gives us a richer understanding of life than we could possibly imagine from our limited existences.

- It extends, enriches, liberates, changes and challenges us. We grow more mature and aware through our reading.

- It gives us a sense of where we have come from, as human beings – of our social and historical past and context.

- It gives us a sense of identity, of who we are, how we can be understood, by revealing to us such a breadth of human beings and appealing to our understanding of them.

- It connects us with others emotionally; it breaks down our sense of isolation.

- It feeds our imaginations: story telling is central to human existence.

- It gives us an appreciation of the power, potential and beauty of language and form.

- It represents truth as the writer sees it. Writers reflect more deeply upon their societies and environment than the average person, and have deeper insights. By sharing these, we become more aware of human and social problems and perspectives on these.

> *Reflection:*
>
> Which of the above echo your own experience with literature?
>
> Which of the points relate to particular texts you have read?
>
> Which of the points seem most valuable or interesting to you?

6. Why writers write, and how this helps our reading experience

Literature is the writer's response to his or her personal world, and to the wider world or society with which s/he is connected. In other words, there is a particular, personal and human impulse behind the creation of any work. The text is a product of human experience and the individual writer's impulses and drives. If you have a sense of this human connection, you will be able to experience the text in a more meaningful way, rather than as a troublesome, impersonal item for 'study'.

There are many different reasons why writers write. If you recognise at least some of these, it will contribute to your understanding of particular writers, your grasp of individual texts and 'unseen' passages, and it will (hopefully) bridge the gap between the world of the text, and your own world. Writers may write, for example:

- To express the truth – as s/he sees it – of human life and behaviour in his or her particular society or group. To raise awareness of this, and change perceptions

- To celebrate the power and beauty of the natural world as s/he experiences it

- To record the heroism, failures, poignancy, struggles and triumphs of human beings

14

- To create new worlds and experiences from the imagination

- To delight (and sometimes provoke) readers through the form, style and language in which the writer expresses his or her vision

- To explore, shape, and share ideas and personal experiences

- To give voice to marginalised people, or those without a 'voice'

- To give permanence to or immortalise significant moments of human experience, of others or the writer's own

- To honour his or her particular society and its heroes; to express its identity and values

---

Reflection on literature in your personal experience:

Which of the above reasons might have inspired a particular text you have enjoyed? (Think of novels, short stories, autobiographies, song lyrics, travel writing, plays, poems, etc.)

Which of the given reasons for writing do you personally think are most important?

Does any literature you have read NOT fit any of the reasons given? If so, what seemed to be the purpose of the work in your view?

If you have written anything creative, by choice, which of the above bulleted reasons (or other reasons) best describe your intention or purpose in writing?

---

7. What 'studying' literature means and how it relates to your personal 'reading'

You will come to this course with some background in reading literary texts (for school and/or pleasure), and may want to know how the course relates to your previous reading experience. You may have a life-long general love of reading, or enjoy particular texts, authors and genres. You may feel that a certain text has changed your life in some respect. Your enjoyment of reading (if you have that) may have to do with, for example:

- The excitement or significance of what happens in a novel and how it happens
- The particular imagined world created by the writer
- Your identification with a particular character
- Your emotional response to stories, poems or plays
- Pleasure in the style in which the work is written

These pleasures from reading will continue to have a place in the course: in your literary development and your success in the course. Your capacity to connect with situations and characters in any genre, and to experience emotional responses, will play a part in how well you do. The 'study' of literature will build on these and deepen your understanding in other ways.

Literature, as studied at IB level and university, is an academic *discipline* (a recognised branch of learning or instruction, with its own methodologies or ways of studying). This can seem problematic, as we read 'for pleasure' in our leisure time, we attend plays for entertainment, and we may read (even write) poetry and listen to songs to connect with or express our moods and emotions.

The 'discipline' of literature permits us to enlarge our awareness of the significance and impact of what we are reading, and to read with greater knowledge and understanding. This contributes to our emotional and mental maturity, as well as to our own creative potential. It is also personally empowering, because the following processes will bring confidence together with competence.

You will begin to understand and appreciate more of the:

- *Contexts* – cultural, social, political, historic and personal – in which writers produce and set their work
- *Genre* in which they are writing (novel, graphic novel, short story, poetry, drama, etc)

You will also be asked to:
- Reflect on what you read
- Develop ideas about and standpoints on texts through discussion
- Consider the views and perspectives of others on aspects of the texts
- Express your considered personal response to and judgment on literature, both orally and in writing

---

Reflection:

Which of the bulleted "pleasures" of reading (in the first section) connect with yours?

Which of the "disciplines" of literature (in the second section) interest you?

---

8. Why different 'critical perspectives' on literature have developed

Literature has throughout history played a powerful and valuable (sometimes subversive) role in human life and society. One indication of this is how literature – the essence of which is 'free' speech – gets suppressed or heavily censored under strict or oppressive political regimes. Because of the centrality of literature in societies, ways of evaluating it have been continuously evolving since ancient times. Historical, political, social and cultural developments have also forced us to look differently at how reality is presented in literature.

For example, writers emerged in newly independent (formerly colonised) countries in the mid-twentieth century, and wrote about their societies from their *own* perspective. This perspective differed considerably from that of their colonisers, whose point of view had dominated in literature before, and changed the way we read the 'colonisers' literature. E.M. Forster's 'classic' novel *A Passage to India* (1924) cannot be read today in the same perspective it might have been read by Westerners in 1924. India is a very different experience seen through coloniser's eyes (however sympathetic), and through the eyes of Indians themselves. The 'postcolonial' perspective on literature was thus made necessary by historical and political changes.

Similarly, the 'Feminist' movement of the 1960s and 1970s in America and Europe led to an explosion of writing by women all over the world, and a new interest in women's points of view. The resulting greater awareness of women's perspectives and rights made us look more closely and sensitively at the way women had been represented in earlier literature, both in texts written by men, and by women. This focus is a 'Feminist' perspective, which again has been made necessary by social and political changes.

In some instances, developments in ways of 'reading' literature (like the 'Marxist' perspective) stem from original and influential thinkers or academics. Their ideas are then followed, mainly in universities, and this influences the way literature is taught in schools.

8.1 Do we need to know and use these different critical approaches?

The IB expects you to develop your own standpoint and ideas on texts, and specifically assesses this in the Higher Level Discussion (Part Two). It wants to see how you position yourself in relation to the views of others, but does not *specifically* ask for or assess knowledge of critical perspectives. Knowing what some of these are, and working with them, however, can enrich and develop your responses to texts.

Your teacher may or may not work with critical perspectives in class. If you want to inform yourself about them, Peter Barry's book *Beginning Theory* provides a clear and helpful introduction to what they are, why they have developed, and how they work.

First, however, you need to start building your skills in independent reading and response. This is the key to everything you do in the course, the foundation for all your assessment tasks. Chapter Two helps you with this skill.

9. The 'range' of literature: genres

'Genres' have already been mentioned many times in this chapter. 'Literature' comprises many kinds of writing, and you will be exposed to a variety of *genres* or kinds of literature in your course. It is therefore important to understand the *differences* between these kinds or genres of literature, and what to look for and discuss when reading and writing about them. A further step is to understand how different genres have evolved in particular social and political contexts. Chapter Eight, Section Two, and Chapter Four, Section Two address these issues.

The range of genres includes:

- The great **epics** of ancient times, like Homer's *Odyssey*, composed orally
- **Lyrics**, expressing the speaker's personal emotions, both sung and written
- **Prose fiction and non-fiction** of many kinds –letters, novels, diaries, autobiographies, essays, short stories
- **Plays**, written for public performance, and arising out of public occasions
- **Graphic novels**, that combine the potential of visual images with the art of a sequenced narration

---

Chapter Reflection:

Which statements have altered or enlarged your understanding of literature and the study of literature?

What point do you especially want to remember from this chapter?

CHAPTER TWO

How to Read and Study Your Texts

Chapter Overview

The end of Chapter One emphasised that reading is the foundation for everything you do in this course, and the key to successful performance. The *process* of reading at this level presents problems for many students. Two of the most frequent concerns they express are about 'getting the meaning' of texts, and knowing 'what to look for'. This is understandable because most of your reading takes place when you are by yourself. Your teacher may discuss or refer to passages in class, but the continuous act of reading is something you mostly do independently.

If you are hoping to reach the highest levels in your work for this course, this can only be achieved by the quality of your personal reading, or how you respond to what you read. Your teacher may suggest what is significant in a text, provide you with much of the knowledge you need, and prompt your thinking about it, but your *personal grasp* of the whole text is what counts in the end for your assignments and exams. This cannot be overstated.

This chapter is a starting point for your independent reading. It is divided into three sections, which aim to help you:

- 'Get the meaning of texts' and 'know what to look for' (Section One)

- Read more effectively using special strategies (Section Two)

- Feel better prepared for assessed tasks and exams (Section Three)

Section One: how you 'get the meaning' of texts

1.1 What 'meaning' means
Many students express anxieties about not 'getting the meaning', or 'missing the point' of what they read. They may rush to the Internet or study notes to 'find the answer', or to understand 'the message'. They are afraid of not being 'right', and hope the teacher will 'give' them the meaning.

There is no single meaning of a text
The most important thing to know at the beginning of your course is that *there is no one final and exclusive meaning* to a literary text, no one 'right' answer or way to read the text. There is no one person (or body of people) who has that answer or who 'owns' the meaning, even the author. All good literary texts have aspects and passages that can be interpreted somewhat differently by different people, and all texts shift in significance over time.

Your task as a reader is to question the texts you read (a way to do this is provided later) and to look carefully at passages and aspects that are complex or ambiguous. Rather than expecting your teacher to 'provide' you with the 'meaning', you must appreciate that *you help create your sense of the meaning through close reading and discussion with others*.

The teacher's role in meaning
Teachers present you with knowledgeable viewpoints, and these should be respected, but the IB expectation is that the teacher's role – through activities, discussion and assignments – is to facilitate your active participation in your learning and enable you to *shape your own interpretation*. This skill is valuable for all assessed components, and specifically the Higher Level Oral Discussion in Part Two.

Your part in the meaning
This does not mean you should propose an eccentric or provocative view just to be different from others. You need to read texts carefully and responsively, with attention to context, so that you can *support* your ideas persuasively through your references to the text. Among close readers of any text, there tends to be a certain consensus of what it is about, but with varying interpretations of, for example, characters or events or author's intentions.

This approach to reading should be liberating, because it allows you the space for your own voice and personal response; but it could also leave you feeling challenged or insecure, because it is handing you some responsibility for constructing meaning from your reading. This chapter and subsequent chapters aim to provide you with strategies for approaching texts with greater confidence and awareness.

1.2 The limitations of 'meaning'

Readers sometimes use 'meaning' to signify the idea or impression they think the writer intended to convey: ("What Shakespeare means here is.."). But we usually have little or no idea what the author had in mind, especially if s/he is dead. How did Shakespeare wish to convey the character of Shylock the Jew, or Macbeth? Both characters are presented with some ambivalence, and this ambivalence is true of many great works of literature. All we can do is work as closely as we can from the clues of text and context, and from the pattern of the whole work.

Even where authors have stated what they intended to convey, *their* 'meaning' may not be conveyed to *us* when we read the text. We may read the text differently, conditioned by our time and circumstances. Authors cannot control the way in which the many different readers read and respond to their work. If we know and understand the context of the author we may be able to make intelligent inferences about his or her possible intentions, and by reading closely we can see patterns, points of emphasis, and possible significance. However, neither context nor close reading can establish *definitive* 'meaning'.

We also use the word 'meaning' to signify what is conveyed to us (as individuals) when we read, or how we interpret the texts: "What this means to me is..." But texts convey different things to different people. One person might say that the dominant impression s/he gets from reading *Hamlet* is the futility of revenge. Another might say that s/he is above all aware of the difficulty of honesty and sensitivity in a political context. Both viewpoints are valid and can be defended.

1.3 How meaning shifts with time, circumstances, and the reader's context

Shifts in meaning through time
'Meaning' is not a fixed and final thing, established definitively by the author when the text is written, or by teachers and critics. Shakespeare may have had one meaning in mind when he wrote *Richard the Second* in 1595, about an unpopular king in English history. The same play, translated into Arabic and performed by Palestinians in 2012, carries a sharp new meaning related to their own current political and cultural circumstances, yet it follows the text closely.

Texts read at different times in history, in different contexts, by different kinds of people, can carry subtle shifts in significance. Yet each 'meaning' can be a valid response to the same text, provided the text has been closely scrutinised. This sense of fresh and particular significance is what makes the reading process exciting and valuable. Some books of literary criticism on a particular text provide accounts of different reactions to a text over centuries or eras. These demonstrate clearly how different times and contexts affect the way people read, respond to and interpret works of literature.

Meaning or significance also shifts through time for the individual reader. When you read the text several times, at different points in time, you will extend or even change your responses, especially after discussion and further contextual and critical reading. This is why the Four-Stage Reading Process outlined below is so important for your progress. Your understanding will grow with each reading.

The impact of reader's context and circumstances

Readers' circumstances also impact on their sense of a text's significance. Their responses to a text are conditioned – consciously or subconsciously – by their personal experiences, temperament, knowledge, background, status, gender, beliefs, and values, amongst other factors. If you come from a disadvantaged background, for example, you might be more sensitive to the struggles of a central character and more negatively aware of the writer's representation of those in power over the character. If you are a girl, you will probably read a novel about a young man a little differently from a boy.

1.4 How meaning shifts with discussion and hearing others' viewpoints

When students and other readers share and compare their responses, in discussion or in writing, they find that others have different opinions or responses, because each person is coming from a different set of experiences and background. This sharing should lead to a careful re-evaluation of your viewpoint. The multiple responses also contribute to the evolving and infinite meaning of a text. The Interactive Oral in Part One illustrates and assesses this process.

As we saw in Chapter One, meaning is also shaped through critical perspectives that evolve over time and affect our responses to texts. We cannot read Conrad's *Heart of Darkness* in the 21st century with the same view of Africa that readers had in late 19th century England. The Post-Colonial perspective has given us a framework for approaching such texts, in addition to our own responses to them.

Ultimately you must create your personal standpoint in relation to that of others, for all your texts. This is best achieved by reading a text several times (as shown in the Four Stage Reading Model below). This will make a difference in *every assessed component* in this course.

How meaning is created in texts

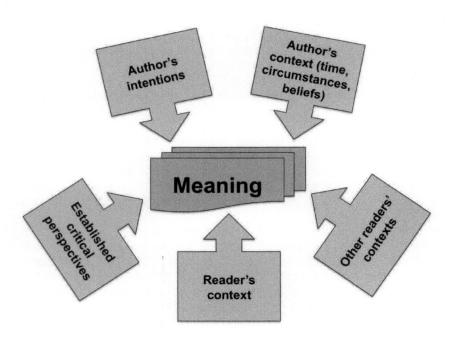

Section Two: How to read more effectively using special strategies

2.1 Ways to improve your reading and understanding

A second problem many students encounter is that they are unsure of 'what to look for', in their reading of texts. This is understandable because without guidance you cannot be expected to know what to look for. Effective reading and study methods can make a huge difference to your success. Five ways to improve your skills and performance are summarised here and expanded in the subsequent sections (and chapters):

- Expect to **read texts three to four times** to understand them sufficiently, and know how to use each reading stage productively

- Develop your **note-*making* skills** when reading independently

- Develop disciplined **note-*taking* skills** in class and filter these notes as suggested

- Understand the ways different *genres, their features and conventions* work (see Chapters Four and Eight), and the terminology for these literary aspects

- Appreciate how **the perspectives of others** can enhance your reading of texts

2.2 The Four Stage Reading model

The section on 'meaning' above emphasised that your understanding of a text develops *through discussion, and over time.*

Experiments conducted in classes, have shown how students move from just two or three responses to a text (or part of a text) when they first read it on their own (Stage One), to six or seven when they exchange ideas in small groups in class (Stage Two). This number can double when all the small groups exchange ideas and the teacher provides more input.

By the end of the class (during Stage Two), students can move from two to three responses or ideas, to fourteen to fifteen. They become more engaged and empowered in consequence, because they can now see so many possibilities. These will enrich their reading in the next stages and also the later texts. However, you need to take and make good notes through this process, as 2.3 and 2.4 below demonstrate.

Read the following model carefully to see what it involves and how your work can especially benefit from the Stages.

The Four-Stage Reading model

Reading Stage One: Initial Independent Response

- This is when you first read your text or part of your text for homework, before your teacher discusses it in class.
- Section 3 below will help you with ideas for *how to respond independently* at this stage. Learning to do this is vital to your entire course, yet this is often neglected or poorly covered.
- You need to generate as many responses as you can because there won't be time in class to discuss everything, or to explore all the text's possibilities.
- If you produce questions, responses and ideas at this stage, you are better prepared to help generate good discussion in class, and to ask the questions that you need answered.

Reading Stage Two: Class Notes

- This stage usually takes place soon after Stage One.
- When your teacher and the class discuss the section of text in question, many more points of view and ideas should emerge. You need to note down the most interesting of these (without this stopping you from participating in the discussion).
- Don't try to take everything down. Develop your own shorthand to make note-taking easier.
- Use the 'Class Notes Model' in 2.4 below to sift out the most significant ideas.
- Notes based on in-class discussion can seem muddled and random. Go through your notes soon after the class noting: 'what have I learned? What do I still need to understand?' Make three to four points.
- By comparing Stage Two notes with Stage One, you can begin to see how your understanding has developed, and how you position yourself in relation to others. This is where you begin to take ownership of the text.
- "Evernote" (note-taking software with keywords) could be helpful in rationalising your notes.

Reading Stage Three: Re-Reading with a particular focus (Parts 1 and 4)

- This stage takes place when you are asked to produce an essay or oral presentation on the text read, either on a given topic or a topic you choose. It is also the preparation stage for the Oral Presentation for Part Four and the Written Assignment for Part One. This may occur within days or weeks of the class study of the text.
- To prepare for this (for example, for an Oral Presentation) you will *re-read* the text with the benefit of Stages One and Two, but will develop your personal understanding of the whole text further, as well as gathering particular evidence for your assignment. You will find patterns and emphases in the text more clearly with this third stage perspective.
- You may also need to do some reading of relevant 'secondary' texts (introductions to the text, internet sites, library resources, etc.)
- This carries you forward to a higher level of understanding, necessary for an IB 6 or 7.

Reading Stage Four: Revising for exams – how to know the whole text

- This stage prepares you to know the *whole* text (for exam Paper Two and the H Level Discussion in Part Two) where you need to be prepared to show knowledge and understanding of any aspect of the text that you may be asked about, without the text to hand.
- It may be significantly later than the previous stages
- At this stage you have the benefit of all the discussions on all the other texts read. Your awareness of 'how to read' will be much enriched and your competence greater. A re-reading at this stage brings everything together. It sharpens your awareness of the role of the parts of the text, as well as giving you a firmer sense of the whole.
- During this re-reading, you should be making *more* notes, identifying key ideas and quotes (see Chapter Eight, Section Three for further ideas about how to revise) You will want to look back through the earlier stages and will certainly find some knowledge and ideas that are still valuable. But you have moved on since then, and your new notes should reflect this. Asking yourself Level 3 questions on the text (see section 3.1.4 below) is a good way to ensure you have understood the text.

2.3 Reading Stage One – first reading of the text: four ways to respond

There is no one best way to respond to your independent reading of texts, or to take notes. It depends on your personality and preference - what works for you. You may wish to try out different approaches as described in the following subsections, which have worked for other students, or develop your own. What each method has in common is that these notes are created ('made') from your own responses to the texts you are working on, not 'taken' from another source.

    i.   Responding to a text by asking questions

    ii.   Responding to a text with spontaneous writing

    iii.   Responding to prompts provided

    iv.   Creating headings for significant elements

2.3.1 Responding to a text by asking questions

Why it's effective
Asking questions of a text is one of the most effective ways to develop your understanding of a text, at each stage. At the first stage, it can be easier to ask questions - and often makes more sense to do this - than to make comments or formulate statements, because there is much that you may not understand and genuinely need to know. Making meaningful statements, in comparison, can be hard, because you are unsure of what it all means anyway. A statement sounds too confident and final. Asking questions suggests an interest in exploring and finding answers. It also defines the areas of difficulty or complexity that you need to address.

It suits each reading stage
Making the effort to formulate appropriate and good questions will lead you on not only to greater *knowledge* about the text but also deeper *understanding* of the text. The first time you read the text, you will have many different kinds of questions. These first questions are very valuable because you will probably not read with such fresh and clear eyes again. Reading further in the text –even a few pages – will often provide you with some answers. On a later, second or third reading, you should have some more complex ("third level") questions to ask, which will develop your grasp further. Doing this has transformed students' performance.

How to find answers
But how do you find the answers? This will involve different routes depending on the kind of question. You can find some answers by referring to a source or authority such as a biography or encyclopaedia. You will find other answers – or develop your interpretation – from your own subsequent reading and thinking about the text, and from discussion with other people. Remember from section 1.2 above that in some cases there are no 'right' answers.

Asking questions and knowing how you can find the appropriate answers gives you much more control over your learning, and ensures that you are playing an active part in it.

Sample Exercise: Questions in response to a first reading of *Blood Wedding*

Look at the opening page of Lorca's *Blood Wedding* (translated from Spanish). Remember that the more you know about the genre (in this case, drama) the more you will know what to look for. Approaching the text through questions is especially helpful when reading works in translation for Part One, as the specified process for the Interactive Oral asks you to identify what is difficult or unfamiliar to you.

ACT ONE

Scene One
A room painted yellow

BRIDEGROOM (*entering*): Mother

MOTHER: What?

BRIDEGROOM: I'm going.

MOTHER: Where?

BRIDEGROOM: To the vineyard.

(*He starts to go.*)

MOTHER: Wait.

BRIDEGROOM: You want something?

MOTHER: Your breakfast, son.

BRIDEGROOM: Forget it. I'll eat grapes. Give me the knife.

MOTHER: What for?

BRIDEGROOM (*laughing*): To cut the grapes with.

MOTHER (*muttering as she looks for the knife*): knives, knives. Cursed be all knives, and the scoundrel who invented them.

BRIDEGROOM: Let's talk about something else.

MOTHER: And guns and pistols and the smallest little knife –and even hoes and pitchforks.

BRIDEGROOM: All right.

MOTHER: Everything that can slice a man's body. A handsome man, full of young life, who goes out to the vineyards or to his own olive groves – his own because he's inherited them...

BRIDEGROOM: (*lowering his head*) Be quiet.

MOTHER...and then that man doesn't come back. Or if he does it's only for someone to cover him over with a palm leaf or a plate of rock salt so he won't bloat. I don't know how you dare carry a knife on your body – or how I let this serpent (*She takes a knife from a kitchen chest.*)

BRIDEGROOM: Have you had your say?

Reflection:

What questions do you have about this text when you read it closely? Provide as many as you can, and at least three, before moving on.

Sample questions from a student reading the play for the first time:

1. The stage directions are minimal. What kind of a room and where? Does this minimalism matter? Would a stage director put other things on the stage?

2. Why is the room painted yellow? This sounds as if it means something. Does it have some significance?

3. The very short sentences in the opening lines seem strange and jerky. Would this sound more natural in the Spanish? Or does Lorca want this to sound jerky and edgy for some reason?

4. Why don't the characters have personal names? Aren't we supposed to see them as individual characters? How will we relate to them if they are just roles?

5. Why does the bridegroom laugh when his mother asks why he wants the knife? Does he know what she's thinking?

6. Why does the mother speak about the 'handsome man' without identifying him? Is she related to him?

7. What's the significance of inheriting your olive groves? Is this supposed to be a good thing?

8. Why does the bridegroom lower his head and tell his mother to be quiet?

9. Why would you cover a dead body with a palm leaf or a plate of rock salt?

10. Why does the mother describe the knife as a 'serpent'?

11. Is Lorca inviting us to be sympathetic or critical of the mother's obsessive attitude?

Identifying the kind of questions asked

The student's questions do not cover all the questions that might be asked of this page of text, but they represent a range of questions, which should give you a good idea of how to use this technique. Now look at them carefully and see how many kinds of questions you can identify, and how you would set about finding answers for each category. This will also help you see what to do with your own questions.

Task:

How many kinds of questions can you find here? How might you find the answers to them?

Which are the easiest questions, in your view, and why?

Which are the hardest, and why?

- Some of them (1-3) require **knowledge of the author**, his ideas and tendencies and context: for example, Lorca's approach to drama and his personal symbolism (the colour yellow). These have to do with 'context' and biography, and answers could be found from secondary sources on Lorca's life and work.

- Some (7, 9) touch on **specific cultural allusions** (the palm leaf and rock salt) that would need explaining by someone familiar with the culture and context, or verification from an appropriate secondary source dealing with the culture.

- Some (10) like the 'serpent' allusion, need **encyclopaedic** (Biblical) knowledge.

- Some (3, 4)) need the **reader's imagination** and judgement about the dramatic effects that may be created in the theatre (the short sentences)

- Some (5, 6,) need **inferences** that can be made after reading more of the play and understanding the characters and circumstances (why the bridegroom wants to silence his mother).

- (11) Needs careful **evaluation** of the play, which can only be done when the whole play has been read at least once.

The easiest questions should be those you can answer by means of a verifiable source such as a biography.

Harder ones such as 3-6 require close reading and bringing bits of evidence together to analyse and make inferences about. Responses to these profit from discussion with others, and will be a matter of personal judgment rather than a definitive 'answer'.

The final question (11) is likely to seem the hardest because it needs a careful weighing up of the impact of the whole play and the choices Lorca has made.

You may think the teacher should be 'telling' you these things. The teacher's role is to be knowledgeable, but also to be exploring with you and asking his or her own questions too. Teachers cannot always know what students don't know and need to know. This is why you must be responsible for your own questions. Many students are afraid that their questions will seem 'silly'. Remember that the only silly question is the unasked question.

Levels of difficulty in questions
Each stage of your reading and learning will lead to different 'levels' of question as well as different kinds. You are more in control of your learning when you can identify these levels, and understand how you can progress by asking good questions. They do not fall neatly into the reading stages, however. You may ask a level three question in the early stages of reading.

Level One Questions * ("Where is _Blood Wedding_ set?")
This kind of question tends to occur on a first reading, and needs a _specific, factual_ answer that can be found through asking or locating an authoritative source. Level One questions are not foolish questions. Without an answer to them you cannot continue to read with reasonable understanding of the action and context. Lorca set the action of his play in 1930s Andalucia (in Southern Spain) where he came from and knew well. It is important to know this because the landscape and the culture of the region play an integral part in the meaning of this text.

Level Two Questions ** (What kind of relationship do the mother and son have?")
This is the kind of question that you can answer after reading and studying the text or part of the text fairly closely and when you have a broader perspective on it. It requires a certain level of analysis and is a matter of _observation and judgement_. It is the kind of question a teacher might ask at the end of a few chapters or an act, or at the end of the study.
You need to be able to ask and answer this kind of question in order to test your power to think about your text, to test your knowledge and understanding, and to prepare yourself for essays and assignments, at Reading Stages 3 and 4.

Level Three Questions * (Is Lorca sympathetic or critical of the mother's obsession?")**
Such a question demands a very good level of understanding of the text as a whole, and a sense of the author's purpose. It may tackle ambivalences or ambiguities or gaps in the text. It should represent the highest level of thought you can achieve at this stage of your reading and learning, as needed for your assignments and exams.

This level of question is best asked when you can look at the whole text in perspective, for example, at Reading Stages 3 or 4. It does not have a definitive answer. You approach the question through exploration, interpretation, evaluation, and ideally, the different perspectives of others, and it may raise more questions. This level is less about finding clear answers than in exploring possibilities.

2.3.2 Responding to a text with spontaneous writing

Some students prefer a free personal response to their reading. They like writing spontaneously in continuous prose (on a computer or by hand in a notebook). This follows the free flow of thought and can lead to valuable analytical and 'deep' thinking. This can be honed and structured into an assignment later.

The following sample illustrates this method. It is a response to Chapter Nine of Dickens' *Great Expectations*. Notice how the continuous prose allows *development* of thoughts, *exploration* of ideas. The best levels of student work in the Literature programme need the capacity for this kind of exploration of texts.

Great Expectations: Chapter Nine – my response

Pip's first visit to Satis House and Miss Havisham in Chapter 8 is so extraordinary and transforming that I wondered if there would be an anticlimax after that, but instead, I found Chapter Nine a kind of comic relief and also psychologically interesting.

Pip gives us his reasons for lying to Pumblechook and Mrs Joe about what happened to him at Satis House, but are these the real or at least the only reasons? He says he had a 'dread of not being understood' and that there would be 'something coarse and treacherous' about describing Miss Havisham as she really was, but I don't think either of these are true because what he actually describes is just as fantastic.

What I think is happening is this. First, Pip has experienced something overwhelmingly life and mind changing, and he cannot go back to where he was before. He has changed beyond return. Miss Havisham has in a way made him feel special, like a kind of *confidant*, and Estella has totally changed his feelings about himself, emotionally and socially. He is attracted to her, but also humiliated. This is all too complex and personal – he couldn't begin to try to explain it, especially to two such unsympathetic people.

But second, it's also (in my opinion) that for once, he has something of his own, and I can see why he wouldn't want to share this. It's not just that he dreads not being understood. For once he is in a kind of position of power. He has something these horrible bullies want to know. We, the readers, know what happened and can enjoy watching these unpleasant adults being made fools of. Dickens must have enjoyed making them look foolish and letting Pip give rein to his imagination. Maybe here we can make a distinction between what Pip the narrator tells us, and what the author is doing?

2.3.3 Responding to prompts provided

Some students prefer more structure and suggestion about what to look for at this stage.

(a) *First impressions*
Write down briefly anything that stands out to you, about mood, style, attitude, character, whatever, on your first reading.

(b) *Interrogating or questioning the text*
Jot down what difficulties you have in understanding any aspect of the passage (what the author seems to intend; why s/he used that expressions, etc.).

(c) *Making connections*
Does any of the reading remind you of any other text that you have read (for example in subject matter, style or language)? Does it connect with anything from your own experience?

(d) *Identifying striking stylistic elements and possible patterns*
What words, details, aspects of style, etc, stand out to you? What do you see, hear, think, feel, in response? Why do these elements stand out? Why might they be significant? Are there any patterns (for example words of a similar kind, such as to do with war)?

(e) *Selecting interesting lines or short passage as quotations*
These need to stand out to you for some reason. Try to determine what that reason is. Close reference to the text is important in this programme, so familiarity with phrases, lines, and passages will help you later too.

(e) *Responding through art*
If you can draw, you might make a cartoon or sketch of a character or moment, and decide how this reflects your response to or your interpretation of what you have read. Or you might create a series of panels as in a graphic novel, and reflect in the same way.

2.3.4 Creating order through 'headings'

In contrast with 2.3.3 above, some students like to identify what *they* feel are significant aspects of a reading assignment, for example the action or event, characters, relationships, setting, style, themes, etc. Providing your own title (as the student does below), pulls it together.

This process gives them a feeling of control over the material and the sequence of the narration, and is a useful basis for revision for exams at a later study stage. You can add more insights to these headings and notes at the later stages.

Dickens: *Great Expectations*

Chapter Two: "The forge and the theft of pie and brandy".

The forge, Joe and Mrs Joe
- Contrast warm home setting with lonely marshes
- Characterisation methods (speech traits: "Rampage", "by hand"; actions: bread cutting; clothes: the apron with pins; accessories: "tickler" cane)

Joe-Pip relationship: comic and serious
- Dickens' starting point for the novel (bread and butter sequence; Joe's moral influence)

The discussion of convicts and hulks
- Pip's questioning: bright child
- Authorities (law, army) versus wretched individual

Pip's conscience about the theft
- He identifies with criminals

Food significance (convict versus forge)
- Each item takes on significance later; food to do with relationships and attitudes

---

Reflection on Reading Stage One:

Which of the four suggested methods of responding to a text appeals to you or suits you most, and will be most helpful to you? (You may want to try them all, or invent others).

2.4 Reading Stage Two: A model for taking and making notes on class discussion

If knowing how to respond when you read is the first crucial skill for success, knowing how to take and make effective notes at the discussion stage is the second. Many students confess to the following statement in a survey on study skills:

I find it too much effort to take notes in class and have never really developed the habit, though I think my work would be better if I did. I would appreciate advice and models of note-taking.

Section 2.3 (Reading Stage One) above has provided models for taking personal notes on your first reading of a text. The following model helps you process the second stage (class discussion). Recording class discussion is vital for the development of your personal grasp of the text. You need to make sense of the part of the text you are working on, in order to grasp later parts, and to avoid feeling progressively overwhelmed and confused as you go on.

This is also the stage at which you hear a variety of other responses to the same part of the text and need to position your ideas in relation to these. If you take just a little time to record and filter this as you go along (as shown below), you will find the study of the text much easier and the eventual assignments and exams more manageable. You are likely to achieve a better grade, as there is a high correlation between effective notes and success.

Step One – class notes: (*write text; chapter, pages for easy identification late*r)

Step Two – Reflection: significant ideas emerging from notes (what have I learned?)

What have I not understood or still need to find out?

There are two steps to the note process:

- **The 'class notes' box** invites you to jot down (or *take* notes on) the main ideas that come up in discussion with the teacher and students in the class. This is a matter of listening and *recording*. At the same time you should be following the discussion and contributing your own ideas. It is the stage at which you are seeing your own ideas in a forum, in relation to those of everyone else.

  Some students take a photo of the teacher's board of notes written during class, but this may not be a complete record of what others have said. The photo helps, but take your own notes too. Similarly, even if your class uses an electronic method of combining everyone's notes, the personal reflection box (below) is still important in building that personal grasp.

- **The 'Reflection' box** takes more thought and effort, but is the important point at which *you begin to take ownership of the text*. This is the stage at which, having heard a variety of other responses to the same part of the text, and 'taken' notes, you need to establish your own ideas through 'making' notes. The box asks you to take a few minutes to reflect on what has been discussed. This should be done soon after class, on the same day, or towards the end of the class if the teacher provides the time for this.

  You sift through the mass of notes taken, make some sense and pattern out of them, identify and write down key ideas and points of significance, preferably *in your own words and in whole sentences*. This process should also make clear to you what you have not fully understood and need to ask or find out about.

If you stop at Step One ('class notes'), you will accumulate a mass of un-sifted notes that are hard to work through later, and may not then make much sense to you. If you have formulated your own ideas (Step Two), you are much more likely to write persuasively about the text.

A sample of a student's use of the model:

Step One: class notes: *Heart of Darkness.* **Part 1. Pp 29-30**

"rivet": unique job (in airplane) ⇒ key to salvation
"caper" = skip. "motionless in the moonlight: a world beyond the vegetation .
juxtaposition "rivet and vegetation ⇒ time is forgotten
Why is the environment, setting and rivet important? Clings on to civilisation
* *"Little" -this world has put little attention on us*
Rivets are disappearing and other things are appearing -the narrator accentuates their negativity.
Rivets: connotation -the need to grasp.
Rivets try to connect the crisis by condemning the environment causing it.
End of Part One, rivets obsession silly, because instead of slinging, one should just move forward.
* *What is Marlowe recognising in this expedition?*
p. 27 passage feels pretentious.
The core attempt to tell the story is always fruitless, counterproductive, impossible.
Implication of readers. Can't convey the truth.

Step Two: Reflection: significant ideas emerging from notes (What Have I learned?)

1. Rivets connote civilisation and the need to hold on to what is 'normal'. For Marlow they are control vs chaos. (Foreshadows 'darkness', probably).
2. If Marlow becomes riveted to the past, he won't be able to move forward. He gives a lot of his effort to maintain his control but eventually must fall into chaos if he is to understand.
3. "Every little man of us out of his little existence" Marlow is pulled in two different directions: one to control and be part of civilisation; the other is from control to chaos.

What have I not understood or still need to find out?
1. Identify evocative words (writer's choices)
2. Interpret chaos vs control more deeply
3.See what the end of Part One brings: will Marlow be in chaos and will that take him to the 'heart of darkness"?

This model clearly shows the movement from a mass of notes without order from discussion, to the student's (numbered) processing of the notes in his own way. Step Two was completed in the last eight or so minutes of class time, but could also be done soon afterwards.

Section Three: reading for assignments and exams

3.1 Reading Stage Three: re-reading 'with a focus' for Parts Four and One

Reading Stages One and Two have been about initial personal response and response to class discussion, usually following the narrative sequence of the text. Stage Two has been about enlarging understanding through class discussion, but equally about the establishment of your own standpoint. This is a necessary foundation for Stage Three.

At Stage Three, as you prepare for the Oral Presentation, the Written Assignment, mock exams and other assignments, you move to a more independent and analytical level. Both the Oral

Presentation and the Assignment call for *your personal exploration of a topic you have chosen.* Chapters Five and Six take you through this process in detail.

3.2 Time-Managing the Oral Presentation (Part Four) and the Written Assignment (Part One)

Another key to your success is time management. An assessed assignment often looms very large in students' minds, and can be daunting. This results in stress, late work and sometimes a lower grade than hoped for. The secret to managing your time (and mental state) for such tasks is to:

- Break the big task down into smaller tasks (as in the student model, Chapter Five, Section 2.2.1)
- Decide on the best time to work on each of these tasks and enter this on a timetable (as below)

When the task is broken down into component or smaller tasks, and when you have dedicated a specific time slot for each task, the project becomes much more manageable. Seeing it visually on a plan like the sample (Chapter Five) helps you realise you can accomplish it step by step. You can devote more quality time to each part of the task and feel more in control of what you are doing. Tasks often take longer than you plan, so allow for an extra hour or two.

The following weekly model works well for assignments of one to three weeks such as those given during the study of a text (essays, presentations, orals). You can adapt it for bigger tasks such as exams, and even the Extended Essay. Begin by asking yourself the questions:

- *How much time do I have to complete this assignment? (eg: two weeks)*

- *How many hours will the assignment probably need? (eg: five to six hours work)*

- *How many smaller tasks or aspects does it break down into?*

- *Do these need to be done in a particular order or place?*

- *When can I create the time-slots for these tasks – realistically -over the next two weeks? (free periods, evenings, weekends, etc.)*

Once you have designed your time plan and start putting it into action, it is encouraging to see the smaller tasks completed daily and crossed off. Keeping on top of your daily list gives you a good sense of control. There is a model time plan for the oral presentation in Chapter 5, Section 2.2.1. If you refer to this model, you will see that by breaking the main task down you can establish what it really involves and how much time it will probably take. Once you have done this, fill in a timetable as follows:

Creating a timetable for the parts of a bigger task

	Mon	Tues	Wed	Thurs	Fri	Sat	Sun
Morning							
Afternoon							
Evening							

3.3 Reading Stage Four: revising for Discussion (HL) and Paper Two

These two exams require you to have a good grasp of *several* whole texts at once. You will not know what questions you are going to be asked, and must be ready to turn your mind to any aspect of those works without the texts to hand. There are strategies to make this a manageable process, as follows.

The most important thing you do is to re-read your texts. Prioritise this over going through old notes or reading secondary sources. Nothing substitutes for this third or fourth reading of the text.

(i) Getting a sense of the whole
Where the text is of manageable length, re-read it carefully for a sense of the whole. A good answer to a question involves understanding how the question topic fits into the whole text.

You have probably read and discussed the text in *parts,* bit by bit. It makes a very different impact when you read the entire text again more or less at a sitting. Everything comes together. Things that you laboured to understand when the text was new to you should now be absorbed into your reading and make sense. Conversely, certain things may stand out to you with new force. Jot those things down. Finally, write down one or two sentences that for you encapsulate the whole work.

In the case of poetry, read your poems as a sequence. Whatever their qualities as individual poems, each takes on more significance in relation to the others when read in sequence.

(ii) Seeing how parts fit into the whole; revisiting detail
Your exam essay, especially, will explore a particular aspect of the work (like setting), so in addition to having a sense of the whole, you need to remember in some detail what happens in the parts. You also want to remember what is significant. The way you prepare this is a matter of preference. One helpful strategy is as follows. While you are re-reading the work or poems:

- Prepare a sheet of card or paper (not too large) for each poem, or part of a bigger text (Act, scene, chapter or part, depending on the genre)
- Create your own title for that section (except the poems) that brings its essence together. (For example: *Blanche's arrival at the New Orleans apartment and her impact on Stella and Stan*)
- Bullet the main features of the scene, chapter, etc., as you see it –perhaps 6-8 points
- Create one or two 'level 3 questions' on each section that make you think more deeply about the section (as illustrated below on *Death of a Salesman*)
- Write a quote or two from that section that carries particular meaning for you
- For poems, make sure you see how each one works individually as a whole

Creating a visual sequence of the contents
Arrange these in sequence on a table or on a wall, so that parts and whole relate clearly. Add in symbols or colour code to connect parts where you had not seen connections before. Remember that the fourth note-making method in Reading Stage One ("Creating Order Through Headings", can be the basis for this revision strategy.

For mock exams and other tasks where you need to know the whole text, this "God's Eye" view allows you to see the design of the author much more clearly. For example, you might see how often a particular setting occurs, or a particular kind of encounter between characters. You might also see the patterning of the plot in a new way. Instead of the text just being a 'story', you see it as a carefully designed and created whole.

When you see the sequence visually, with a bulleted order to the contents, it will imprint itself better on your memory and provide a quick way to remind yourself of the contents of the texts shortly before the exams. It can also be a way to see comparisons between texts.

(iii) Creating 'Level Three' questions to consider the implications of the work
Reading and noting (as in (i) and (ii) above) to remember the contents is a basic revision strategy. A way to gain more understanding and insight into the texts (for the highest levels of mark) is to create 'Level Three' questions (see 2.3.1 above). These will centre on passages that are ambiguous in implication, or that involve stylistic techniques. For example (on *Death of a Salesman*):

"How far does Linda believe in Willy's dreams at the start of Act Two?"

"Does Miller invite us to have any sympathy for Howard?"

"How should we respond to the Dave Singleton story?"

"Why does Miller have both Biff and Willy experience disasters on the same day and try to tell them at the same time?"

Creating such questions involves thinking about the text in a different way from (ii) above. It helps to do this in a pair or group where more minds are involved.

(iv) Using your past notes efficiently
Read back or skim quickly through your past notes to highlight anything you especially want to remember, and *incorporate this into your new compact plan* of cards or pages as in (ii). You will not want to be wading back through sheaves of notes more than once, but the notes may clarify some points or remind you of some important ideas.

(v) Using secondary sources
Read a good introduction to the author and his/her context. (Texts often have useful introductions.) It is an advantage to have a perspective on the context of the writer and the text.

Exercise discretion with secondary sources if you read them. As you will know from this chapter, you should not be expecting them to provide you with 'meaning', but they may have some interesting observations that make you examine your own position more clearly.

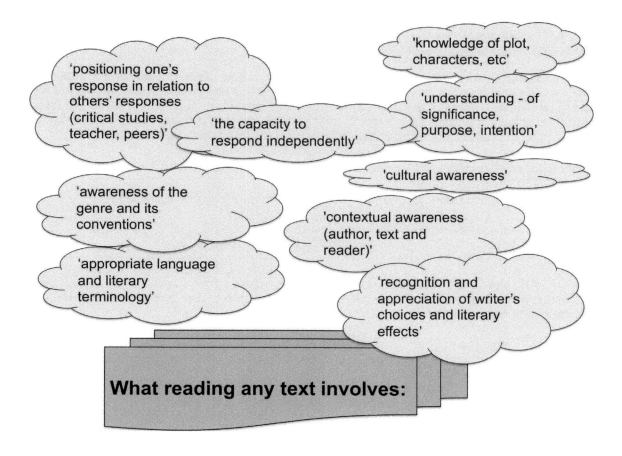

'knowledge of plot, characters, etc'

'positioning one's response in relation to others' responses (critical studies, teacher, peers)'

'the capacity to respond independently'

'understanding - of significance, purpose, intention'

'cultural awareness'

'awareness of the genre and its conventions'

'contextual awareness (author, text and reader)'

'appropriate language and literary terminology'

'recognition and appreciation of writer's choices and literary effects'

What reading any text involves:

Chapter Reflection

The main ideas I want to remember from Reading Stages Two, Three and Four above?

CHAPTER THREE

Developing your writing in the Literature programme

Chapter Overview

Chapter Two emphasised the importance of knowing how to read effectively. Writing in this course *develops out of* your reading; it is not a separate activity or skill. The way you read and study (as described in the previous chapter) will impact positively on your writing skills. 70% of your total mark in this programme is based on your writing, so you should understand the ways you can help yourself become a better writer from the beginning.

In addition to being central to this literature programme, the ability to write well is personally, academically and professionally empowering. Writing affects your confidence and capacity as an individual: if you are able to express your ideas and opinions, you feel more secure, and can perform more effectively, whatever the context. It is still the dominant mode of expression in our global society, and is the most highly valued professional skill, so for many reasons it benefits you to develop your writing abilities.

Many students see 'writing' as a major challenge or difficulty. They feel that they lack the ability to 'express ideas' and to 'structure' essays. This can make sitting down to write an essay a very discouraging experience. The ability to write well also seems mysterious and inaccessible. The good news is that people become good writers *through their own efforts*; they are not born with the gift. The other good news is that you can improve your writing by breaking down the mystery and seeing clearly what goes into the skill.

This chapter aims to show how good writing comes out of a *process* based on knowledge, practice, and attitude, all of which are within your grasp. This process begins at the start of the course, and at least some of the skills can be strengthened *daily* through your reading and class work. The chapter identifies the components of good writing and the steps to a good essay. It should make the task of improving writing both understandable and more manageable.

1. Writing in the Literature programme: the three essays and their assessment

In the Language A Literature programme you will write *three* essays for assessment:

- The Written Assignment for Part One: 25%
- The Literary Commentary/Guided Literary Analysis (Paper One): 20%
- The Exam Essay (Paper Two) 25%

Between 40% and 50% of the marks on each of these essays (ten marks per essay) specifically assess your writing and language skills. The other marks are about your knowledge, understanding and appreciation of the texts.

Each of the essays (apart from Standard Level Paper One) is described as a 'formal essay' and should reflect an understanding of the characteristics of this form. However, the task of each essay is approached a little differently.

- For the Part One (Works in Translation) Written Assignment you choose *your own* literary topic on a single text (one of two or three studied) and you write the essay *in your own time*, to be sent to an examiner.

- In contrast, the exam essay on Paper Two is a timed *answer* to an exam question, and is based on a comparison between at least two texts of the same genre, studied in Part Three. The essay is written without the texts to hand, unlike the Written Assignment

- The exam Paper One is a literary commentary or (at S Level) a guided literary analysis. This is an essay based on your interpretation of a passage (provided in the exam), which you will not have seen before. You have thirty minutes or so to work out your interpretation and plan your essay.

The Standard Level Guided Analysis is not strictly called an essay, but benefits from an understanding of the essay form.

As you will understand from these differences, you *prepare* for these essays in different ways. Chapters Four, Six and Eight are dedicated to demonstrating the process involved in each respectively. However, the writing is assessed on almost identical qualities in each of the three cases, as follows.

The two writing *aspects* assessed in the essays: Organisation and Language

(i) Organisation
An organ is a part of an organism, vital to its functioning. When you "organise" your ideas you group and arrange them in such a way that the reader sees their individual value and relevance (their vital function) to the whole essay. "Coherence" is a word usually used in association with organisation, meaning that the parts "stick together" in a clear and meaningful way. Organisation of ideas is a challenging aspect of the process (hence it is rewarded), and a way to develop the skill is demonstrated later in the chapter. It relates to those aspects of the formal essay that enable a reader to follow the argument or point of what you are writing;

- Clear introduction with thesis statement
- Coherent organisation of content through paragraphs with 'topic sentences'
- Logical *sequencing* (structure) of paragraphs
- Appropriate conclusion
- Integration of quotations or supporting evidence (specifically in the case of the Written Assignment) as part of the argument

(ii) Language is multi-faceted. It comprises:

- clear expression
- precise vocabulary and appropriate literary terminology
- accurate grammar, sentence construction and punctuation
- appropriate register

What these all mean, and how you improve them, is detailed below.

2. Ten ways to develop good writing

You build good writing in a variety of ways, some of which are less obvious than others. As you work through the following list, note carefully which ones are especially relevant to you, and record these in the Reflection box at the end.

(i) Attentive individual reading and active response to your reading
Almost all good writers begin by being good readers, attentive not only to what is said but to *how* it is said. Good writing in this course come out of engagement with the literature, of being interested in it and genuinely having something to say about it. Content is where your writing process begins: the essays you have to write are based on your knowledge and understanding of your *texts*. Chapter Two covers ways to read and study your texts effectively. In addition to your reading for your literature course, you are also reading complex texts – advertisements, journal articles, etc. – on a daily basis, which contributes to your reading experience and skill.

(ii) Taking and making effective notes
Chapter Two also discussed the importance of good notes. These contribute in two main ways to your writing:

- Writing notes in whole sentences helps you articulate your thoughts fully, and therefore improves the quality of your thoughts. It also helps to develop your *independent* thinking; the ideas have come from *your* head. There is a high correlation between your progress, and the effort you make in making notes. Writing the odd word or phrase on the text itself (such as "image!") does not really develop your thinking.

- The second way that notes aid your writing is that, if you follow the Four-Stage reading model in the previous chapter, specifically the "class notes" model, you are making more sense of what you read *at each stage*, so that your *ideas* will be clearer, and thus easier to shape and present when you come to write essays.

(iii) Developing your oral skills through discussion

Good oral work helps your writing. When you work with other students in small groups, or contribute thoughtfully to whole class discussion, you force yourself to articulate your ideas and you develop your power to think. Through discussion and listening to others, you also negotiate your own standpoint, which helps you to be clearer and more persuasive about what you want to say in your writing. Clear thinking helps lead to clear writing. If there are few opportunities for discussion in your class (for example because of small size) you can compensate by working with a like-minded student or group, or with an online conversation group, such as some teachers set up.

(iv) Knowing (at least some of) the rules of language usage

Grammatical rules exist for the purpose of clear communication. Sentence structure and punctuation are part of grammar and good use of these is essential to the clarity of your writing. Many students feel disabled because they think they don't understand grammatical rules and terms. They know it is important to be familiar with the rules, but are uncertain about where to begin.

Some of the books on grammar and usage suggested in the bibliography to this chapter will make it easier to recognise grammatical structures and terms. This will help you feel more confident, write better, and also analyse passages for Paper One more perceptively, as you will see how grammatical structures create particular effects in writing.

In fact, students' grammatical mistakes in English tend to be similar, and boil down to a list of 10-20 typical errors. An obvious way to start improving your writing is thus to familiarise yourself with these (see the bibliography) and avoid them in your writing and speech.

Another way to improve your grammar is to list in one place (like an A4 page) the corrections your teacher makes in your work, and avoid them in subsequent work. Students often needlessly make the same errors again and again. You may need to check with him/her to ensure you understand what it is wrong. This only takes a minute or so each time you receive your marked work. Some students are eager to see their grade on their marked work, but don't take time to look carefully at corrections and understand the point of them. The teacher's work and suggestions are valuable!

(v) Building vocabulary and knowing the appropriate literary terminology

Good writing is partly to do with using vocabulary that expresses your meaning accurately. Build your vocabulary consciously by using a dictionary – online ones are efficient and fast – when you come across unfamiliar words. Even familiar words (like "organisation" above) are not always well understood. It is empowering to have a good grasp of precise meaning and its origin.

Writing about literature requires particular terminology for literary features and genre conventions. Use a good glossary of such terms and begin to use them in your written and oral work as soon as you can, to "get them into your head". A glossary is provided at the end of this book.

(vi) Understanding the formal essay components (introduction, paragraphs, etc)

Before you begin to write major essays for this course, you should understand the components of a formal essay and how these function in practice. Formal essay writing is part of the curriculum in some educational traditions and cultures, but not all, so you may not be familiar with the concept. The conventions of the formal essay exist to help you organise and present your ideas clearly. Subsequent sections in this chapter focus on each of the components in turn.

(vii) Selecting and using persuasive evidence (textual references and quotes)

The *way* you quote or refer to the text has much to do with the quality of the essay, and is specifically rewarded in the Written Assignment (Part One). Student essays could often be much improved by gathering and using textual evidence more effectively. Good lawyers cannot argue a case convincingly unless they have good evidence. A legal case arises *out* of the evidence. Similarly your argument should arise out of the *text,* out of your analysis of the best evidence in the text relating to your topic. The evidence is part of the argument.

Using good evidence comes from your reading and study habits at each reading stage. During your first reading you will be questioning and noting bits of text that have interest and meaning for you personally. The second stage of class discussions will often focus on certain words, phrases and passages that carry significance to the whole text. Good evidence is vital for your Written Assignment (see the "grid of evidence" in Chapter Six). Using it skilfully is discussed later in this chapter. Revision of texts for final exams (Discussion and Paper Two) should involve a re-reading of your texts, when certain lines and passages will stand out to you with new meaning. Noting these is part of your revision process, as discussed in Chapter Eight.

Selecting and using evidence works a little differently in the case of each kind of essay, so the chapters on these essays will model this in more detail. As the Written Assignment is done at home you have the time to select and incorporate the best quotes. In an exam you rely on memory, and close reference to the text will usually suffice, except for poetry.

(viii) Organising ideas and evidence into coherent units or paragraphs
All writers find it challenging to break down a random mass of responses and ideas into smaller coherent units, each of which has a clear focus and will form an essential part of the argument or essay as a whole. Organising ideas calls for the skill of analysis, which comes with strategy and practice. The boxed paragraph sequence on *A Doll's House* (below) demonstrates a way to do this.

For Paper One and Paper Two essays, organisation needs to be done quite quickly in the planning time, but you can take more time for the Written Assignment, which you do at home.

(ix) Sequencing or structuring these units or paragraphs into a logical line of thought
'Organisation' and 'structure' are sometimes used synonymously, but they are different stages. Once you have your main ideas organised into units (organs), you can then decide how best to sequence them so as to create the most logical line of thought (argument). Again, the visual model below illustrates this process. Sequencing is especially important with the Part One Written Assignment, as examiners will look closely at your argument. One successful student said she had cut up her Part One Written Assignment into paragraphs like playing cards and moved them around on a table until she felt she had created a clear sequence.

(x) Identifying and understanding good writing from samples and practice
Reading good samples of work is one of the best ways to help you understand what a good essay should look like. It should inspire rather than depress you, because you now know how you can improve your writing. It is important to know the source of the sample you use, and whether, for example, it is an officially marked IB sample. Chapters Four, Six and Eight contain sample essays for the different writing tasks, with comments on their qualities.

Obviously, your own writing for class essays and assignments should be done with awareness of the above list of things to strive for. Recognising what good writing consists of is important, but this doesn't (usually) lead *instantly* to good writing on your part. Good writing develops over time, but can be accelerated through the use of strategies and samples. Each time, it will get easier.

Reflection:

Which of these ten elements of good writing do I particularly need to work at?

What steps am I going to take to improve my writing skills, as a result?

---

3. The Formal Essay: definition and components

The essays you write for this programme, as stated above, are described as 'formal' essays (with the exception of Standard Level Paper One) so it's helpful to start with a definition. The formal essay is concerned with *ideas*, and the clear, persuasive presentation of these ideas through the way they are sequenced and substantiated (using 'evidence'). The sequence of ideas through the paragraphing should constitute a clear line of thought or argument. The register and style of the essay are 'formal' as opposed to colloquial and personal.

The formal essay has an **introduction** that makes your thesis or standpoint clear, and/or signposts the direction you will take in the essay. The subsequent **paragraphs** or 'body' of the essay *develop* and *demonstrate* that thesis through the logical sequencing of supporting ideas and evidence. The **conclusion** arises out of -and synthesises- what has been said in the body of the essay.

Apart from this definition, for the purposes of the three essays in this IB programme there is no *rigid* set of rules about the form and style of the formal essay (for example, the exact shape of the introduction, the number of paragraphs or words, or the avoiding of the first person pronoun 'I"). Individual teachers and cultures may favour a particular model, but the IB has always maintained that as a global programme the Diploma embraces different conventions of writing practice, *provided* they meet the criteria.

These criteria, as stated in section 1.1 above, have to do with clarity of organisation and with accuracy and appropriateness of grammar and language. The three main components of the formal essay (**introduction**, **paragraphs** and **conclusion**) all play part a part in the assessment of 'organisation'.

3.1 What an introduction is and what it should contain

The introduction is the *end product* and sum of your scrutiny of the text and your thinking and note-making about it. It is not the place where you *start* to think. You can only write the introduction when you have worked through the whole process and clearly formulated and organised your ideas and standpoint. The introduction should give the reader a clear idea of the *focus* or main idea of the essay, and the direction the essay will take (as in samples 1 and 2 below). *You* already know the direction. The rest of the essay flows from that.

How the introduction is written and exactly what it contains will vary a little depending on which of the three essays is under consideration, but it must always:

* Provide a focus or thesis
* Define terms that are crucial to the topic (where necessary)
* Indicate how the topic will be explored

The following sample introductions demonstrate the possible variations.

3.2 An 'inductive' approach in an introduction

This kind of introduction states what the essay will explore, and how it will do this, but does not give the resulting thesis at this point.

An analysis of Torvald's language in his conversations with Nora, in Ibsen's *A Doll's House*

Towards the end of *A Doll's House* Nora remarks bitterly to her husband Torvald that they have never had a "serious conversation" (p80) during their eight-year relationship. A 'conversation' implies an equality of participation, and the lack of this equality is one reason that Nora has come to find her marriage untenable. This essay will explore the 'conversations' of Nora and Torvald – specifically examining Torvald's language – to throw light on the nature of their relationship, how Torvald's attitude to his wife is reflected in how he speaks to her, and what impact this eventually has.

This introduction:

- Shows how the topic has come out of a close reading of the text, specifically from attention to a particular phrase in the dialogue, which is captivating for the reader because it is focused and concrete.

- It defines the key word - "conversation" - and shows the importance of the context of this word: where it occurs in the text, how it is related to the significance of the play, and thus why it is of interest to develop this topic.

- It provides a clear focus for the essay: *Torvald's language in the conversations*, and directs us to the body of the essay where we expect to be shown the nature of that language in specific conversations, and what that reflects or implies.

- Makes the direction and development or structure of the essay clear: showing what will be investigated (their relationship, Torvald's attitude, the impact). This reflects the student's analysis of the 'evidence' found in the conversations, and the organisation of this into three main areas. This three-pronged thesis is typical of many formal essays and is helpful as a tool of organisation, but is just one of a number of ways to approach the essay.

Although the student does not state in this introduction *what* she has concluded from the evidence (in other words she does not state a thesis directly), she has, of course, already worked out her ideas and conclusion. This type of introduction is sometimes called 'inductive', because it tells you what is to be explored in the body, and *leads* you through that investigation to the conclusion.

This type of introduction works for the Written Assignment, but in the exam Paper Two the time limit makes it desirable to state your thesis at the beginning, so that it is clear to the examiner how you are addressing the question and what your main line of approach is. The second sample (on "Earth and Sky Imagery" below) does this, working in reverse order to the introduction above.

3.3 What is a 'thesis' and how do you create a good one?

A thesis is the main idea of the essay, presented in the introduction and often (but not always) expressed in a single declarative sentence. It is not the *subject* of the essay. It is a *specific personal view or standpoint* on that subject, or an *interpretation* of the subject. This standpoint or interpretation will be developed and substantiated in the body of the essay. You arrive at the standpoint or thesis through first analysing your evidence and deciding what the main thrust of this is. The "grid of evidence" in Chapter Six shows how you can do this.

Your personal standpoint or thesis (your declarative statement) might be, for example that:

> Torvald's language controls, demeans and silences Nora, leading ultimately to her decision to leave.

You can only arrive at such a statement of thesis after close examination and analysis of the evidence. These examples were your starting point. In the body of your essay you would need to argue *how* this statement can be seen as true, through discussion of carefully chosen examples demonstrating *how* Torvald 'controls', 'demeans' and 'silences' Nora. The reader needs to see how you arrived at your thesis. This second model is sometimes called 'deductive', because you begin with an assertion and then show in the essay how you reached it, or 'deduced' it from the evidence.

A good thesis is one that has an interesting and specific edge because it arises out of your personal close examination of the text. As each reader reads in his or her own way, close reading should always lead to something a little individual. It is not a matter of being 'right', but of being persuasive, using your evidence well, like a good lawyer.

3.4 A sample of an introduction with a "deductive" thesis

> **Earth and Sky Imagery in Sophocles' *Antigone***
>
> Humans exist in the natural environment and so are bound to respond to and interact with it. Writers often show their characters in relation to the natural world, but use the setting to highlight their own particular theme in the work. In *Antigone* there are many references to the earth and the sky. These draw our attention to the connection between humans and Gods but also the distance between them. They remind us of human limitations and inferiority to the Gods, and underline a serious issue at the heart of the play: the need to respect the Gods and recognise the danger of pride.

- We see here the process of textual exploration that leads to her personal thesis. She first notices the many references to earth and sky. Looking closely at these in context she observes that many of them draw our attention to the relationship between humans and Gods. Then looking at them as whole she can then draw the conclusion that they contribute to the overall purpose and significance of the play, as stated in the thesis. This is a promising indication that a specific aspect of the text will be used to illuminate the whole text.

- As readers we now expect that the body of the essay will be an examination of the imagery to 'prove' the thesis. However, we do not know at this point how this evidence will be organised and developed into an argument. (Contrast this with the introduction on Torvald's Language above, where the organisation we are to find is clearly stated). We might expect that significant examples of imagery will be explored to illustrate the thesis, which is the glue holding all the evidence together.

- Unlike the first sample, this does not begin with a direct reference to the play. It opens with a *general* statement about human life and the environment, followed by a narrower general statement about how writers often use this subject, followed by a direct but still quite broad observation about the text (imagery). The penultimate sentence connects these broader statements with a significant theme of the play. The final sentence (the thesis) establishes a personal statement or thesis connecting imagery and theme. In other words, this introduction shows a gradually narrowing, sentence by sentence, to the thesis, which is like the point of a triangle.

- The two first sentences may seem general, but are in fact connected with the topic and are also statements that arise out of the evidence.

Which approach you take to your introduction is a matter of personal preference. Both types demonstrated here show careful study of evidence, and a clear focus. You are not marked *specifically* on your introduction, but it is part of good 'organisation', which *is* assessed. In addition, the process you go through to write a good introduction means that you know where to go in your writing, and the essay is likely to be persuasive.

Note that the examples above have specifically *literary* topics, which is appropriate for the essays in this programme. It can be helpful to look at a less successful example, to understand more clearly the difference between a weaker and a stronger essay.

3.5 An introduction with no clear direction

> **The male oppression of the female in Ibsen's A Doll's House**
>
> Since the beginning of time, women have suffered oppression at the hands of the male species, and Nora, in *A Doll's House*, is no exception. Throughout the play she is oppressed by the patriarchy of her husband Torvald until she is forced to abandon her home and children. In this essay I will be showing how Torvald uses his power to oppress Nora and how this pushes her to reject her status as a wife and mother.

This introduction:

- Makes a broad and general claim about the relationship of men and women in the opening sentence, rather than leading us towards a subject with a specific angle

- Makes a sweeping claim about the play itself. (Closer reading would have helped avoid this).

- Provides no personal literary angle on the *text*. What the candidate 'will be showing' sounds as if it will be a narrative of the plot, from a sociological or psychological standpoint, rather than an analysis of an aspect of the text. It does not look as if the candidate has read the play closely and assembled evidence out of which comes a thoughtful individual standpoint.

3.6 What is an 'argument'? Is it the same as a 'thesis'?

Although these terms are sometimes used synonymously, 'argument' refers to the *line of thought* or reasoning that runs through the essay, developing and substantiating the main idea or thesis. This line of thought connects all the paragraphs with the introduction and creates coherence or logic in the essay.

Each paragraph should clearly be a link in the chain of the argument, showing how the main idea develops. The way you structure your argument – the *sequence* of your paragraphs – has a lot to do with how persuasive and coherent your argument is. The following model should demonstrate this.

3.7 How to come up with an argument in seven steps

The biggest challenge for students in the essay writing process is to come up with an argument. It is a leap in the level of skill from gathering and clustering evidence, to shaping the *implications* of this evidence into a thesis. Seeing the creation of argument as a series of steps makes it more manageable.

The following model is designed for the Written Assignment but most of the steps apply to Paper Two as well. Remember that a secure grasp of the whole text is essential for a good argument, so this should be based on your second or third complete reading.

Seven Steps to an Argument and thesis

1. **Re-read the text** (as in Reading Stages 3 and 4) with a focus on topic.

2. **Select evidence** that is pertinent and interesting.

3. **Organise the evidence** into meaningful groups (as in the boxes below)

4. **Analyse** the significance of each of the units of evidence (as below in italics). Inferences must make sense in terms of the whole text.

5. **Synthesise** that analysis as a whole, and formulate a thesis that brings the units together.

6. **Sequence** the units of evidence in the most logical order.

7. **Write a topic sentence** (see below) for each unit. The topic sentences link your ideas and express your argument.

3.8 Organising and analysing the evidence to create an argument and thesis

The following plan expands on Step 3 above:

- As the student re-reads the play, she gathers evidence about Torvald's language (note how she cites the page numbers).

- Then she examines the evidence and *groups it under headings* as shown in bold in the boxes. The groupings will form the basis for the paragraphs, each with its own topic.

- She thinks about each group of evidence and comes up with an analytical comment about it. It is this analysis that will help provide the spine of her argument, and will constitute the 'discussion' element of the paragraph. This bit of the process takes some hard thinking.

41

- She cannot use all the evidence, so she must select what is most interesting. Although only one piece of evidence is provided per box here, more examples could be used in the actual paragraphs of the essay (as shown in the sample paragraph below).

---

1. Complacent rhetorical questions
Torvald "Has my little spendthrift been out squandering money again?" (p2)
Analysis: *Torvald in control, sure of the answers.*

⇩

2. Possessive pronouns in relation to Nora
Torvald: "Can't I look at my most treasured possession? At all this loveliness that's mine and mine alone, completely and utterly mine." (p69)
Analysis: *Torvald sees her as a fixed possession rather than an evolving human being*

⇩

3. Animal/bird imagery to describe Nora
Torvald: "I shall hold you like a hunted dove I have rescued."(p78)
Analysis: *This objectification of Nora diminishes her; reinforces T's sense of her helplessness, his protector/owner role. It diminishes her.*

⇩

4. Exclamations!
Torvald "I pretend that you are my young bride, (that I am) quite alone with your trembling loveliness!"
Analysis: *T is carried away and excited with his own fantasies and sensations. Further objectification*

⇩

5. Outraged rhetorical questions and exclamations/commands
Torvald. "Do you want me to make myself a laughing stock in the office?"
Torvald: "Don't come to me with a lot of paltry excuses!"
Analysis: *Torvald cannot understand Nora's action and does not seek explanations because only his viewpoint matters to him.*

⇩

6. Proclamations/pronouncements (usually moralistic)
Torvald: "You are betraying your most sacred duty"(p82)
Analysis: *By pronouncing (throughout the play until close to the end), T exercises control, imposes his established view.*

⇧

Cumulative implication: all of the above modes of speaking are 'closed' or limited to the speaker's views and reflect his sense of control. This shifts with Nora's decision to leave.

⇩

7. Open, 'needing to know" questions (final pages only).
Torvald: "Can I never be more to you than a stranger?"
Analysis: *The openness and tone of these questions contrasts strikingly with all above evidence. Hopeful sign.*

⇩

THESIS:
Torvald's language to Nora is consistently controlling, demeaning and egocentric, allowing her no separate identity or voice in their relationship, driving her finally to assert her voice and needs. This results in a complete change in Torvald's speech patterns, and creates hope for change.

Once you have your thesis, you can start the essay confidently, because each evidence box has the makings of a topic sentence and paragraph. You know what the body of your essay is going to contain. If each paragraph contains about 150 words, the above model (adding in introduction and conclusion) would yield around the limit (1500 words) for the Written Assignment.

3.9 What exactly is a paragraph and what should it contain?
The importance of the paragraph is generally not well understood, but good paragraphing is vital to good essays. Paragraphs are the building blocks of the argument: each one has a significant place in advancing the line of thought. As they are *visually* separated from each other, they make it easier for the reader to process the argument, section by section. They are the outcome of the 'organisation of evidence' stage of the essay, as in the model above.

Each paragraph should contain:

- ***One*** **main idea**, clearly stated in what is often called a '**topic sentence**'.

The topic sentences carry the thread of the argument and allow the reader to move through the essay with a sense of its coherence (the line of thought and idea that holds it together). The main idea or topic is the *focus* of each paragraph and *everything else* in the paragraph should clearly relate to this. The topic sentence is often, but not always, the first in the paragraph. In the sample paragraph below the focus or topic is 'questions' (introduced in the first sentence); but the topic *sentence* carrying the argument (underlined) follows a little later.

- **A link with the introduction and the other paragraphs**
  As paragraphs carry the thread of the argument, each of them should show a relation to the introduction and the thesis or statement of intent in that. You need to show that you are doing what you set out to do, and that each paragraph is relevant. The student's comments in Chapter Six about how she organised her Written Assignment clearly shows the effort to make everything relate.

- **Illustration of the main idea** (in quotations or references to the text).
  A main idea or claim should *always* be substantiated, showing what you are basing your claim on. Illustration may be in the form of one or more quotations or references, or in a statement that 'embeds' a reference, as illustrated below. There you see one *'stand-alone' quote* (line 6), one *embedded quoted sentence* (line 4) and *two quoted phrases* embedded (line 12) in the penultimate sentence. Illustrations should be placed in context. For example, in the sample introduction below, the student introduces the quotation about questions by placing it in "the opening dialogue between Nora and Torvald".

- **Discussion or interpretation of main idea or illustrations.**
  The main idea itself, and/or the illustrations, usually requires some discussion, which is all part of your argument. In the sample paragraph below, lines 8-9 interpret or discuss the significance of the quotation in relation to the topic: *"His questions do not need answers, because he thinks he has the answers"*. The quality and interest of your thought in your essay is most clearly illustrated in your discussion and interpretation.

Summary of what a paragraph contains:

- Claim (as in the topic sentence);
- Substantiation or illustration of that claim (quotes and/or references to the text)
- Discussion of the illustration to make its relevance to the claim clear
- Relevance/link of all this to the thesis or statement of intent (contribution to the argument)

These four elements should appear in a good paragraph, but not in any precise order.

When you write assignments in your own time you can develop each paragraph individually and then decide on the best order. This breaks down the task of writing into manageable units. If you think of an essay as one long logical block of writing, this can be daunting, but broken down in this way, you can perfect one paragraph at a time.

3.10 A sample paragraph

The following paragraph develops the first 'evidence' box in the section above (based on *A Doll's House*) and is the first paragraph in the body of the essay, after the introduction. The main idea, or topic sentence of the paragraph, is underlined.

Much of Torvald's speech in the play consists of questions, which are mainly rhetorical. In the first few pages of the opening dialogue between Nora and Torvald, when Nora has just arrived home from Christmas shopping, Torvald asks her as many as *sixteen* questions, almost all about money and her behaviour. These questions control, demean, and effectively silence her. When Norah excitedly wants to show her purchases to him: "Come on out, Torvald, and see what I've bought!" (p 2), he does not join in her mood but taunts her playfully with *three* rhetorical questions:
" 'Bought', did you say? All that? Has my little spendthrift been out squandering money again?" (p2)
Although the language seems strong ("spendthrift" and "squandering"), he is not really critical of Nora, and his questions do not require an answer, because he thinks he has the answers. He enjoys the image of Nora that he has constructed, as it gives him a sense of superiority, and reflects his control of the household and his wife. His language mirrors the middle-class marital pattern of his time, where the woman's role had been reduced, servants effectively ran the household, and the husband was the sole wage earner. Torvald's language in his questions – referring to Nora in the third person as his "*little* spendthrift" (p2) and his "*little* singing bird"(p3) - objectifies her, demeans her, and stifles dialogue, though it is not until much later in the play that Nora recognises this. At this early point in the drama she plays along with her husband and appears happy.

The paragraph:

- *Develops* the main idea set out in the introduction to essay (3.2 above) about the inequality of the conversations between Nora and Torvald
- *Creates a clear focus and topic ('questions')* to which everything else in the paragraph relates
- *Substantiates or illustrates* the idea with a clear example of a conversation
- *Illustrates* with both 'embedded' quotations and a 'stand-alone' quotation
- Introduces the *context* of the conversation discussed
- *Interprets, analyses and discusses* the effect of the way Torvald speaks
- Refers to the *broader context* of the play, anticipating the later impact on Nora

3.11 Embedding or integrating quotes and references

Your essay process begins with your close reading of a text, and the text should remain at the centre of the essay, by means of quotes and references. A quotation from the text that supports your ideas vividly is *a lively part of your argument*. It is not something that is stuck on to your essay as decoration. It is part of your thought process. It brings the text to life in your essay, and reflects your engagement with it. The selection of quotes shows your individuality. Students often have difficulty incorporating quotes or references smoothly. However, when you know and understand the text well, it becomes easier and more natural to do this. Mastering this art will enhance your essays significantly.

As said earlier, quoting is particularly important in your Written Assignment because you have the text to hand. In exams, close reference or quoted phrases will suffice, with the exception of poetry, where you do need to quote.

There are several ways to quote or refer to the text:

- **Stand-alone quotes** as in line 6 of the paragraph sample above.
  These bring our attention to focus on the text itself, and to register its effect. Such quotes are most effective when given a context. In this case the previous sentence leads us into the impact of Torvald's questions, by describing Nora's excitement and desire to share this with him. The stifling effect of Torvald's three questions, as quoted, has more impact because of the way it is contextualised and introduced.

- **'Embedded' quotes,** as in line 4 of the paragraph sample.
  Here, the quoted *sentence* "Come on out, Torvald, and see what I've bought", is embedded in the student's sentence, and into the grammar of her sentence. This works well here because the sentence is driving on to focus our attention on Torvald's response. We need to know Nora's mood, but we don't need to pause on it. The quote is also short enough to keep the whole sentence clear.

- Similarly in the conclusion in the section below, the last sentence embeds a quoted *phrase*: "make a real marriage". It is part of a discussion. The student could have used her own words here but using a few of Nora's words makes the statement more relevant and brings the life of the text into focus.

- **References to the text,** as in line 2 of the paragraph sample: "Torvald asks her as many as sixteen questions". Referring to a detail of the text is another way to illustrate a point. Here, the point to be emphasised is the significance of money, and the excessiveness of the questions. In Paper Two, where you are working from memory in the exam, quotations are not essential, but *referring* to specific moments in the text is a good and acceptable way to show knowledge and understanding. In the case of poetry you should be quoting as far as necessary, but can also embed words and phrases and refer closely to parts of the text.

3.12 Conclusions: what should they contain?

Students frequently say they find conclusions difficult. It may be helpful to read back over the introduction and through the topic sentences of the paragraphs to remind yourself of the essence of your argument. Your conclusion is the *outcome* of your argument, bringing your ideas to a close. It should show the reader that you have done what you set out to do, but not by repeating exactly what you have said in your argument.

Throughout the play, until the last few minutes, Torvald's speech patterns in his 'conversations' with Nora have reflected his assumptions about the superiority of his status in the marriage. The questions, the proclamations, the commands and other features of his conversation have all tended to limit the dialogue to his point of view, and blind him to the real Nora who is struggling with her own life. His change at the end is radical, once Nora has asserted her 'duty' to herself. It is this change of Torvald's – reflected in his 'open' questions – that is the focus of the final moments, as much as Nora's departure. The shift in his language and attitude is a positive and hopeful sign. It shows that even if they cannot "make a real marriage" (p86) in the future – and Ibsen does not rule that out – they have both come closer to understanding what "real marriage" means. This is what Ibsen was concerned to convey to his audience.

This conclusion:
- Refers back to the introduction and its mention of "conversations". It shows that the student has addressed her "statement of intent" in the introduction (to investigate what Torvald's speech patterns are and the impact they have, etc.).
- Reaches conclusions about that investigation
- Shows the significance of the topic to Ibsen's overall purpose (or the student's interpretation of that purpose) and the development of the play.

Chapter Reflection:

Which of the aspects of the formal essay do I most need to work on?

What parts of the chapter do I want to return to in the future?

Some resources on writing

Books, articles and websites about essay writing are often targeting a particular audience within a particular system. You may pick up some useful tips from these sources, but remember what the IB is asking you to do. The expectations may be different.

Crystal, David. *Rediscover Grammar with David Crystal.* Revised Edition. Harlow: Longman 1997
Strunk and White. *The Elements of Style*
Trask, RL. *Mind the Gaffe*: *The Penguin Guide to common Errors in English.* London: Penguin 2000
http://www.fas.harvard.edu/~wricntr/documents/Overvu.html
http://owl.english.purdue.edu

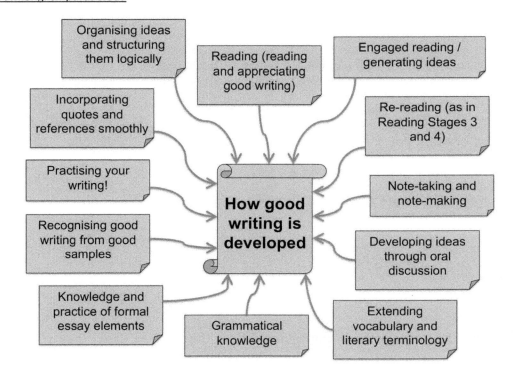

CHAPTER FOUR

Paper One: Literary Commentary/ Guided Literary Analysis

Chapter Overview

"Paper One" often seems a bit a mystery to students and teachers alike. "Commentary" has been a part of some school and university exams for over a century, but it is not common to all educational systems. For most IB students it is a new kind of task. In one sense commentary skills are the foundation of everything you do in your literature classes. This is why this chapter is placed early in the Guide. On the other hand you need to understand:

- What Paper One asks you to do
- How you build the skills for the task
- How you approach the exam itself and what a good paper looks like

The three sections of this chapter aim to address these three needs.

Section One – Paper One: What you do

1.1 What is Paper One?

Paper One is one of two examination papers taken at the end of your two-year course, and is worth 20% of your final grade. The Paper requires you to choose ONE of two passages (poetry or prose), and to write a *literary* response to that passage or poem. The exam has often been referred to as 'Unseen Commentary', because it is intentionally based on poems or prose passages which you are unlikely to know.

The prose passage may be taken from a range of prose genres – the short story, novel, biography, autobiography, journalism, essay, or drama. Both the poetry and the prose may be contemporary or from an earlier period. You thus need to be familiar with a wide range of writing styles and forms in preparation for the exam.

Higher Level candidates are given two hours to do this; Standard Level candidates are given one and a half hours. The exam is marked externally.

There is a difference in the way that the Higher and Standard tasks are defined and presented for this exam, reflecting the different levels of skill required. The way you *build* skills for the tasks is, however, similar in each case.

The Paper is a unique test of your *independent* powers of close reading and interpretation, because no one has prepared you for these specific texts, unlike in the other Parts of the programme. It invites your *individual* perception and responsiveness to the craft of literature. It is this that gives Paper One particular value.

1.2 Higher Level "Literary Commentary": what this is and what you do

A definition

"Literary Commentary" involves the close reading of a previously unseen poem or prose passage, without guiding questions. 'Close reading' means paying attention to all the significant elements in the text and the part they play in the meaning and impact of the text: for example: the content, form, structure and language of the passage or poem. Specifically it requires you to identify and explore the *purpose and effects* of the literary features.

"Commentary" is not a summary or paraphrase, or a list of identified literary features, but *your interpretation* of the passage or poem with a focus on your appreciation of the choices and *craft* of the author. "Interpretation" is a key word in the assessment of this Paper. It means explaining the meaning or significance of something in a way that shows how you understand and feel about it, and how you think the writer thinks and feels about his/her subject. Individual responses to a text may vary a little, especially to the effects of literary features, but you must support your interpretation carefully from the evidence in the text.

What you do: the essay

You are given the title, author and date of the work, and sometimes a note explaining an unfamiliar term, but *you* are responsible for the way you interpret the passage, and for the details you select and discuss to support your argument about the significance of the passage. You are not expected to know anything about the writer and his or her context, though sometimes you can make an appropriate inference or connection from the date of publication or the title.

The IB advises that your response to the poem or passage be presented as an *essay*. This means you should establish an overarching argument or thesis in your introduction – in one or two sentences – containing your interpretation of the purpose and effect of the passage. This should be followed by a coherent sequence of paragraphs developing your argument with close reference to the text; and a conclusion. Chapter Three demonstrates these conventions of formal essays, and samples of commentaries that illustrate their use are included in Section 3 of this chapter.

Although you should use this formal essay *structure*, there is no single way to organise the *ideas* in the essay. Various principles of organisation – such as the linear or aspectual – are acceptable, and are discussed in later sections of this chapter. The specific challenge of this Higher Level task is deciding on your interpretation and ideas, and then organising them into a coherent whole. A strategy for this process is demonstrated is provided in Section Three.

1.3. Standard Level "Guided Literary Analysis": what this is and what you do

The term "*Literary* Analysis" means understanding and discussing the literary techniques that make a work effective. "*Analysis*" is the skill of identifying and appreciating how the literary aspects of the passage help create the whole meaning and effect. The Literary analysis is "*guided*" because the poem and passage provided are each accompanied by two questions that *guide* you to an analysis of the passage.

One question will usually help you focus the significance of the *content*; the second will ask you to consider how literary features help *create* that significance through their effects. The two questions (content and style) are usually inter-related. For example:

---

a) What do you understand of the situation and state of mind of the narrator?

b) How do details and other literary techniques convey the situation and feelings of the speaker?

You are asked to answer both questions, but your response should not consist of two separate 'answers' to the given questions. The questions are not supposed to be restrictive or to *limit* your thinking. They are designed to guide you to an appropriately focused response in continuous prose. This should *address* the questions but may also reflect further personal exploration of the text, relevant to the questions.

Although the IB intentionally does not describe this as an 'essay', you may paragraph your response, as in an essay, to emphasise the aspects you select to discuss, and you may include an introduction and conclusion. The sample later in the chapter illustrates this.

1.4 The difference between Standard and Higher Levels in Paper One

The main difference is that Higher Level candidates must decide for themselves *what* the poem or passage is about and what the focus is, and then show, in a coherent formal essay, how literary techniques work to create that focus. This is a significant challenge.

Standard Level candidates are already provided with a focus by the questions, and already provided with a basic structure by the requirement to address the questions. However, like Higher Level candidates they still need to read closely, interpret, and think carefully about the contribution of literary features to meaning. They also need to articulate these ideas clearly in writing. These are still challenges to be met in the time frame.

1.5 How is Paper One Assessed?

Criterion A: Understanding and Interpretation /5
To what extent does the student's interpretation show understanding of the thought and feeling of the passage, and are the ideas supported by appropriate references to the text?

Criterion B: Appreciation of the writer's choices? /5
To what extent does the student show appreciation of how meaning is shaped by the writer's choices of language, structure, technique and style?

Criterion C: Organisation /5
How well organised and coherent is the presentation of ideas?

Criterion D: Language /5
How clear, varied, grammatically accurate and stylistically effective is the language used?

1.6 How is Paper One taught? Is there a textbook?

Although, as said in the Overview, commentary writing and literary analysis can be seen to some extent as the sum of all you do in the literature course, there are many ways in which you can improve your skills for the specific task of the exam. These are summarised below and developed in Section Two of this chapter.

There is no specific way commentary is taught, and there is great variation in the way teachers approach it. Some 'teach' commentary skills; others may not tackle them specifically, but constantly draw attention in class to interesting literary effects in whatever text is being covered. There are textbooks on commentary, usually aimed at students, which provide practice in the necessary skills. Some of these have been written for other, non-IB exam boards that also 'do' unseen commentary. These cover the same *skills* but may expect a different approach in the essay.

Many teachers approach commentary by working with past papers and with model responses to the passages set. Whatever approach your teacher takes to commentary, you will want to know how to build your competence. Your route involves:

- **Knowledge** (of kinds of texts and their literary features)

- **Skills** (in close reading and literary analysis, and in writing responses)

- **Attitude** (willingness to engage with texts and develop a response to them). This has been identified as a key component in success at this task (the X factor)

> **Reflection:**
>
> *Is there anything still unclear to you about this task?*
>
> *From your reading of the above sections, what skills may present the biggest challenge for you?*

Section Two: How to build your skills for Paper One

2.1 Overview: students' need for suggestions

The 'unseen' aspect of Paper One is often daunting for students. It makes them perceive this exam as harder than other components in the programme. In fact, candidates have often performed better on this task than others. However, many students are unclear about how they can improve their skills and prepare themselves for the exam, and are eager for solutions. As one student expressed this:

> There is a feeling, both within my own mind and the minds of others with whom I speak, that there is no real way to revise for commentary. Other than what we do in class, we do not know what it is that we can do to revise effectively for something as broad and fluid, as open-ended and intangible as commentary. To write sheaves of practice essays to be marked by the teacher does not seem to be the only answer, and it is in the silent hours of the revision period, that we wish for something to – at the very least – give us a comforting sense of preparation akin to mathematics problems or the simple regurgitation of a physics formula.

The following sections aim to explain what commentary skills involve, and to provide some 'tangible' ways to develop them.

2.2 There is no single formula for approaching literary analysis

There is no one formula or 'approved' method for approaching literary commentary/analysis, or one that fits *all* passages and poems. *Each passage is unique*, with its own particular characteristics, and needs to be approached with open-mindedness and flexibility, on the basis of the experience and knowledge you gain from the eleven-point process described below. If you use a single 'formula' for all passages, this can limit you to predetermined and isolated aspects of the text rather than grasping the whole text and appreciating how its own *distinctive* features contribute to its impact.

Most students, however, need some kind of concrete framework or map, both to approach the task of analysis and the exam itself. This chapter provides this through:

- A list of suggestions as to how to build skills (Section 2.6)

- A list and discussion of some essential tools of analysis for any text, and of features of specific genres that may be used for Paper One (Sections 2.7-2.10)

- A recommended method of tackling an exam paper (Section 3.6) that helps you to meet the assessment criteria appropriately

2.3 'Getting good at" literary analysis is a cumulative process

The skill and art of writing a good commentary is the end product of a multi-faceted *process*. You need to understand what the skills are and to practise them. But your *personal* understanding and appreciation of a text is also a creative act.

The process of 'getting good' at commentary is snowballing or cumulative. Each poem or prose passage you read with attention along the way, each literary technique you are introduced to, each piece of literary writing you do of any kind, contributes to a sum of knowledge and experience you will draw upon in the exam. It is not a matter of simply practising endless past papers (though this helps, nearer the exam). The list and the graphic below shows how it is all these things (plus an x factor) working together.

2.4 Skill in Literary Analysis develops through a multi-faceted process (like football)

An analogy with a skill (and art) like football may help describe the process. If you want to play a great game, there is no one formula or set of instructions that will ensure a great performance each time. Each game or match you ultimately play will be different in a variety of ways, and each will test your flexibility of thinking and playing.

You need to understand what skills are involved, and to build those individual skills over time. You need to be shown (not just told) what these skills are - like ball control, striking, passing, and so on- and must practise them endlessly. You will play practice games to get a feel for the game and how much more you need to work at the skills, but you will not be ready for a big match yet.

You will watch games and start being able to identify and analyse striking features of the game. You will listen to media commentators illuminate a particular game, and your enthusiasm for the sport may be inspired by their perceptions and the passion of their discussion. The same kind of process is true of commentary.

2.5 The X factor: personal engagement

'Engagement' is a quality much prized by examiners and teachers. It facilitates learning like no other quality. Engagement (or personal commitment) combined with skill is the vital component of success in sport and in commentary (and all important aspects of life). The student who enters into the exercise of commentary with fascination for the art of language and how writers use it to communicate, will often learn more and go further than the bright student who 'gets' the passage but isn't motivated to look into the text more deeply and develop a detailed analysis. Research and results have shown this to be the case. What distinguishes the best commentaries is *personal insight*, and this insight tends to come through engagement.

2.6 Eleven suggestions for building good commentary skills

The following activities do not represent a *sequence* of separate activities to build your skills, but are continuously overlapping ways to develop commentary skills throughout the programme. Some items have to do with learnable *knowledge*; some with skills acquired with *practice*; and others with *attitude*. They relate to both Standard and Higher Levels. Some facets may be covered in class, others you can pursue for yourself. Even if you do not become aware of these suggestions until shortly before the exam, you can use many of the ideas in the last months or weeks of revision.

The list is designed to help you avoid some of the main weaknesses of candidate performance in this exam. It needs to be used in conjunction with the "Five Starting Points" in Section 2.7 below, and the following subsections on "What to look for" in genres.

(i) Widen your range of literature reading
Paper One may present you with a passage from a 19th century novel, a 17th century poem, a piece of contemporary travel writing – the range is endless. You should thus be familiar with different genres and styles of writing from different time periods and contexts. Other texts in your course will help broaden your range, but may not cover all the genres that could be on the exam, such as autobiography, essays, journalism or travel writing, for example.

- Textbooks on commentary and poetry analysis (see Bibliography) often provide an interesting and broad range of short passages – a quick way to acquaint yourself with different kinds of writing. Some of the texts provide useful *analyses* of passages (Lodge, for example); others provide *practice* in literary analysis by setting leading questions on passages.

(ii) Learn the terminology for literary features of genres and how they shape meaning in texts
To analyse literature of any kind effectively, you need the tools or terminology.

- To see this in practice, read the **samples** in Section Three of this chapter. Such detailed and precise discussion of the features of the text would not be possible without knowing the language (caesura, enjambment, diction, metre, etc).

- Suggested **textbooks** (Lodge, Fry, Perrine) introduce features and terminology accessibly *and* show techniques in action. Teachers also do this in class. Apart from being able to *identify* a wide range of literary features, you should especially be aware of how *creatively* these can be used and how they shape the meaning of a text.

- Use the **glossaries** (in recommended texts and in this Guide) nearer the exam to remind yourself of the range of terms and their meaning. However, a good exam commentary should not merely identify features but demonstrate how they contribute to the meaning and effect of the text.

- Sometimes **websites** yield useful material but beware of websites that are not attached to reputable academic institutions. Some Internet sites on commentary and literary terms misspell, mispronounce and mislead.

(iii) Know the rules of grammar (including punctuation, sentence construction and syntax)
You might think that grammar only has to do with your writing and speech. However, much of your literary analysis of both poetry and prose is to do with grammar, especially the effects created by the writer's choice of punctuation, sentence construction, and syntax. Writers' uses of these can be highly creative and distinctive, in all genres, and if you become aware of them you have an effective and very concrete tool of literary analysis.

- Section 2.7 below and the Bibliography supply ideas on this

(iv) Develop the habit of close reading and note-making in and for class
Exam commentaries are exercises in close reading. Chapter Two demonstrates ways to develop close and effective reading and note-taking/making habits. The close reading you do for all other parts of the course, especially the Oral Commentary, will develop your skills for Paper One.

(v) Practise generating ideas about interpretation and language in class discussion

- Insight into language and meaning – part of the X factor in commentary performance – develops through the habit of being active in discussion and pushing your thinking through oral work (as well as your notes).

- Establish your own interpretation of poems or passages by comparing yours with those of other students in the class, with your teacher's, or with interpretations in secondary sources. Revise Chapter Two of this book and what it says about establishing 'meaning'.

(vi) Read poetry *holistically* for a sense of the whole meaning and effect
A difficulty with candidates' performance on poetry in Paper One is that they often read poems in individual lines or phrases, or even build 'meaning' out of random words, rather than establishing a sense of what the *whole* poem means and how it hangs together.

- Find poems you connect with and enjoy (as in the collections recommended); read them *holistically*, and give some thought as to what makes them memorable or appealing. Practise writing an overview or thesis in a sentence or two about your chosen poems. The Internet is a great way to find interesting poetry but quality is variable.

- *Listen* to poetry on CDs and the Internet (see the bibliography)

(vii) Know the assessment criteria and (viii) assess good sample commentaries
The criteria are summarised in Section One of this chapter

- Know key assessment words and concepts in the criteria and what they mean ("interpretation", "writer's choices"; "how language shapes meaning", "coherence" etc).

- Study good IB student samples on past exams (as in Section Three) to see commentaries that meet the criteria at a high level.

- Remember that commentaries in some textbooks, though useful in terms of how they analyse literature, are not written for IB purposes and are not developed to meet the specific IB criteria.

(ix) Practise writing past papers to get a feel for the length, challenge and type of passage given

You need practice in the *stages of the process* of reading, analysing and writing about a passage (as outlined in Section Three), in order to perform well in the exam. It is best to start by practising in your own time, and later in a timed situation, nearer the exam. Section 3.5-6 provides samples of exam commentaries with the students' plans of the process.

- Your school or teacher is able to access past papers through the IB Online Curriculum Centre. You may be given some of these to do as 'mock exams' or as homework assignments. If not, you should try to procure some.

- Writing practice on all and any literary texts helps towards this Paper, including note-making strategies as illustrated in Chapter Two.

(x) Revise by practising *planning* commentaries in the recommended time

What you do in the *planning time* of the exam is vital for a good result (as shown in Section Three of this chapter) and you need to practise working in this time frame. It's an ideal way to consolidate skills shortly before the exam, because a plan will only take 30 minutes, but the concentrated reading and response is excellent revision.

- Nearer the exam (or your mock exams) work over unseen passages with the suggested planning model in Section 3.6 in about 30 minutes per passage.

(xi) Remember the X factor: keep engaged!

This is within your control and doesn't take skill – it's a matter of decision and attitude, and it makes all the difference.

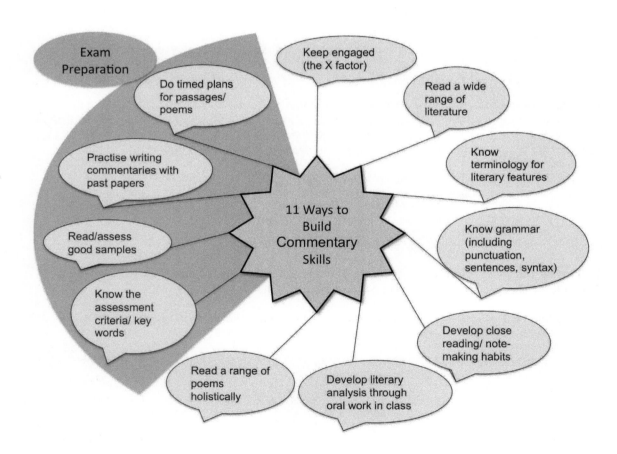

52

2.7 Five starting points for literary analysis of any passage or poem

When you first attempt a literary analysis or 'unseen' commentary, you may well wonder where on earth to begin. The five numbered items below, dealing with some of the most essential elements in close reading and literary analysis, should provide a concrete and revealing approach to most passages or poems. They will take you a long way. The student samples in Section Three illustrate how these elements play a strong part in a good analysis.

They move from the 'basic tools' of analysis (sentences and words) to the broader picture (structure, tone and contrast). All are essential for a sound understanding of any passage or poem, and help you develop a systematic close reading. *Failure to do this is the most common shortcoming in student performance on Paper One* and affects almost everything else in the essay.

Close reading involves:

- Identifying the subject or content clearly
- Appreciating how the art and craft of language, in many different ways, help shape the meaning of the content and our response to it

"**Missing the meaning**" – something that students express fear of doing – is the result of not reading closely and systematically. It happens because students sometimes think that whatever the poem or passage *appears* to be about, (for example, a fish, a fan, or two hands) the 'real' meaning must be deeper and elsewhere, something *other* than what is actually said. They are afraid to trust the text to mean what it says.

The 'meaning' resides *in* the object or experience described, which is given significance through the *way* it is told. No comment on style or features has much value unless you first establish the actual (not imagined) content, and then show how content and language inter-relate. All the illustrations in the subsections below aim to convey this vital point.

2.7.1 Starting points: Words and sentences - the writer's basic tools (and yours)

Students often think that literary analysis is about the more exotic-sounding devices such as metaphor, onomatopoeia, and so on, but awareness of *sentences* – their content, construction, style, and the *words* in them – is a vital tool of analysis. Using this tool is also a way to ensure that you see how content and style work together, whether in prose or poetry.

Words and sentences are the most basic tools of the writer's trade, and literature is about the extraordinary things that writers do with just these two elements. The right words and word order can make a simple sentence memorable forever. What makes Hamlet's most famous sentence memorable? *" To be, or not to be, that is the question"*.

What if he had said: "The big question is, whether to go on living or to take your own life"? No one would have remembered or quoted this, but on one level it means the same thing. Literary commentary is interested in how words – their connotations and denotations, their sounds and combinations – make one sentence memorable and another not at all memorable.

Sentences in prose: what they do (content)

If you are to gain knowledge and understanding of the content or a poem or passage, you need to follow the development of the text, *sentence-by-sentence*, to see *what* each sentence is saying, and how it links with the next one, developing or changing direction, or playing a different role. Sentences anchor you to sense; to what a piece of writing is actually saying and doing. They are the basic units of narrative and the development of thought. They help you navigate through the text, revealing its structure or architecture. They move the poem or passage along.

If you look at the opening sentence of the *Frankenstein* passage (in Section Three below) you see that it is an expository sentence that tells us where and who the narrator is, what time of day it is, and the decision he is contemplating, which will impact on the rest of the passage. It conveys important information.

Sentences in prose: (craft)

Writers take infinite care over the construction of their sentences, because sentences make all the difference to the way we read. The *way* a sentence is written and the *effect* it creates on us as we read is as important as the content. In lines 23-4 of *Frankenstein,* Shelley conveys information and moves the narrative along, but she also achieves a number of significant effects in the same sentence.

"I trembled, and my heart failed within me; when, on looking up, I saw, by the light of the moon, the daemon at the casement".

She moves slowly in one narrative arc, from having the narrator describe his extreme physical, emotional and mental state, to what he sees, slowing the process down by means of commas and pauses, and deferring the horrific part until the end. We see the moonlight first, and then the daemon, whereas the narrator would have registered the daemon first, and maybe not even the moonlight.

Thus, punctuation and syntax (word order in the sentence) combine to take us vividly into this experience, as it were, in slow motion. Four commas force us to read slowly what would have been seen in a fraction of a second. Further, by not separating the content into two sentences, Shelley links the narrator's fragile emotional state with the sight of the daemon, and so increases our awareness of its impact on him.

Sentences: content and craft (poetry)

Students do not often think of sentences as the core of a *poem*, but they are often the key to understanding the logic of the development of the content (the narrative or thought). They also create significant effects through their construction.

The poem "The Black Lace Fan" (Section Three below) contains 25 sentences in its 29 lines. Most of these contribute to telling the story at the heart of the poem. Some are short; some only fragments, some longer. The way these are written influences the way we read and receive the story. They help create its meaning. The sample analyses this well.

Sentences: grammar (parts of speech; tenses)

There are other aspects of sentences to be aware of in analysing a passage or poem, for example the way grammar works. Look at part of a sample paper to determine:

- Do any *parts of speech* predominate in a sentence or sequence of sentences (for example nouns, pronouns, or adverbs) and does this have an effect on our response? Many nouns, for example, might help build a scene visually and concretely.

- *Pronouns* often create particular effects such as the 'he' and 'she' in "Black Lace Fan".

- What *verb tense* or tenses are used, and to what effect? Look at the conditional tenses in the narrator's thought sequence in *Frankenstein,* or the effect of past and present tense in "Black Lace Fan".

- Are there declarative, imperative, or interrogative sentences in *speech*? What do these convey?

- If verbal adjectives ('gerundials' or adjectives formed from verbs) are used, what impact do they have? For example the sentence fragment with its gerundial, "A man *running*." in "The Black Lace Fan" is an image of arrested motion, the last image of an unfinished story. The action is incomplete. Gerundials are quite common and very effective in prose passages and poems and it is worth looking out for them.

- Is there a deliberately *ungrammatical* element that produces an interesting effect? (see Auden's "Lullaby" discussed below).

Sentences: pauses

The impact of pauses is often overlooked. Reading a poem or passage aloud (or in your head), or listening to a recording with attention to the pauses helps you recognise their impact. Pauses can be indicated by the:

- Punctuation of sentences (commas, dashes, colons and semi-colons, etc.)
- Line breaks in poetry
- Caesura (a pause within a line of poetry)
- Effects of metre and rhythm in lines of poetry

All these can create powerful dramatic and emotional effects, or indicate shifts in a thought process.

> **Study Activity on pauses (caesura):**
>
> Consider the pauses (as defined in the bulleted points above) in almost any line or sequence of lines in "Two Hands" (Section 3.10 poem sample). Come up with at least two ideas about the effects they produce.

2.7.2 Starting points: words (diction) and how they can work

Words can have a powerful effect because of:

- *Where* they are placed in a sentence
- How they *sound*, alone or combined with other words
- What they *mean* (denotation)
- What they *suggest* (connotation)
- Whether they are being used in an *unusual* or unexpected way

For example, look at the opening lines (sentence) of W.H. Auden's poem "Lullaby", and try to decide which of the words 'have a powerful effect", and for which of the above bulleted points.

"Lay your sleeping head, my love,
Human on my faithless arm."

It is obvious that "human" and "faithless" stand out in a shocking and unexpected way, especially after the expectations aroused by the title ("Lullaby"); by the tender first line – tender from what is said *and* the sound of the words; and the soothing regular metre. The words stand out partly because of where they are *placed* – in the second line, but also because of the syntax, where "human" is placed in the sentence.

Grammatically, we are expecting an adverb in the second line, telling the lover *how* to "lay" his head (for example, "softly"). Instead, we get an adjective ("human") that seems to be describing the "head" but doesn't make clear sense. Of course the head is (literally) "human", so why use the word? And if the speaker is so loving, why does he announce that he is "faithless"?

"Human" and "faithless" are connected. To be human is (sadly) potentially to be "faithless". The imperfection of human beings means that one cannot guarantee faithfulness, but as the poem goes on to show, this does not mean that love in the here and now is not genuine and deep.

The brilliance of the poem is how it holds 'in tension' (see 2.7.5 below for this concept) the idea of faithlessness *and* the idea of tender love. The two words connecting these ideas (human-faithless) provoke attention and point to the unusually honest idea and feeling at the heart of the poem. Present tenderness is celebrated, but in the sober awareness that it may not last.

Study Activity on words (diction):

Take a poem/short passage you enjoy and look at just one part of it from the angle of the diction or words. What words stand out? Refer to the bulleted points above for ideas about how the words work.

2.7.3 Starting points: the bigger picture – structure

Structure has to do with the way the material is shaped, organised or sequenced. The structure of a text may seem obvious to us when we read it, but the writer has wrestled with the best way to order his or her material, and this has a huge influence on how we respond to it and what it means. (Imagine "the Black Lace Fan" beginning with the speaker looking at the fan, *and then* going on to tell the story, rather than *starting* with the story).

The 'Three to four readings' planning model in Section Three below emphasises the importance of looking at the structure (the bones) of the poem or passage *early* in the process of analysis, before examining the fine details. The point and purpose of the passage or poem is only clear when you have identified a structure (though there can be variation in the way individual readers perceive the structure). This process gives you a sense of control over the text. The plans of both the Higher samples in Section Three below show how the students work with structure.

- What are the points of focus in the unfolding of the narrative or argument or thought process of any prose passage or poem you select? (Identify these by numbering or boxing them)

- Are these points of focus or topics organised into paragraphs in the prose?

- In a poem, is the material developed through stanzas? If so, what stage does each stanza represent? What focus is there to each stanza?

- If the prose or poem is presented in a larger block of text, what divisions or stages can you see within that block?

2.7.4 Starting points: the bigger picture – tone

Students often struggle with the concept of tone. It can seem elusive, difficult to define, and much less obvious in some texts than others. Tone in everyday *speech* is a matter of how *sound* conveys the speaker's attitude. "I don't like that tone of voice", means, "I don't like the *attitude* the sound of your voice expresses." Tone in *written* literature also reflects a speaker or narrator's attitude or feelings towards his or her subject, but without the benefit of *hearing* the words, how do we determine the tone? How can we be sure we 'hear' the right tone?

We become aware of tone through close attention to *what* is said in the context of the whole passage, and to *how* this is being said. In other words, we determine tone through close reading. Establishing tone comes out of how we interpret or identify the speaker's or narrator's *thoughts and feelings*. This interpretation comes out of our response to *words*.

An exercise demonstrating how tone is created in literature (Owen's "Futility")
Read carefully Wilfred Owen's short but complex poem "Futility" (below), written in World War One. Identify the f*eelings* it expresses. How do you determine those feelings?

The poem expresses the speaker's *feelings* of sorrow, anger, incomprehension and despair at a young soldier's death. It conveys his *attitude* of anger and frustration about war. It is *what* he says, and the *language* he uses, that enables us to 'hear' the tone (discussed below).

Move him into the sun -
Gently its touch awoke him once,
At home, whispering of fields unsown.
Always it woke him, even in France,
Until this morning and this snow.
If anything might rouse him now
The kind old sun will know.

Think how it wakes the seeds, -
Woke, once, the clays of a cold star.
Are limbs, so dear-achieved, are sides,
Full-nerved - still warm - too hard to stir?
Was it for this the clay grew tall?
- O what made fatuous sunbeams toil
To break earth's sleep at all?

We sense the gentleness of the speaker's tone, as he appears to instruct others to move the dead soldier 'into the sun'. He does this in the poignant but futile hope that the sun, which gives life to everything and has always daily woken the soldier until this point, might wake him now. This *idea* or thought, in this situation, helps create the tone of compassion.

The gentle and sorrowful tone is also created through the personification and diction describing the 'kind old sun' 'gently' awaking the boy in the past, and 'whispering' to him of his farming tasks. It is further created because he is imagined in his rural home, which gives him a human and natural context, so different from the battlefield.

The next stanza continues the argument about the power of the sun, which wakes 'seeds' and also once woke the whole planet earth. This idea of the power of the sun contrasts with its inability to 'wake' the soldier. The way Owen expresses this contrast through a rhetorical question (lines 10-11) emphasises his incomprehension and grief at the death. This is accentuated by the broken syntax of his question, with its dashes and interruptions, and by the three compound adjectives describing the body as "dear-achieved", "full-nerved" and "still warm". Owen's adjectives give meaning and life to a body that is dead. The final rhetorical question is a sudden outburst of the speaker's grief and despair. What was creation for if it leads to such a senseless death?

Thus we see that by reading closely and determining the speaker's *thoughts and feelings*, through the impact of words and sentences, we may sense the *tone*, or in this case the shift in tone from sorrow to anger and despair. Not every piece of literature reflects tone as clearly as this poem. In such cases, instead of hunting through the passage or poem looking for 'tone' and trying to find an adjective to describe this, focus on the thought, feeling and apparent purpose of the piece. Any discussion of tone should be integrated into discussion of the content and style, rather than being addressed as a separate issue, in a separate paragraph. Reading aloud and finding the vocal tone that seems to fit the literature is one way to develop sensitivity to tone.
Mood and tone are often confused, but are different. Tone is to do with the *speaker's* or narrator's attitude to the subject (or specifically the writer's attitude in the case of non-fiction). Mood is the feeling or atmosphere that a piece of writing creates in the *reader*.

2.7.5 Starting points: the bigger picture - contrast, tension, opposition, conflict

Most literary works will contain at least one of these (somewhat similar) elements, because they create interest but also because they reflect the complexity of life itself. They relate to the structure of a work or passage and can helpfully open up what is happening in a text and the ideas or meaning the writer wants to express. Look for these in your texts.

'**Contrast**' is where one thing is placed in opposition to another *to emphasise differences*. For example, we could say that the *Frankenstein* passage opens up the *contrast* between the tortured interior world of the scientist-narrator, and the harmonious world of nature and the human community outside, from which he has separated himself by his actions. This is emphasised by placing the narrator inside and at a window, from which he observes the outside.

'**Tension**' in literature is a more subtle principle that denotes a balanced *relationship or interplay between two opposing elements*. For example in some poems about death one finds a tension between grief, or refusal to accept death, and on the other hand, the effort to accept it. In "The Black Lace Fan" one could argue that there is a tension between the life of the past, and the life of the speaker's present. Both have meaning and give value to each other.

In both *Frankenstein* and "The Black Lace Fan", we see that the contrast or tension is part of the structure of the text, and part of the central purpose or meaning.

'**Opposition**' is the pairing of opposites so that one is more sharply defined by the other. In Owen's "Futility", quoted above, the reference to the dead soldier's happy rural home and boyhood is thrown into sharper definition by the poem's context of war, and *vice versa*.

'**Conflict**' creates tension and interest in literature, and may be found in any of the genres, especially drama. It involves *an incompatibility between the motives of two forces*. It can be *external*, between two or more characters, or a character and a force or event.

Internal conflict involves an ethical, emotional or other challenge within a character or speaker. The *Frankenstein* passage reveals an *internal* ethical conflict within the narrator's mind, as well as an *external* conflict with the 'fiend'. This constitutes much of the interest of the passage.

Study Activity on 2.7.4 – 5: starting points for literary analysis

Take a short poem or prose passage and explore it from one or more of the above angles, (contrast, etc) to see how it helps you understand how the text is working.

2.8 What to look for in unseen prose fiction passages

The following suggestions are reminders of some of the many literary elements of prose fiction that you should be aware of as you read. They should be read in conjunction with the "Five Starting Points" above. Many of them also apply to prose *non*-fiction. Not all the items will be relevant to every passage; and any given passage may contain features not mentioned here. For that reason you should give a passage your own sequence of Three to Four readings first (as in Section 3.6 of this chapter), and *then* look at the list. The list is not intended as a way to structure a commentary, but to give you some pointers for your reading.

Almost all prose fiction passages will be taken from a larger work. It won't matter that you don't know the wider context. The passage will have been chosen to have some kind of interesting focus and shape, and to have coherence as an extract. We may not know exactly why, for example, a traveller is making a visit to his friend in the night; what we focus on is just what the passage *presents*: his state of mind and his reaction to his environment. Occasionally a candidate may know the work from which the passage is taken, but this may only give a marginal advantage. Your task is to analyse the passage itself, not to set it in context.

To see what a prose passage looks like, refer to the *Frankenstein* sample in Section 3.9.

Content and focus
You need to start with a clear idea of what is happening in the extract. What is this passage about? Who is involved? Where (and perhaps when) is it set? Does the context (which we might glean from the publication date provided) affect the way we approach the passage? What seems to be the significance or focus of the narrative? For example, does it centre on a decision a character takes, or an event, or a particular moment, and what that reveals?

Narrator and point of view
Every narrative is told by someone, so narrator and point of view require particular attention in prose. It is also important to distinguish between the writer and the narrator. The writer has created the narrator, who may or may not represent the views and perspective of the narrator.

From whose point of view is this narrative told (usually either first or third person)? What kind of person does this narrator seem to be? Is the *attitude* of the narrator towards his/her subject significant? What kind of voice and *tone* comes across, suggesting that attitude? What might the writer intend by creating that narrator, with that tone? How are we being invited to read the passage? With amusement, empathy, critical judgement, or some other response?

Is there a shift in narrative perspective during the passage? If so, why do you think this is done and what effects are produced? Is anyone else's point of view represented at any point, as in 'free indirect speech'? (See Glossary for this term.)

Characters
Is there one central character? If so, *what* we do we learn about him or her? How do we learn this (through description, his/her thoughts, others' comments, the dialogue, language, attitudes and opinions, or something else)?

If there is a third person narrator, does s/he appear to have a particular attitude towards this character? If there is a first person narrator, remember that the writer has *constructed* this narrator/character. Do we seem to be invited to take a particular attitude towards the character – sympathy, admiration or criticism, for example?

If there is more than one character, what is the relationship between them? How are they characterised? What role do they seem to play?

Narrative structure
How is the narrative shaped? What stages does it move in (for example, stages of a journey or of an experience, or stages of thought? What is the significance and impact of these stages (for example, do they build to suspense or climax, or do they reveal more of character and situation)?

Narrative time
Is the narrative chronological, or are there shifts backwards or forwards in time? In either case, why is this done and what does it achieve? Is time of significance? Does the passage represent a long or brief period of time? How are we given a feeling for the passage of time?

Setting, imagery and detail
What kind of setting is there and what role does it play? Does it constitute a challenge for the character(s) in some way? Does it create a certain atmosphere or carry particular associations? How is the setting created – through detail, sound effects, symbolic associations, or other means? What details seem especially important? How do they contribute to the significance of the passage?

Dialogue
What purpose does dialogue play in the passage? Does it help characterise, reveal details of plot, move the narrative forwards, express conflict? What is the impact of any piece of dialogue or the dialogue in general? What is the tone in which any part of the dialogue is spoken? Does the speech of individual characters have identifying traits?

Language (diction, syntax, punctuation, sentence construction)

As with poetry, language may be a matter of diction and its sound effects, or grammar (including syntax, sentence construction and punctuation).

- Are there words that especially stand out and carry a lot of meaning or suggestion?
- Are there any interesting effects of syntax (unusual word order in sentences)?
- Is punctuation striking at any point? Does it draw attention to meaning or create particular effects?
- Are there variations of sentence length or construction that emphasise ideas or create particular effects?

Beginning/ending of the passage

Is there anything notable about either of these? Remember, however, that this is usually an extract, so beginnings and endings are 'artificial' here.

Task:

Take any page of fiction text and examine it from some of the above points of view.

2.9 What to look for in prose 'other than fiction'

Definitions of some sub-genres of non- fiction

'Non-fiction', as it is often called, comprises many subgenres such as travel writing, journalism, biography, autobiography, memoir, and essays. These categories often overlap, and share many of the same literary features. However, each has its starting point in history, its reason for existence, and its conventions. Many writers of fiction also write 'non'-fiction. As you may well be given such a passage, it is helpful to know the definitions of the terms and the expectations you should have of some of the kinds of non-fiction.

- *Journalism* (feature writing as distinct from 'news') focuses on significant aspects of what has happened, selects and reflects on 'telling' details, and *ponders the implications of the events*, setting the story in a wider human, social or political context. It is a combination of solid underlying fact, the interpretation of these facts, and reflection upon them.
- *Autobiography* is the writer's account of his or her life that puts the life *as a whole* into some perspective, tracing a development. It is a kind of history, and facts are significant. Traditionally (but not always) it is written when the writer has achieved or experienced something notable in later life.
- *Memoir* is also autobiographical but tends to be more flexible (often focusing on one particular aspect of the life such as childhood). It creates a narrative rather than a history, and is more of a personal essay or exploration through memory.
- *The Personal Essay*, a genre with a distinguished history, is a vehicle for exploring thoughts on any topic of interest and significance to the writer. S/he may start with a personal moment or reflection, but a good writer will transform this into something of broader appeal and human significance.
- *Travel writing* (like the Essay, Feature Journalism, even Memoir) transforms the particular and personal experience of the traveller into something of wider human significance, about the traveller in relation to where s/he has travelled, as well as something memorable about the place itself. It is concerned with the inner as well as the outer journey.

Some Literary features of Non-fiction

You might think that because non-fiction is concerned with reality and truth, it is less 'creative' than fiction, with fewer 'literary' aspects. However, writers of non-fiction are compelled by the same desire to communicate something of personal importance, and to draw the reader in to that experience by the way the work is written. The craft of their writing is supremely important to them, and many of their 'tools' are similar to those of fiction. Some aspects of non-fiction to look out for are:

Narrator/ Point of view

What seems to be the writer's attitude (and emotions) towards his or her subject? How critical, sympathetic, complex or ambivalent is it? What kind of narrator emerges? With what intentions and tone? Sometimes a writer, having interviewed his/her subject (a criminal, perhaps, or famous person) adopts the subject's point of view in telling their story. What kind of impact does this have?

Story telling

This lies at the heart of much non-fiction. When the facts and the untidiness of experience are artfully shaped into a compelling story with a purpose and point, they become memorable. What seems to be the significance or purpose of the narrative in the passage? What aspects have been especially selected?

Structure

Writers pay close attention to how they shape their material. What is the structure? What seems to be the purpose and what is the effect of the way this is done? (Relate this to point of view above.)

Use of detail

The significance of an experience can be conveyed in the selection of details and how these resonate. They may be about place, people, or events. What meaning and impact do details have in the passage? What do they reveal?

Characters/people

People are an important part of the non-fiction writer's work. Encounters with people impact upon their consciousness and give rise to new realisations. What role do people (and their words) play in the passage? What significance do they carry? What is the writer's attitude to them?

Ideas

Non-fiction is typically concerned with ideas, opinions, convictions, and reflections – what the writer has *made* of his or her raw experience and facts. What ideas are implicit or explicit in the passage? How surprising, provocative or fresh are they, and how has the writer made them compelling to us?

Context

How important is the sense of time and place to our appreciation of the passage? If the work is of another time period, how does this affect how we approach the material and the way it is written? Was the writing intended for a particular audience, and how is this reflected in content and/or style? If the writing is contemporary, how does the writer layer in context to the experience presented?

Language

How are sentences, punctuation, syntax, diction, imagery, figures of speech and other aspects of language used to fulfil the writer's apparent intention?

2.10 What to look for in a drama passage

If you are given a passage from a play, you are likely to be making more inferences than with narrative prose, and "listening" to the dialogue carefully. This calls for sensitivity to tone, interpreting the implications or 'subtext' (see Glossary) of what is said. It also calls for *imagining* the stage space and the movement or placing of the characters within this space. It requires a different kind of response in many ways from poetry or prose.

Situation and context

What does the dialogue convey about the situation? Is there any indication of what has led to this situation, or what might ensue from it? What questions does it pose? Does the passage give a sense of context: of place, setting and time?

Dialogue

What does the dialogue convey about the relationship between the characters? Does either character appear to have authority or status of any kind (psychological, familial, sexual, social, etc) over the other? Does this shift during the passage?

Does the dialogue express any conflict? How would you describe this? How is it suggested? What desire or goal does each character seem to be trying to achieve?

How would you describe the nature and tone of the dialogue and does this change? Does each character's speech convey a different tone? Does one character speak more than another? If so, does this suggest anything about the characters, the relationship or the situation?

Characters and their language

How is a sense of each character conveyed? Does the language of each character say something about them, in terms of diction, grammar, sentence structure, register, etc.? Do any words or images or phrases in any character's speech convey particular meaning? Is there a telling line or phrase or word spoken by each character in this scene that might epitomise his or her attitude, values or goal?

Does the speech or discourse of the characters respectively reveal patterns of discourse, such as imperatives or commands, assertions, questions, etc? Given the speech, actions, tone and any other cues to each character, what adjectives and adverbs might describe him/her/them?

What do any actions or movements suggest about a character?

Do we seem invited to respond to any of the characters in a particular way, for ideas, personality or other aspect?

Stage aspects

What do stage directions about sound, light, space, objects, movement or action contribute to our understanding of atmosphere, character, conflict and situation? If it is not indicated, how do you see the characters using the space on the stage? Where are they in relation to each other in your view?

Overview

How do you respond to this dialogue? Does it arouse unease, curiosity, concern, or what? What does the author seem to want to convey or create in the passage?

Study Activity on prose or drama:

Take a page or short scene from one of your prose or drama texts and look at it in the light of the above points in 2.9-10.

2.11 What to look for in poetry

Poetry is the most ancient and universal of literary genres, and has evolved over centuries in a great variety of *forms*, such as (in English literature) the lyric, the ballad, the sonnet, blank verse and free verse. It has also developed a great number of features or 'devices' such as metaphor, alliteration, etc.

This variety can make it a little more challenging to approach than prose, and you will need to build your skills further through texts specifically devoted to poetry analysis. The best way to start, however, is to read and *hear* as many poems as you can of different forms and historic periods. It also helps to see how poets and others have defined poetry. It has evolved for different purposes and each poet has his or her own relationship with the genre. The Internet is a huge resource for this.

The poetry samples in this chapter and Chapter Eight (Paper Two) provide good examples of writing analytically about poems.

Determine the human impulse and apparent purpose behind the words

A poem is a *shaped and carefully crafted communication*. Candidates can go astray on the poem in this paper by not 'hearing' the poem as primarily a unified *human communication*. In comparison with prose and drama, a poem is usually intensely individual and *personal*, with the focus of a single voice and vision.

Your aim should be to 'hear' and grasp this focus, and then to examine in more detail how effects of language shape and create the nature of the communication. (The sample "Two Hands" is a good example, in Section 3.10). What is said and how it is said are so intertwined that it takes several readings to distinguish the two. It is this sense of focus that should be established in your introduction.

To help you think about the kind of communication a poet may be making, and his/her starting point, remember s/he may, amongst *many* impulses:

- Give form and expression to a deep emotion
- Give permanence to or celebrate a significant experience
- Explore an experience from a fresh, probing, or critical angle
- Express wisdom or raise consciousness about an important idea or aspect of life
- Experiment with language and form to suit the topic

> **Study Activity on poetry:**
>
> *Find one poem you enjoy and decide which of the above suggestions (one or more) fits that poem; and if not, what you think the poet is communicating.*
>
> *Look back at Wilfred Owen's "Futility" above. How many of these impulses combine in his poem?*

The title

The title can be an important clue to the *literal* subject of the poem and how to read it. The poem "The Black Lace Fan My Mother Gave Me" (Section 3.8) would not make sense without the title. Titles can work in other ways, for example ironically, or metaphorically. Think about the relation of title to poem but do not force a meaning.

The situation

You need to be able to give a clear overview of what is going on in the poem. Who or what is described? Who is speaking? What is going on? Where and when (if relevant)? A sense of the situation is essential and it may take a couple of readings to establish. A discussion of literary features has little relevance without the sense of situation.

Form

Form is the *physical structure or organisation* of a poem: the length, arrangement and rhythms of **lines** and **stanzas**; the system of **rhymes**; the repetition of **rhythms** and rhymes. Unlike prose writers, poets tend to work within a tight framework of form and pattern. This gives coherence and meaning to the subject. You need to be able to establish how the form is used to suit and enhance the topic.

Avoid simply noting the rhyme patterns (such as abba) as this is of little value in isolation from the *effects* of the sound and their relation to the subject.

How do lines and stanzas develop and express the thoughts, feelings and/or ideas in the poem? How do rhythm, rhyme and metre emphasise the thoughts and feelings? (Make the habit of reading aloud to find the sound patterns and their effects).

Read slowly aloud the first stanza of Tennyson's famous poem "Break, Break, Break", reflecting the death of his closest friend. You see how the stress patterns (the 'beat' of the sound) underline his bleak isolation and sadness, but also suggest resentment that the sea goes on regardless. The three heavy stresses (underlined) in each line suggest the heaviness of his heart (sadness and bitterness), as well as the rhythmic unstoppable breaking of the waves.

"Break, break, break,
On thy cold grey stones, O sea!
And I would that my tongue could utter
The thoughts that arise in me."

Kinds of form

It is helpful to have some familiarity with established forms like the ballad, the sonnet, the ode, the pastoral, the elegy, and blank verse, to be well-prepared for your paper. Although many Paper One poems have been 20th century, there have also been poems from previous centuries.

Two broad forms that you should know are the lyric and free verse. The majority of Paper One poems tend to fall into one of these categories. 'Lyric' describes any poem that primarily expresses a state of feeling, and has a rhyming scheme and rhythm that gives it a song-like quality. "Free verse" has no strict metrical or rhyming scheme. It is a flexible form for exploring personal experience, as it tends to follow the rhythms of speech, and the movements of thought and feeling.

Sound

Poetry originated in the spoken or sung word, and sound still has an important place in poems, underlining or *enacting* the thought or feeling or situation, as seen in "Break, Break, Break". There are many ways in which sound effects are created, for example, through rhyme and metre, through punctuation, through combinations and kinds of vowel or consonant sounds. Take the opening lines of the famous war poem "Dulce Et Decorum Est":

"Bent double, like old beggars under sacks.
Coughing like hags, we cursed through sludge"

The difficult combination and alliteration of harsh 'explosive' consonants (b, d, k, c g), and the details separated by commas, enact the difficulty and pain of the soldiers' movements.

It is well worth understanding how metre works (iambic and trochaic, especially), as it creates pronounced and interesting effects in any one line of poetry, as well as in a poem as a whole.

What sounds are prominent or striking in your poem? How are they created? How do these contribute to the subject and meaning? (See the poetry sample in Chapter Eight, Section 3.)

Imagery

How do descriptive words and phrases appeal to our sense of sight, hearing, touch, smell or taste? How do they create meaning in the poem as a whole?

Lines

Awareness of how lines work is a powerful tool of analysis in poetry. Poetry is distinguished from prose in being arranged in meaningful and expressive *lines*, more or less rhythmical. The poet's use of the line, and combinations of lines, can be very forceful. A line may be a complete statement ("end-stopped") as in "The Black Lace Fan" in Section 3.8 below: "They stayed in the city for the summer." Conversely, a line may flow over to the next line or lines ("enjambment"). Or it may be broken in the middle by a pause or full stop (caesura) for a particular effect.

Each of these three ways of using a line can be very expressive, and impact on the way you read the poem. However, although you should notice how lines are working, you should *not* read them in isolation from each other or neglect to see how *they are part of sentences and the whole sequence of thought and feeling.*

Diction, sentences, grammar, punctuation, syntax or word order, contrast, tone

These essential aspects of poetry are discussed in "Five Starting Points" above.

Section Three – In the exam: reading, planning and writing Paper One

3.1 Student concerns on approaching the exam

Students' concerns as they approach the exam tend to be similar. They are primarily concerned with:

- How to revise
- How to avoid "missing the meaning" of the text
- Having enough time to read, plan and write the essay
- How to get started on the exam paper
- Organising ideas effectively

Section Two of this chapter addresses study and revision activities or strategies; what to look for in literary analysis; and how to approach different genres. The planning model (Sections 3.5-6 below) helps you use your time in the exam room effectively. The sample essays (Sections 3.8-10 below) demonstrate what good essays looks like and the planning process that went into them.

3.2 Should Standard and Higher Level students approach the exam in the same way?

The exam room reading and planning processes are very similar, but there is a difference between the two Levels in how your *structure* the response or essay. This difference is outlined in Section One of this chapter. You should consult the regulations described there before you take your exam, so that you know exactly what is expected of you.

The recommended reading and planning process for the exam (the "Three to Four Readings" model below) indicates how it should be used for each level.

3.3 Is it better to focus on either prose or poetry in the revision process?

It is unwise only to be prepared for one type of passage. If you decide ahead of time that you will only choose poetry, you might find that the given poem is much less appealing and accessible to you than the prose passage, or the reverse. Your choice should be based on which of the two given passages *appeals* to you most in subject and style, because you will write more effectively if you respond to the passage positively. Neither prose nor poetry is inherently easier or more interesting.

There is much overlap between the way language works in both prose and poetry. The "Five Starting Points" in Section Two of this chapter discusses some features common to both (grammar, diction, contrast, tone, structure), and there are many others, including imagery and sound effects. Close reading and good awareness of the features of one genre help you with the other, although you also need to be aware of what is *distinctive* about each genre.

The poems and prose passages are chosen to be interesting to students, as well as to present sufficient challenge to test your skills. To give yourself the best advantage, work with both in your revision, and enter the exam with an open mind.

3.4 Two important differences between a poem and a prose commentary

(i) A poem on Paper One is usually a complete work (not an extract). This means that it has a coherence and purpose *in itself*, which you must determine. The fact that it is a whole work *does* affect the way you approach it. Reading a poem tends to be a more circular process than reading prose. The purpose of different parts or details may not be obvious on a first, or even a second reading. Language in poetry is more concentrated than prose, so that the sense or meaning only emerges with successive readings.

By contrast a prose passage is usually an extract from a longer work. It will have a focus, structure and interest *as an extract*, and it is your task to identify this, but you are not expected to know or guess the meaning and purpose of the *whole* work from which it is taken. Even if you happen to know the whole work, your task is to discuss the passage itself and its features, not to contextualise it.

(ii) Prose fiction passages usually have a narrative thread, which forms the spine of your interpretation, and can often be identified on a first reading (compared with the circularity of reading a poem). Literary features may also be an obvious part of the narrative (like the setting in the *Frankenstein* passage below). The challenge with prose can be to see just how *crafted* it really is. The greater straightforwardness of narrative can sometimes make its art less visible. Non-fiction prose will work differently, but the type of subgenre (travel, etc.) will determine how you read it (as suggested in Section 2.9).

In contrast to fiction with its narrative thread, each poem works *differently*, and part of the challenge is to establish *how* it is working. One poem may build its meaning largely through imagery, and you will need to think about the connotations of its images and how they are working together. Another poem may develop an argument (for example in the sample "Two Hands" below), and you will need to identify how that is built through the parts of the poem. A poem may even contain a narrative, as in the poem sample "The Black Lace Fan" below, in which case you will need to apply some of the approaches normally used for prose, and think about the structure of the story line.

3.5 Why the 'reading' and 'planning' time in the exam is vital

Many students feel that because of limited time in the exam, they should start writing as soon as possible. This is very unwise. When you see *what it is that you actually do* when you 'read' and 'plan', you will understand why this time in the exam is vital to your success. The different mental processes involve:

- **Reading to understand** the situation (who, what, when, where, why, etc.)

- **Responding** to the passage, registering what is striking, interesting, problematic to *you*

- **Identifying and analysing** literary aspects and their role and effect

- **Organising responses** into a structure, on which your writing will be based

- **Synthesising responses** into a thesis or overview reflecting a grasp of the whole

It should be clear that these are complex aspects of 'reading' and that the brain cannot (usually) operate in all these ways simultaneously. They need to be separated out into stages and each stage needs time. This is why a "Three to Four Readings" model is proposed for the planning time, outlined in the next subsection. There is also *logic* in the process; you need to establish what a passage is about before you can closely examine details of style. (In practice, you may find that the stages overlap a bit).

The quality of the reading, responding and thinking that you do in the planning time determines the quality of your essay. What you eventually write about is *what you have already thought out* as far as possible. When you have thought it out, the writing tends to flow quite easily. It is not efficient or effective to try to respond and think as you write. The responding and thinking part of the process is more of a challenge than the writing, and needs concentrated time. You will be well aware of this if you have practised 30-minute timed plans, as highly recommended in Section 2.6.9.

In the exam room you will be given a few minutes reading time to look through the paper before the exam time begins, and to decide which passage to select. Once you have decided this, you should spend at least 20-30 minutes reading and planning before you start to write. (Higher Level students might plan for a little longer – up to 40 minutes.) To some students, this might seem like an agonisingly long delay before writing, but taking this time, and using it effectively is crucial to a good result.

3.6 A reading and planning model for the exam ("3-4 readings")

Section Two of this chapter emphasised that the most common weakness in performance on Paper One is the lack of a close and systematic reading. This is best achieved through several careful readings. Many candidates would write better exams if they had a more solid sense of the whole text and how it fits together.

The multiple readings approach allows for a *personal reading* that registers the *distinctiveness* of the content and style of any given text. If you use a formulaic model, and approach a text, for example, with a checklist of 'features' to identify, you may risk too narrow and artificial a reading, missing the essential communication of the text.

No one model suits all texts and students neatly. Even the '"Three to Four Readings" will be adapted to each individual student and passage, as seen in the variations of student plans for the poetry and prose samples below.

Each time you read, you deepen your understanding of the whole text and notice more of the parts or details of the text and how they contribute to the whole. This is very hard to achieve in one reading. This model works by looking first at the big picture, then the parts or details, and finally the big picture again to appreciate how it all fits together.

Stage One: holistic first impression – reading for a "feel" for the whole

Remember to *start* with **the title and details of the author and the publication date**. Without this (sometimes vital) information, your reading could take you in the wrong direction and waste time. On the other hand, don't struggle to make a date or title mean more than it does. Do not worry if it is not clear to you whether the author is man or woman. If this is going to affect the understanding of the passage, the IB will normally supply a note of clarification.

If the publication date is of an earlier century, you may need to approach the text with a different set of expectations. Sentences may be longer and punctuation more complex; attitudes may be less familiar. However, a classic text can yield excellent responses and its age is not an impediment.

Your first reading is for **an overall "feel"** for the particular text: what it is about and how it works and what the outstanding features are. This is vital to your interpretation and sense of focus (as assessed in Criterion A). Is there an ironic or other tone? Is a particular feature such as dialogue or setting outstanding? What kind of person does the central character or narrator appear to be?

Write down **some key words that express this "feel"** or write a sentence that describes what it seems to be about. You will almost certainly refine or adjust this later. This is not the stage for details about features, but for an *overall impression*. You may need to read the text more than once at this stage to figure out the content. Don't expect to understand it completely on the first reading. A fuller understanding will come with the later stages.

Identify "trouble lines" or words, difficult bits that don't make sense to you, which you will give more thought to later. Put question marks against what isn't clear.

Stage Two: reading for the structure and development of the content

The second reading should help solidify your sense of the content and situation. Students often overlook or neglect the 'structure' of commentary texts, but in fact it is one of the keys to a strong paper (and is assessed in Criterion B). Any passage or poem will have some kind of structure, and will develop an idea, or narrative, or a feeling, or a combination of these.

Finding the 'logic of development' in a text helps you get to grips with the content itself in a disciplined and *systematic* way, which is often missing from candidates' exams. It will help you find a focus and purpose for the whole text, and contribute to your thesis. The logic will be clearer if you follow the **sentences** one after the other. What is the relationship of each sentence to the next? What happens within each sentence?

Seeing the logic or map of the development and breaking it into sections also makes the analysis of literary aspects (stage three) more manageable. You can focus on one bit at a time. Your appreciation of the structure of the text should be *part* of your analysis. It can also suggest a way you might want to structure your own essay, as you see from the student plans below.

In a prose passage, what are the stages of the narration (or dialogue, if a play)? What is the focus of each of these stages? What are the implications of these stages? Is there a twist or turn in the narrative or thought line? It can be helpful to box or underline or number these stages and give a quick heading for each (as in the student plan for the Higher prose sample below).

Paragraphs will often, but not always, help you find a structure. It is what is *happening* in a piece of prose that suggests structure. For example, in the *Frankenstein* sample below, you might decide that the way the structure works for you is: (i) narrator's situation; (ii) thought process; (iii) action; (iv) consequence. The paragraphs do not reflect that structure neatly.

In a poem, look at how stanzas or other divisions develop the content. If the poem is written in one block of text, what divisions or stages does this fall into, of thought, feeling, event or action? Look carefully at *how punctuation guides the reading*. Does thought flow over into the next line or stanza, or even through several stanzas?

Stage Three: reading for the writer's creative choices and how these shape meaning

This stage specifically addresses Criterion B, which assesses *appreciation* of the writer's choices. The specific challenge is not just to identify the choices or features of interest, but also to recognise the part they play in the meaning. Work through the passage closely identifying and highlighting significant ways in which language is used and how this helps shape the meaning and impact of the text. Quickly note the appropriate **terms** for the features in the margin (as described in the student's poem sample plan below).

Think about the about the way these identified "choices" are working and how they contribute to the meaning and impact, but don't make detailed notes about this. Fuller treatment will come at the writing stage. If you do not know or remember the term for a feature you see, you can at least *describe* the role and effect it has. You will not be penalised for not knowing every literary term. Neither can you discuss every feature. Select for your discussion those that seem most striking and *relevant to the content*.

If there is a word or phrase that you do not understand, even after several readings, try to gauge the meaning from the context as far as you can. Similarly, if there are two possible ways of interpreting a word or image or section of the text, it is acceptable to present this ambivalence, provided each meaning really seems to have validity. Be careful to ensure that any single image or word is balanced with other elements and fits the general sense. It is better to address "trouble lines" as well as you can, than to ignore them altogether.

The more you are aware of the creative ways language and form can be used, and how genres work, the more effective (and faster) you will be at this stage. (Section Two of this chapter helps you prepare for this, also Chapter Eight on Paper Two).

There is no neat progression from understanding the content (Stage One) to seeing how language shapes that content (Stage Three). As you read for understanding in Stage One, certain features may leap out at you, and nothing stops you noting them at that stage. Similarly as you ponder details of language in Stage Three, the whole *meaning* will become even clearer, especially in a poem. Content and language are closely interrelated.

For example, as you look closely at "The Black Lace Fan" below, the image of the blackbird's wing, and the choice of the adjective "flirtatious" should make clearer how the story ends (happily) and what the speaker's feelings are (positive). You might initially have felt that the blackness of the bird had a connotation of death, but "flirtatious" indicates the opposite. However much you like your idea, abandon it if it doesn't fit the general scheme.

Stage Four: planning – finding a focus and structure for the essay

(a) The thesis or focus

If you have time, it can help to read back through the text once more to pull it all together again. Once you have a clear sense of the whole (content and language), this is the moment for finding a way to express this in a sentence or two, as a thesis or overview. Look at the samples below for an idea of how to do this. The description of the commentary as an "essay" at Higher Level implies that an overarching focus is expected in the introduction. This will reveal how well you have understood the *purpose* of the text, as far as you can determine this.

This thesis is personal to you, and represents the way *you* have read and understood the text. When you are clear about your focus you can more easily ensure that the rest of the essay is linked to this. Both Higher and Standard Levels benefit from a sense of this focus but a thesis is not *required* for Standard Level.

(b) Structuring and paragraphing the essay (Higher Level)

This part of the planning helps you meet Criterion C (Organisation). There is no one 'best' way to structure your essay. Your structure is a personal choice. It should arise out of *your* interpretation and should reflect *your* sense of the coherence of the text.

The student plan for The Black Lace Fan" below shows a combination of a 'linear' approach (the essay follows the *chronological* development of the poem) and an 'aspectual' approach which (in this case) bases the paragraphs on key moments or *aspects* of the narrative. She identifies significant aspects within the chronology, and considers the way these are presented stylistically. The plan for *Frankenstein* could be defined as 'descriptive' as well as 'linear' because it *describes* what happens – in sequence – with an emphasis on the significance of this and how it is presented.

The IB has always emphasised that different approaches to the essay structure are accepted so long as the ideas are logically and effectively developed with references to the text, and connected with the thesis. "Effective" and "coherent" are the key words here. It is more important for you to find what works best for you with any given text, rather than trying to mould your ideas to a prescribed approach.

Remember that "effectiveness" will partly be a matter of how well you incorporate your references to the text. As stated in Chapter Three (on Writing), your essay arises out of the text, and a sense of the text needs to come alive in your writing. The student samples provide good models of this through their plans.

3.7 Student concern about timing in the exam

Although students often express concern about running out of time, in practice this rarely happens; the task is manageable in the time. Adrenalin ensures your mind works fast in the exam room, and if you are prepared for the task and what it involves (as outlined in this chapter) you can work efficiently and use the time well.

3.8 Sample Literary Commentary: Poetry (Higher Level)

To give yourself practice in effective reading and planning, read the following poem and try out the planning stages (as above) in a minimum of 20 and maximum 40 minutes. Then read and compare with the student's work, which follows the text. You may want to feel more prepared by reading through the relevant parts of Section Two of this chapter.

"The Black Lace Fan My Mother Gave Me"

It was the first gift he ever gave her,
buying it for five francs in the Galeries
in pre-war Paris. It was stifling.
A starless drought made the nights stormy.

They stayed in the city for the summer.
They met in cafes. She was always early.
He was late. That evening he was later.
They wrapped the fan. He looked at his watch.

She looked down the Boulevard des Capucines.
She ordered more coffee. She stood up.
The streets were emptying. The heat was killing.
She thought the distance smelled of rain and lightning.

These are wild roses, appliquéd on silk by hand,
darkly picked, stitched boldly, quickly.
The rest is tortoiseshell and has the reticent
clear patience of its element. It is

a worn-out, underwater bullion and it keeps
even now, an inference of its violation.
The lace is overcast as if the weather
It opened for and offset had entered it.

The past is an empty terrace.
An airless dusk before thunder. A man running.
And no way now to know what happened then
none at all – unless, of course, you improvise:

the blackbird on this first sultry morning,
in summer, finding buds, worms, fruit,
feels the heat. Suddenly, she puts out her wing-
the whole, flirtatious span of it.

Eavan Bolland. Outside History (1990)

3.8.1 Student Commentary on "The Black Lace Fan"

"The Black Lace Fan my Mother Gave Me"

Beautiful and interesting works of art have often been objects of inspiration for poems (such as Keats' famous Grecian Urn). The contrast between the permanence of the object and the impermanence of the people associated with it can make it poignant, and the mystery of its origins makes it fascinating, in addition to the beauty or interest of the object. In "The Black Lace Fan My Mother Gave Me" Boland reveals the significance of the fan as part of the narrative of her parents' relationship, and examines it closely as a work of art with its own history. Through contrasts and shifts in time and space, and through effects of punctuation and imagery – amongst other techniques – she brings the fan and its history alive, while keeping its meaning and life mysterious.

The title suggests the fan has value because it was a gift from her mother, but the first line, plunging us into the story of the romance, shows that it also has value as the 'first' gift he 'ever' gave her mother –the emphasis of 'ever' making this clear and also suggesting that the 'he' may well have been the speaker's father. The use of the pronouns 'he' and 'she' throughout the narrative, however, keep the narrative more distant and mysterious with a life of its own rather than simply having value because of the connection with the speaker.

In contrast to the imprecision and mystery of the pronouns, the precision of time, place and the original cost of the fan are striking: pre-war Paris, the Galeries, five francs. The tactile imagery of the weather and atmosphere ('stifling' and 'stormy') creates a dramatic and suspenseful setting for the romance, which moves quickly and economically from time (summer) to places of meeting ("cafes") to the significant "that" evening – the climatic moment when the fan is to be given. The narrative moves in short sentences and end-stopped lines, which seem to heighten the breathless drama of the relationship,

> "She was always early,
> He was late. That evening he was later.   7
> They wrapped the fan. He looked at his watch.   8
>
> She looked down the Boulevard des Capucines." 9

The tension of the moment is captured by the caesura of line 7 and the emphasis of 'late' – 'later' at the end of the short sentences. The space between the salespeople ("they", the late 'he' and the waiting 'she' is brought out by the way line 8 is broken by caesura, and the break between the stanzas.

In the third stanza the brittle sentences and caesura-broken lines, and the anaphora of 'She looked", "She ordered", "She stood", "She thought" bring to life the tension of the moment for the woman as the streets ominously empty and the distance seems to smell of "rain and lightning". These dark overtones create suspense about the relationship and possibly the fate of the city.

At this critical moment Boland breaks off the narrative and there is a tantalising time-shift to the present, as the speaker now closely contemplates the fan itself. This takes us back to an even earlier moment lost in time, when the roses that inspired the embroidery were picked or imagined, and the turtle swam in the sea before the "violation" of its capture and use for the tortoiseshell frame of the fan. The diction of this description presents another contrast between the boldness and speed of the person sewing, and the "clear patience" of the "turtle's element", presumably the sea. The diction and images could suggest symbolic links with the lovers and their relationship. The "wild roses…darkly picked" suggest the passion and spontaneity of the love, and "silk" the sensuousness of it. "Darkly picked, stitched boldly, quickly", with its pronounced adverbs, could relate to the forwardness, speed and risk of the relationship in these times. The fabric of the fan also absorbs atmosphere and the "lace is overcast", as if bearing the weather of that romantic summer with it, bringing the past into the present.

The tortoiseshell frame of the fan is by contrast 'reticent'. It resists time and retains its value like gold or bullion. The way Boland describes it, with stressed double adjectives ("reticent, clear", and " worn-out, underwater") and using enjambment to move between lines and the next stanza, suggests the slow passage of time and the history of the tortoiseshell. This contrasts with the intensity of the relationship, which it preceded and has outlived. Perhaps "patience" relates to an aspect of the relationship. Did "she" have to wait for "him" because of the war, or just because he was usually late?

The reference to "weather" in stanza 6 refers back to the narrative, which is resumed with cryptic and ominous images (the café terrace is now empty) and in sentence fragments: "An airless dusk before thunder. A man running". The absence of verbs seems to transfix this suspenseful image in time forever, leaving the narrative unfinished. The gap between past and present that can never be closed is stressed by the double negative, "No way now…none at all".

But the narrator needs to bring her story to closure, and does this by "improvising", bringing us back to the present "sultry" summer of her garden, connecting this with the "stifling" city summer of the romance. She sees a blackbird in the garden. Blackbirds are associated with beautiful song and so this could be interpreted as a symbol of joy. The speaker sees the bird suddenly spread her wing like a fan: "The whole flirtatious span of it", to protect herself from the heat. This visual image connects us with the way "she" (the mother) must have opened the fan upon receiving it from "him", but this is left for us to infer, so keeping the mystery of the narrative.

The poem is effective for the way the narrative is told. Though the speaker is linked with the history of the fan, she keeps herself and her feelings out of the picture, focusing on the story, the fan, and the image of the blackbird. The story is haunting because of its fragments and the vividness of its images. The pressure of the short sentences carries the pace instead of any regular rhythm, and the resolution is satisfying because of the sense of renewal of life, connecting past and present joyfully.

3.8.2 The student's reading and planning process for "The Black Lace Fan"

We had been taught to do a minimum of three readings so this is what I did, but my readings were not exactly like the teacher's plan because of the nature of the poem (the narrative).

First Reading ('Holistic')
I read it through without taking notes, to get a feel for the whole way it worked. There was a lot that I didn't understand but I got the general drift about the story of the lovers and the fan, and wrote down a few key words that said what I got out of that reading. They were: fan, time, narrative, mystery, drama, contrast.

Second Reading (Getting the structure of the content clear –trouble spots)
I then read it through very carefully again with a focus on content to make sure that line by line I could follow what was going on and find the logic of the development. I knew that the criteria emphasised 'interpretation' so I needed to

feel secure about content. At this stage certain words stood out to me that gave me clues about this, like "first…ever" which told me that this was probably a long term relationship and that "he" could have been the father of the speaker.

In this reading for content I identified some of what my teacher calls "trouble spots" where the meaning is tricky and you need to work at it till it falls into place. I put question marks against these difficult lines and words, for example lines 15-18 about the tortoiseshell; the line about the man running, and the blackbird. I needed to work at these before going on to look at style.

For the blackbird, looking at the punctuation helped because I could see the link between "improvise:" with its colon, and what the writer does in the last stanza, which is *her* improvisation. You can't know exactly what happened in the past, so you have to "improvise", and the blackbird idea is the way she improvises. The word "flirtatious" helped make the connection for me. The mother could have opened the fan (like the blackbird's wing) and used it to show her lover how much she liked it. I could see that if the café was empty and the man was running, they must have met up elsewhere, because she got the fan, and the fan maybe clinched the relationship. I never did work out completely what the idea about the tortoiseshell was (especially "inference of its violation"), but I could see from the diction that it formed a contrast with the roses and I decided to stick with that because of time.

I also had other questions like what were the speaker's feelings and what was her purpose in writing this? Her feelings didn't seem to be part of the content, but I thought that they must be part of the creation of the poem so I inferred them and brought them in at the end.

Third Reading (identifying the role of the literary elements)
Now that I had more or less got the content straight, the literary features were easier to identify and it was clearer what they were contributing. I went through the poem again quite quickly in a linear way highlighting features and jotting down in the margin the terms for these, like narrative, pronouns, setting, weather, contrast, imagery, details, diction, climax, punctuation (caesura, etc.), suspense, time shift, adverbs and adjectives, symbol(?) This list meant I could see how much I had to talk about, and that would meet the criterion about literary effects. Later when I was writing and got to each stanza, I would think more precisely about how the features I had highlighted there were working in the poem.

The plan (thesis/focus and paragraph topics)
It seemed obvious to me that as the poem formed a narrative I should follow that in the essay, showing how the features helped make the story stand out and intrigue the reader. But I needed a broad idea about the content and the style first to give the essay a focus and bring it together in the introduction. The fan as an object was the obvious focus of the content, and my original idea about time and space shifts fitted that focus. (The fan reflected different times and places – like when it was made and when it became a present, and then a inherited object).

The way to focus the paragraphs was not immediately clear. The stanzas did not each focus on one thing, so it didn't work to do it stanza by stanza. What I decided was to find a sequence of key aspects that would create the focus for each paragraph, like (i) 'time and place"; (ii) "the movement to 'that' evening"; (iii) "the origin of the fan"; (iv) "the end of the story"; (v) "the improvisation – blackbird". So each paragraph has a focus about a particular moment in the narrative (sometimes spanning two or more stanzas), and about the effects that create that moment. For example, my third paragraph is about the relationship moving to the climax of the giving of the fan. This spans two stanzas in the poem and contains a lot of different effects that create that section of the story.

The reading and planning took around 25-30 minutes.

3.8.3 Comment on the student sample and account of the process

The student's **commentary** has a very clear sense of the poem and its significance as a whole, as she interprets it. Her thesis or overview is outlined in her third sentence in the introduction. The essay is particularly strong on 'interpretation', supported throughout with close references to the text, most of these embedded as phrases into her account of the poem.

She has a very good sense of how the writer's choices of language and style, especially sentence structure and diction, create meaning and effect. She explores a good range of literary effects. She has found a clear way to structure her essay, using key moments of the narrative chronologically, and her language is clear, effective and accurate. The essay fulfils the expectations of a formal essay.

Her **plan** shows how she benefits from the 3-4 readings model, and how she bases her structure on the way the text actually works, not on a predetermined model.

3.9 Sample Prose Commentary Passage (Higher Level) *Frankenstein*

I sat one evening in my laboratory; the sun had set, and the moon was just rising from the sea; I had not sufficient light for my employment, and I remained idle, in a pause of consideration of whether I should leave my labour for the night, or hasten its conclusion by an unremitting attention to it. As I sat, a train of reflection occurred to me, which led me to consider the effects of what I was now doing. Three years before, I was engaged in the same manner, and had created a fiend whose unparalleled barbarity had desolated my heart, and filled it forever with the bitterest remorse. I was now about to form another being, of whose disposition I was alike ignorant; she might become ten thousand times more malignant than her mate, and delight, for its own sake, in murder and wretchedness. He had sworn to quit the neighbourhood of man, and hide himself in deserts; but she had not, and she, who in all probability was to become a thinking and reasoning animal, might refuse to comply with a compact made before her creation. They might even hate each other; the creature who already lived, loathed his deformity, and might he not conceive a greater abhorrence for it when it came before his eyes in the female form? She also might turn in disgust from him to the superior beauty of man; she might quit him, and he be alone again, exasperated by the fresh provocation of being deserted by one of his own species.

Even if they were to leave Europe, and inhabit the deserts of the new world, yet one of the first results of those sympathies for which the demon thirsted would be children, and a race of devils would be propagated on earth who might make the very existence of the species of man a condition precarious and full of terror. Had I a right, for my own benefit, to inflict this curse upon everlasting generations? I had before been moved by the sophisms* of the being I had created; I had been struck senseless by his fiendish threats: but now, for the first time, the wickedness of my promise burst upon me; I shuddered to think that future ages might curse me as their pest, whose selfishness had not hesitated to buy its own peace at the price perhaps of the existence of the whole human race.

I trembled, and my heart failed within me; when, on looking up, I saw, by the light of the moon, the daemon at the casement. A ghastly grin wrinkled his lips as he gazed on me, where I sat fulfilling the task he had allotted to me. Yes, he had followed me in my travels; he had loitered in forests, hid himself in caves, or taken refuge in wide and desert heaths; and now he came to mark my progress, and claim the fulfilment of my promise.

As I looked on him, his countenance expressed the utmost extent of malice and treachery. I thought with a sensation of madness on my promise of creating another like to him, and trembling with passion, tore to pieces the thing on which I was engaged. The wretch saw me destroy the creature on whose future existence he depended for happiness, and with a howl of devilish despair and revenge, withdrew.

I left the room, and locking the door, made a solemn vow in my own heart never to resume my labours; and then, with trembling steps, I sought my own apartment. I was alone; none were near me to dissipate the gloom, and relieve me from the sickening oppression of the most terrible reveries.

Several hours passed, and I remained near my window gazing on the sea; it was almost motionless, for the winds were hushed, and all nature reposed under the eye of the quiet moon. A few fishing vessels alone specked the water, and now and then the gentle breeze wafted the sound of voices, as the fishermen called to one another. I felt the silence, although I was hardly conscious of its extreme profundity, until my ear was suddenly arrested by the paddling of oars near the shore, and a person landed close to my house.

In a few minutes after, I heard the creaking of my door, as if someone endeavoured to open it softly. I trembled from head to foot; I felt a presentiment of who it was, and wished to rouse one of the peasants who dwelt in a cottage not far from mine; but I was overcome by a sensation of helplessness.

Mary Wollstonecraft Shelley
Frankenstein; or The Modern Prometheus (1818)

*sophisms: apparently attractive arguments

3.9.1 Student Sample Commentary

This passage from Shelly's *Frankenstein* focuses on the scientist-narrator's train of thoughts in the moments leading to his sudden destruction of his new creation (a female fiend), and on what immediately follows. By being taken into the narrator's thought processes and his physical situation, we share the moral and emotional terror of his situation, emphasised especially by diction, setting and suspense. Although the passage only covers the events of a few hours, the narrator's history with his creation (the male fiend) and the consequences of his actions are all made clear.

The passage opens with the narrator describing the fateful evening vividly – the atmosphere of the setting and his own situation. Although at first it seems peaceful, with the imagery of "the moon rising from the sea", a closer look at the precise details shows how dark it is, between sunset and moonlight, and too dark to continue his "employment". He is also alone in his laboratory, which suggests an obsession with his work but also makes him vulnerable to his fears and as we see later, to the 'daemon'. The long sentence in which he establishes his surroundings and the choice he needs to make about leaving or continuing work for the night suggests a deceptively leisurely state of mind. He is in a "pause of consideration" as to what he should do, and the choice seems almost a trivial one.

This contrasts with the shocking but almost offhand statement that three years before, he had "created a fiend whose unparalleled barbarity had desolated (his) heart, and filled it forever with the bitterest remorse". This launches us unexpectedly into the horror of the narrator's past and present situation, and his state of mind. The statement is coloured by the forceful diction and sounds – the word 'fiend', for example, and the repetition of dark-sounding consonants like "p" and "b" and "d" throughout the sentence. Additionally, the superlatives ("unparalleled", "bitterest") suggest that his situation cannot be relieved. But it is to become rapidly worse.

At this point he states that his "employment" is the creation of "another being" though at first it is not clear why he is doing this, given the terrible consequences of the first. He begins to imagine how the new creation could add to the horrors of the first one. In comparison with the seeming calm of the opening, there is now a kind of mounting hysteria in the long string of sentences that express his different fears about what the new creation "might" lead to. Hyperbole suggests the terrors of his imagination –"she might become ten thousand times more malignant than her mate". He imagines how different she might be from the present fiend who at least has "complied" with a contract. His question as to whether she might reject the male fiend and make him feel worse about himself emphasises the horror of uncertainty, as do the many repetitions of "she might". The use of the conditional tense makes it seem as if the narrator is experiencing these fears in the present (rather than recalling past fears), and this draws us in to share the mounting terror of his thoughts.

Until now the speculations have all been about the possible nature of the new fiend and the relationship between the two fiends, but in the next paragraph the scope widens to include the possibility of children, "a race of devils would be propagated on earth", and the implications this has for "the very existence of the species of man". The breadth of suggestion in this language, and the tension between "race of devils" and "species of man" brings the narrator to a crucial ethical question that falls in the centre of this passage. "Had I a right, for my own benefit, to inflict this curse upon everlasting generations?" The question not only makes the narrator's dilemma clear but also causes us to think about the narrator and his actions. We are both inside the situation sympathising with him, and outside the situation thinking about the implications of his actions.

The narrator at this point has a kind of moral epiphany about his new creation: "the wickedness of my promise burst upon me". However, although he sees that his actions to buy "peace" from the male fiend would be interpreted as "selfishness", he almost seems more concerned about his future reputation than the future of the "whole human race". He shudders "to think that future ages might curse me as their pest". However, he has not yet made a decision.

Shelley makes outside events interrupt the decision process, accentuating his dilemma. We are suddenly brought out of his appalled train of thought, and back to his physical state and situation. "I trembled, and my heart failed within me". What is striking is that within the same sentence, without a pause, we are told how: "looking up, I saw, by the light of the moon, the daemon at the casement". After the terrors of his imaginings, the sudden and unexpected appearance of the fiend has an extraordinary impact on the reader. The syntax helps create this impact, as we see the moonlight first, and then the daemon framed in the light, which makes the image more eerie and frightening. The indistinctness of the monster, only described by one detail, the "ghastly grin" wrinkling his lips, heightens the horror. That one word "wrinkled", with its tactile suggestiveness, makes the image especially vivid.

The list of places the fiend has followed the narrator in his "travels" – the forests, caves, heaths – fill in more of the back story and show the pressure on the narrator but also suggests the power the fiend has over him, and its tenacity. Now comes the first and crucial action of the passage, which acts as a climax. The narrator suddenly and rashly tears up his new creation out of fear of creating another fiend like the present one menacing him. It is not for ethical reasons such as he had considered earlier, but self-protection. The rapid decision is enacted in one sentence, taking us first through his "thought" about his madness in creating a second being, then his physical and emotional state: "trembling with madness", and then his final irrevocable action when "I tore to pieces the thing on which I was engaged". The force of "tore" after all the deliberation leading up to this moment suggests a new emotional side of the narrator but also the extent of his fear.

Our sympathies unexpectedly shift at this point because the fiend is described as giving a howl of "despair" on seeing the destruction of "the creature on whose future existence he depended for happiness". This is quite shocking as it is the first sound we have heard in the passage. It also introduces a new dimension to the morality of the situation, as this piece of information about the fiend has been withheld until now, and the word "despair" gives the monster human-like needs. But the word "revenge" also increases suspense and the sense of the vulnerability of the narrator.

He leaves his laboratory and his physical and mental aloneness is stressed: "I was alone; none were near me". In contrast to "the sickening oppression of the most terrible reveries", the setting outside his window is peaceful and harmonious. Visual, aural and tactile imagery combine to create a tranquil scene with the "almost motionless sea", "hushed winds" and "gentle breeze". The personification of the "quiet moon" in an almost maternal way, under whose eye "all nature reposed", has an ironic effect as "all nature" excludes the narrator, isolating him even more. The fishermen calling to one another from their boats on the sea suggests the order and comfort of a simple human community from which he has isolated himself by his actions. The window takes on a symbolic role here because it creates a division, emphasising his separation from nature and human beings. He is an outsider, inside. It doesn't even give him protection from the outside, as we see next.

The image of the window also frames the passage because it began with the narrator looking out of his laboratory window, and ends with him "gazing" out of his apartment window. The "profundity" of the silence lulls us, so that the sudden aural imagery of the paddling of oars near the window, the sound of someone landing, and the "creaking" of (his) door, create horrible suspense and foreboding.

In this passage Shelley powerfully suggests the mental and emotional terror of the first person narrator in his complex moral situation, and immerses us in this by taking us through his thought processes and by creating such a sharp sense of his physical surroundings. She especially makes clear to us the horror of a situation that the narrator himself has created and from which there is no way back.

3.9.2 The student plan for the prose passage

First Reading:
I didn't give a quick overall reading for general effect, like the plan suggests, because the prose was very dense and I had to read slowly, following the sentences and trying to work out what they were saying. I had a pencil and marked where I saw little shifts in the narrative, and numbered these on the text as 'sections'. I changed one or two of these on the second reading when I could see the focus more clearly. I also jotted a few words down that seemed to summarise what was going on in those sections, like 'speculation' for the train of thought, or "climax", and I just circled some interesting words and phrases and effects to come back to. Finding the sections or stages of the narrative was very helpful because I could begin to see the logic of the development of the story, but I could also begin to see how the language in the sections was different.

Second Reading
I worked through the passage slowly again, getting more ideas and noting more features. Although I marked up the text itself, I also had a separate sheet of paper where I jotted down the points I wanted to mention for each stage or section (as in my list below). This expanded on the 'titles' I had made in the first reading (like "scientist – pause" for the first one). This second reading helped me see how I could structure my essay.

Third reading
I now had the story pretty clear, but needed to think out in more detail the effects created by the language, so this time I focused on sections like in the second half where there was a lot to say about language, and worked out some ideas.

Writing plan
As it was such a tight narrative it seemed obvious to me to describe and interpret what was happening in a linear way, making comments about style and effect as I went along, because that's how you actually read it.
I read through my list of key words and ideas and highlighted the ones that seemed to me the topics of each section. These became the paragraphs. The list also made it easier to form an overview for the introduction.
It was really helpful just to have key words here because I only needed the reminders while I was writing, and I could just glance at these but keep my eye mainly on the text. If I had only made the notes on the text I wouldn't have had such a clear idea for a plan.

Plan of section headings and key words

(Introduction)

1. (Lines 1-3) **Present moment** – Scientist (lab)-solitary-evening-dark-imagery "sea, moon" "pause" – formal language, leisurely – one sentence. Peaceful or sinister? Narrator

2. (Lines 3-6) **Reflection**-situation-dilemma-past history-shock-fiend-hyperbole

3.9.3 Comment on student sample and plan

The difference between the poem and the prose sample readings and plans

Note how the way students use the plan differs from student to student (according to their different ways of reading and their personalities) and from one type of text to another. The "Black Lace Fan" readings were more circular, gradually building a sense of meaning, as is typical for a poem. The *Frankenstein* (19th century prose fiction) is a reminder that you may be given a text of an earlier period that makes demands on your close reading. This student's use of his readings focuses on the sense of the sentences and the implications of the narrative in a linear way. His prose sample plan was a particularly effective method of moving seamlessly from 'reading' to a plan for the structure of his commentary.

The student meets the four criteria in his commentary at a very good level. His insights into the narrator's character, and some of his exploration of effects of language, are particularly fine, offering a good example of the literary analysis of prose, and how the content of narrative is entwined with its language. The organisation and structure shows the benefit of the plan, and the language is consistently precise, varied and effective.

3.10 Standard Level Guided Literary Analysis (Poem)

Two Hands

My father in his study sits up late,
a pencil nodding stiffly in the hand
that thirteen times between breakfast and
supper has led a scalpel an intricate
dance. The phone has sobbed itself to sleep
but he has articles to read. I curse
tonight, at the other end of the house,
this other hand whose indecisions keep
me cursing nightly; fingers with some style
on paper, elsewhere none. Who would have thought
hands so alike – blunt fingers short
in the joint – would have no more in common? All
today, remembering the one, I have watched
the other save no-one, serve no-one, dance
with this pencil. Hand, you may have your chance
to stitch a like for fingers that have stitched
new life for many. Down *The Lancet** margin
his hand moves rapidly, as mine moves slow.
A spasm shakes the phone at this elbow.
The pencil drops: he will be out again.

Jon Stallworthy, *Root and Branch* (*Phoenix Living Poets*) (1976)

**The Lancet* is a medical journal

Guiding Questions

(a) What is conveyed of the speaker's attitude towards his father's work and his own?

(b) How effectively does the writer present the situation and the speaker's feelings?

Two Hands

In this poem the speaker suggests his admiration for his father as disciplined, hardworking, and expert in his life-saving work as a surgeon. Even after a long day of thirteen 'intricate' operations and an evening of phone calls, he is sitting up making notes on a medical journal, presumably keeping himself professionally up to date, and at the end of the poem, when it must be very late, he is called out yet again.

The speaker seems frustrated and possibly ashamed at his own lack of productivity as a writer in comparison with his father's achievements, and at his indecisiveness in comparison with his father's discipline. His reference to how he 'curses' his indecisiveness 'nightly' suggests he has constant frustration and lack of confidence. The fact that he and his father have the same shape hands seems to make him wonder bitterly that they have "no more in common". Lines 11-16 express his sense of the futility of his writing. He seems quite obsessed with the uselessness of his writing in comparison with the value of his father's work, as he describes how 'all today" he has thought about his father's surgeon's hand saving lives while seeing his own hand in contrast "save no-one, serve no-one".

In line 16 the speaker realises that his writing can have value by immortalising his father and his work, and that the art of their work respectively even has a kind of parallel, in 'stitching life' for others. His poem can give value to the value of his father's work. This positive shift in his perception of his writing suggests that he does not feel resentment about his father's accomplishments but has found a way to appreciate his own talent and to honour his father's work at the same time.

The poet presents the situation vividly through the way he builds a sense of context, and the contrast between son and father, using metaphor and personification, in addition to other techniques.

First, he establishes the parallel between speaker and father, both sitting up late, working, but at opposite ends of the same house, which emphasises the separation and contrast between them. The personification of the "pencil nodding stiffly" in the father's hand suggests the briskness and concentration with which he is working even at this later hour and after a day of "thirteen" operations. The precision of the number 13 underlines his achievement.

The use of present tense throughout the poem gives a sharp edge to the speaker's feelings, to our sense of this being in a moment in time, and to what father and son are each doing. This is also stressed by the way Stallworthy uses lines. He describes in line 6 how the father is up late because "he has articles to read", and within the same line switches the perspective to the son (speaker) 'cursing' his lack of decisiveness in his writing. The movement from father to son, separated by a full stop, makes us aware of the parallel between "he" and " I" in the line, and the repetition of "curse"/"cursing" creates a very strong sense of the speaker's frustration in contrast with the father's focus.

The central image and personification of the "hands" is what gives the poem its unity and structure. "Hand" and "fingers" are referred to directly (or by pronoun "one"/"other") ten times in the poem. The work of both father and son depends on their hand, and each is using his hand to work at the moment the poem describes, so the hand takes on a kind of symbolic meaning. The title "Two Hands" is ambiguous because we first imagine them belonging to one person, or perhaps to two people in unity, whereas the poem makes clear they are identical hands, of father and son, but performing very different tasks, which initially the speaker contrasts to his own disadvantage. The similarity of the hands is made specific by the precise and rather unflattering adjectives: "*spade* palms, *blunt* fingers *short /* in the joint" and makes the difference in their work more striking. However, the speaker finds resolution in the poem through the image of hands. His hand will celebrate the achievement of his father's hand.

In relation to the image of hands the poet uses two metaphors, of "dance" and 'stitching' that help create the pattern of contrast and unity. The speaker describes his father's hand as having "led a scalpel an intricate dance" thirteen times that day. Dance here has positive connotations of precision and expertise, but when the speaker laments that he has watched his own hand all day "save no one, serve no one, dance / with this pencil", he seems to be using the image contemptuously, connoting uselessness. The image of "stitching", in comparison, unites the work of father and son and in both cases it connotes care and creation. The poet stitches with words, creating the life of a crafted work. The surgeon stitches the flesh, giving the body new lease of life.

Thus, through the sound, meaning and arrangement of words and images, the poet takes us into a moment of the speaker's life when he works through frustration to harmony in his feelings about his work in relation to his father's.

3.10.1 Student comments and plan for "Two Hands"

I started by reading the poem a few times to understand it. I did look at the questions first to get a general idea of the subject – father/son/situation/attitude/feelings. This meant that I was on track from the start in terms of the subject, but I couldn't begin to think about a response to the questions before I'd done a lot of figuring out about how the language was working, in order to understand the whole thing.

To respond to the questions I made two columns, because they relate to each other. For example I had to think about what the "nodding pencil" meant in terms of the father's work and the son's attitude, but it made me think about language choices as well. I started off by re-phrasing the questions for myself (*italicised in the table*) so that I could answer them more easily. I then went line by line and sentence by sentence answering the first question. For me the challenge was finding the *vocabulary* to answer the question well – the adverbs and adjectives that described the feelings accurately.

Then I went through the poem again, thinking specifically about the language effects that made the feelings vivid, and noted down the terms for these in the second column. It helped to see how the two questions linked – it enabled me to understand the whole poem better. This meant I could do a better job in the writing. So in the end I had gone through the text four times. The questions make the task a little easier, but you still have to think hard to get a good response.

Speaker's attitude to father's work and his own	How effectively are the speaker's situation and feelings shown?
What are his feelings about his father's work? His own? How do we know this?	*What is the situation? How is this given significance? How are the feelings made interesting and vivid?*
Contrast	**Situation:** father and son working at opposite ends of the house late at night
Father	
Disciplined/ hardworking/ expert/ productive/ decisive/of value (save/serve)	Present tense/ sense of here and now
	Parallels – father/ son working in studies
	Contrast – productive/ valuable
(Full day/ intricate operations/ note-taking/ very late/ 'dance expertly'	(numbers/ 13/ dance)
	Unproductive/ useless
	Brisk decisive pace/ pencil personification
Son	Repetition – (curse)
Frustrated/ ashamed/ indecisive/ unproductive/ sense of futility (save/ serve no-one)	Caesura – father and son
	Personification – hands (central to poem)
	Repetition
(curses/ compares/ 'dance idly')	Symbol
⇩	Dance and stitch metaphor
Resolution of son's feelings/ attitude	(Save/ serve in new light)

3.10.2 Comments on student sample and plan

The sample and plan indicate that the student has given the poem a very close and disciplined reading, and has made good use of the guiding questions. She outlines very clearly the speaker's feeling about his father and his work. This is a good illustration of the act of 'interpretation', built from the evidence of language and detail. She arrives at this understanding of the situation through a close scrutiny of the language.

This is a good demonstration of how language 'shapes' meaning, and how 'content' and 'effects" of language choices are intertwined. Consistently close reference to the text and the use of quotations in her analysis demonstrate her attention to the way language is working and how it 'shapes' meaning.

For purposes of answering the questions she separates out this process (of establishing content by attending to language), with the aid of the plan and her prompts for the plan. She identifies a range of literary effects but they are always shown in relation to the content and the meaning they shape. There is a particularly fine discussion of the title image of 'two hands' and of the central metaphors of 'dance' and 'stitching'.

The sample illustrates well how this guided literary analysis responds to the two questions in continuous prose (the second question beginning in the fourth paragraph) but also has a brief overview that pulls the poem together and a brief conclusion. Each paragraph has a focus and purpose.

The student's careful choice of her own language ensures that the analysis is clear and precise. All the criteria are thus met at a very good level.

Reflection on Section Three:

Which advice in Sections 3.1-7 do you most need to remember?

What have you learned from the sample work?

Some resources:

Commentary

Fry, Stephen. (2005) The Ode Less Travelled. Arrow Books, London
A very accessible and friendly introduction to the art and terminology of poetry
Lodge, David. (1992) The Art of Fiction, Penguin
Gives examples of and discusses 50 different terms and concepts in fiction
Perrine, Laurence (Revised 1997) Sound and Sense: An Introduction to Poetry
Clear, classic introduction to major aspects of poetry
Prose, Francine (2006) Reading Like A Writer, Harper Collins
Illustrates close reading of the fiction writer's art, with many examples

Books of poems to enjoy and to enhance understanding

Poem for the Day (Volume One), 2001, ed. Nicolas Arbury. Natural Death Centre
In three volumes. Excellent collections of poems to help you enjoy and understand poetry
Poems on the Underground, 2012, ed. Chernalk, Benson, Herbert. Penguin Group
Brilliant collection of short poems to appeal to everyone

CHAPTER FIVE

Part Four and the Individual Oral Presentation

Overview of Part Four and chapter

Part Four is where many schools begin the Literature programme. This is partly because its freedom of choice and approach for both teacher and students is appealing and liberating. It is typically seen as an excellent way to build the skills for the rest of the programme, and as an opportunity for individual creativity. The assessment process is also 'friendly' as it is teacher-managed and is the only assessed task in the programme not directly seen or moderated externally.

Students can see Part Four as a little daunting, however, because it focuses on oral skills, which are often new to them. It also involves building new skills in independent reading, study and planning, to develop a good individual topic and effective plan for the Presentation.

This chapter specifically addresses these two student concerns (the oral aspect and the independent topic) in preparing a Presentation. Many of the sections are based on students' own questions about the Oral.

This chapter should be read in conjunction with Chapter Two on independent reading skills. The sections in Chapters Three (Writing) and Six (The Written Assignment) about the process of constructing a thesis and argument out of evidence may also be of help when you are preparing your Presentation. Chapters Four and Eight provide ideas about what to look for when you study a particular genre.

The chapter is organised in three Sections, to:

1. Define Part Four, what you have to do, and how this is assessed
2. Suggest ways to build the skills and prepare for the Oral Presentation
3. Provide tips for the day of your Oral

Section One: what you have to do and how you are assessed

1.1 Features of Part Four

The texts are freely chosen
Part Four consists of three texts of literary merit, freely chosen by the teacher, at both Higher and Standard Levels. The selection may include (or even consist entirely of) works in translation. Texts may include a range of kinds of literature including graphic novels, anthologies, and non-fiction. Texts may also be studied in relation to films based on them, if of literary merit.

This freedom of choice differentiates Part Four from the other three Parts in the Literature programme, where teachers must select the author or text from IB Prescribed Lists of authors and texts, and where the task or outcome is more prescribed and regulated.

The assessed outcome is an Individual Oral Presentation
The outcome of the study of these texts, for each student, is a 12-15 minute Individual Oral Presentation to the class. The presentation is based on a focused aspect of one or more of the texts, selected by the student and prepared in his or her own time.

The assessment of the Oral is 15% of the final mark
The Presentation is assessed through three criteria, covering: knowledge and understanding of the text(s); presentational skills; and use of language.

How teachers choose the texts

As Part Four is often taught early in the course, the teacher may choose works that serve as a good introduction to the study of literature, and that will lead to stimulating topics for the Individual Oral Presentation. Choices might include:

- Texts they think significant and appealing to students in terms of subject and style
- A new type of text like a graphic novel or hypertext novel to introduce students to ways in which the idea of 'literature' is developing in the 21st century
- A text that has relevance to the region or country where the school is situated, or that is part of a national requirement
- A text that has been made into a film, to study the way in which the text is adapted, and how these media work in relation to each other
- Prose works other than fiction (autobiography, diary, essays, etc) that may stimulate creative writing
- An anthology of poems or short stories or essays, so as to introduce students to a wide range of authors and style

1.2 What you do for the Individual Oral Presentation

The choice of topic

At the end of your study of the three texts for Part Four, you will be asked to prepare an Individual Oral Presentation on a topic you have chosen, based on one or more of the three texts you have studied.

You can choose an aspect of one text, or compare an aspect of two or more texts. The respective benefits of comparing texts or using a single text are discussed later in the chapter. You are free to choose the text and topic, but the topic must allow you *to meet the criteria* and to be manageable in the time allowed. Your teacher will discuss your proposed topic with you to ensure this. You are also free to choose the *style* of presentation that will convey your topic most effectively.

How the Presentation works

The Presentation should last 10-15 minutes, with your class as audience. Questions from the audience follow your presentation for a minute or two. You can design a Presentation with another student (a 'pair presentation'), though it is more common to do an individual Oral. In the case of a pair, each student is assessed separately and must present for at least ten minutes.

1.3 What a 'Presentation' means in this programme

It's useful to know what the concept "presentation" means in this context. Students sometimes think they are taking the teacher's role or even that of a lecturer, but these roles are not the same as a presenter's. A 'presentation' in this Literature programme has a specific meaning and function, distinguishing it from, for example, a presentation in a business or media context (where presentations are increasingly used to inform and persuade).

A definition of 'presentation'

A presentation is a formal, strategic act of introducing and explaining a topic to an *audience*. Communication with the audience is a key aspect of this task. In the context of this Literature programme you *convey an argument or point of view that is the result of your individual engagement with an aspect of a text or texts*. The emphasis is on this *individual* approach, which you *offer for the consideration of the audience*. It is part of your own learning process.

There is a *tight focus* to the presentation and, as in an essay, there is a main thread of thought or argument developed through a few main ideas. This is to help your audience follow the logic of your ideas. A presentation is not read, but may be accompanied by visual or other aids to support and illustrate the main ideas and to keep the audience engaged.

The difference between your Presentation and teaching or lecturing

'Teaching' has a different role and intended outcome. It involves systematic instruction to *enable* a person or group to acquire skills and/or knowledge. It usually involves a cumulative process over time. The teacher is one who already has the knowledge and skill, and is passing this on, not one (like you) who is *in the process of learning*. The focus of teaching is the impact on the learner. *Your* presentation is to show and share what *you* have learned.

A lecture is a formal discourse of some length (usually read) on a subject to a group. A 'lecturer' is an expert in his/her subject, and the emphasis is on transmitting knowledge to the audience. There may or may not be questions afterwards. This is very different from your role.

1.4 When the Oral Presentation takes place in the programme

Many teachers cover the three texts as one unit within the first three or four months of the first year, and organise the Oral Presentations shortly afterwards. Students sometimes feel that it could disadvantage them to do the Presentation early in the course. A benefit of the work being covered early is that you have fewer pressures and deadlines in the first year, and so have more time to work on a good presentation. Anther benefit is that the skills and confidence you build through your work on this task stand you in good stead for the rest of the programme.

Some teachers set a later date so that students have more time to develop their skills and confidence, though that advantage comes with the pressures that accumulate later in the course. There are benefits either way, and students tend to perform well on this component whenever they do the Presentation. This may be due to the stimulation of choosing their own topic and presentational style, and having the time to work on it.

1.5 What you gain from the Oral Presentation

(i) Your experience with the Oral Presentation will build skills for *all* other parts of the Literature programme and additionally for TOK and the Extended Essay. The independent close reading, literary analysis and research (the first three stages of the Reading model in Chapter Two); the development of a personal viewpoint; and especially the construction of a clear line of thought out of your evidence will benefit all your assignments for this programme.

(ii) As this exercise takes place in class and you see a number of Presentations, you gain enormously in your knowledge and understanding of a range of texts, viewpoints on them, and ways of approaching them. In supporting your peers as an attentive audience member and possibly questioner, you assist in collaborative learning, where everyone helps everyone else achieve as highly as s/he can.

(iii) The skills you develop in oral communication – expressing ideas effectively in speech to an audience – will build your personal confidence and provide you with a distinct advantage in your future academic and professional life. Students have seen this task as one of the most valuable in their IB programme. Presentational skills – engaging with an audience – are increasingly in demand in contemporary life.

(iv) Oral skills developed for the Presentation contribute to the Oral Commentary in Part Two (or the reverse, depending on when you do them). Together, they combine to make up a substantial 30% of the marks in this course.

1.6 How the Presentation is assessed

The Oral Presentation marks are different from all the other assessed components in the course, as there are only three criteria, and each is worth ten marks. It is important to understand what each criterion involves for you, as this should impact on how you prepare for your presentation.

A: Knowledge and Understanding of the work (Total = 10 marks)
How much knowledge and understanding of the content and implications of the work does the student show?
This criterion is common to all your assessed components. Your competence in this is built through a conscious study process. Even thought you are presenting on one aspect of a work, you need to reflect understanding of the whole text through brief contextualisation, or by implication.

- **'Knowledge'** involves knowing well the relevant details of *content* (plot, character, situation, context, etc.), in your chosen text.

- **'Understanding'** reflects the writer's purpose, point of view and themes. It also comprises the purpose and effectiveness of the writer's choices of event, character, language, and so on.

B: Presentation (Total = 10 marks)

How effective are the delivery of the presentation and the strategies used to interest the audience?

This focus on effectiveness of presentation is unique to this Part. The criterion assesses:

- How well you **organise and structure your content** for clarity of idea and argument. You may have brilliant ideas, but if they are not arranged or sequenced effectively the point of your presentation may be lost.

- How effectively you present this content in terms of **voice** (volume, pace, expression, tone, etc). If good ideas are mumbled or rushed, their quality may be diminished.

- How effectively you **engage and communicate with your audience** in terms of 'strategies'. These include: eye contact, body language, gesture, shifts of approach to hold interest, absence of dependence on notes or script, and relevant illustrations (slides, photographs, music, quotations, images, etc).

- How appropriate your choice of strategies are for the choice of topic

C. Language (Total = 10 marks*)*

How clear, appropriate and effective are the language, register and style for the occasion?

"Language" is common to all your criteria in this programme but carries some particular emphases here such as the awareness of audience. It covers:

- The clarity and precision of your language – whether what you want to say comes across clearly and concisely in terms of your sentence structure, expression and vocabulary.

- The appropriateness of your choice of vocabulary, tone and style for your audience. It should neither be too rigidly formal nor too informal (colloquial).

- Your use of the appropriate terminology when discussing your particular work. This may include literary terms used to talk about poetry, drama, novels, etc or technical terminology for graphic novels and films.

Reflection:

What challenges do any of the above sections pose for you? Which skills are new for you?

What do you especially want to remember from Sections 1.1-1.6 above as you work towards your Presentation?

1.7 What makes an effective topic for the Oral Presentation?

If you know what topics are possible and appropriate, you can begin to come up with ideas as you study your texts. An effective topic is one that:

- Is **individual**, arising out of your own close reading of the texts and your engagement with them
- Goes further than class work and the teaching, and brings the audience a **fresh angle** on the work
- Is **focused**, and capable of clear and interesting development in the time available. It should not be too ambitious

This could be:

An aspect of style or technique
- "The relevance of the film references in *The Reluctant Fundamentalist*" (novel)
- "The meaning of objects in Tennessee Williams' *The Glass Menagerie*" (play)
- "The visual presentation of the father in the graphic novel *Maus*"

An aspect of theme
- "The role of social class in *Persepolis*" (graphic novel*)*
- "The implications of language in Primo Levi's *If This is a Man*" (autobiography)
- "The meaning of 'darkness' in some of Robert Frost's poems"

An aspect of character
- "Blanche DuBois interpreted as a strong character in *A Streetcar Named Desire*"
- "An interpretation of Mr Darcy in *Pride and Prejudice*, comparing text and a film version"
- " 'Bad People': the attraction of bad characters in two Robert Browning dramatic monologues" (poetry)

An aspect of culture, setting or context
- "The significance of traditional Nigerian culture in *Purple Hibiscus*" by Chimamanda Adichie
- "The role of country walks in Austen's *Pride and Prejudice*"
- "The use of the *Death and the Maiden* motif in Dorfman's play of that title"

Creative Writing in the style and form of one of your texts
The emphasis here must be on your knowledge and understanding of the original text. Your own writing and presentation must reflect your knowledge and understanding of the text in question. You could, for example:

- Compose and justify a conclusive ending in comparison with an open-ended one in texts like *The Reluctant Fundamentalist* and *Death and the Maiden).* Compare yours with the effectiveness of the author's original and its impact on you.
- Try your hand at writing a sonnet, ballad or other poetic form, comparing your choices and intentions with one or more other poems you have studied in that form
- Write a section of your autobiography and compare your intentions and choices with those of a memoir or autobiography you have studied

A reading of one of your texts through the lens of one or more critical perspectives
You could take, for example, a Feminist, Marxist, Structuralist, Post Colonial, Eco-critical or other recognised critical approach and look at a short text (a poem or short story) in this perspective; or compare two perspectives on the text.

Reflection:

What kinds of topics and approaches in the above lists appeal to you?

Can you think of a suitable topic for a text you have appreciated?

Which of your particular talents or interests might you want to use to develop a presentation?

1.8 Is it better to focus on a single text or to compare texts?

Single texts, and two or more texts compared and contrasted, can work equally well depending on the topic, the time you are prepared to devote to this, and the way you develop and present the topic.

Using a single text
If you select a single **short** text like a poem, ensure that you have an interesting angle on it (taking it further than class discussion), and that you can develop and present it in an effective way for your audience in the required time. Ideally it should not resemble the Higher Level Oral Commentary task in Part Two (on a single poem). If you have found a poem that is complex

enough and of personal interest to you, which perhaps has an interesting context or has generated very different interpretations, this could well be captivating.

A single **longer** text may allow for the exploration of an independent, personal and unusual angle, but it will need to be clearly focused and capable of persuasive development in the time frame. For example, flower and plant imagery in *Hamlet*.

Using comparisons

A comparison and contrast can be stimulating for you to explore, and interesting to your audience. The other students will enjoy hearing something that takes them in a new direction and makes original and unexpected connections between texts. You will benefit from the comparative exercise when you come to the exam essay (where you compare two or more texts of the same genre).

Short works like poems, short stories or essays, can lend themselves to imaginative comparison and sharp, analytical development, especially if genres are mixed. For example, the significance of snow in James Joyce's short story "The Dead" compares interestingly with snow in Robert Frost's poem "Desert Places". It can also be highly effective to link two poems in an unusual way, such as the use of the object in Sylvia Plath's "Mirror" and Stephen Dunn's "The Room".

Two longer works can be effectively compared if the topic is highly focused: for example, references to the sea in Sophocles' *Antigone* and Lorca's *Blood Wedding*, or the comparison of the effect of the waltz music in Primo Levi's Auschwitz memoir *If This Is A Man,* and Tennessee Williams' play *A Streetcar Named Desire*.

Working with two long texts requires time and more work, and there is the challenge of keeping a balance between the two texts. This is where a 'pair' presentation might be a solution, as discussed in the next section.

1.9 Are there advantages in doing a 'pair' Presentation?

The decision to do a pair presentation should be a matter of *content* rather than of lack of confidence and the need for support. It suits a larger topic on a substantial text, and could offer opportunities for stimulating collaboration. For example, two students might decide to explore the presentation of the escaped slave Jim in *Huckleberry Finn* through the eyes of the reader, and the eyes of the central character Huck, respectively. Such a topic would require a combination of independent close study *and* exploratory discussions between the partners.

The benefit of the 'pair' presentation comes from this collaboration on the topic rather than the Presentation itself, as each student must perform for ten to fifteen minutes and is marked separately. The Presentation will thus fall into two separate halves. The first student might introduce the topic and the second student could conclude it.

1.10 What makes an effective presentational approach?

The presentational aspect is important because it is given particular emphasis in Part Four and carries ten marks. It is also a good opportunity for you to develop this skill. Students are often more concerned about their content than the presentational aspect, but the two are entwined.

The presentational strategies emphasise and enhance *content*. You begin with content, and then think how best to put this across and engage the interest of your audience. Strategies should not be something hastily added on at the last moment, but considered during the process of researching the content and planning the structure (see the model plan in Section 2.2.7 below).

Your choice of presentational style should depend on how well it suits your content and, above all, helps your audience understand and appreciate the topic. It can give you scope to use your particular strengths or interests, which may be technological, dramatic, photographic, or musical, amongst other possibilities, as in the following:

Dramatised debate or interview

You might consider this as the best approach for an evaluation of Chinua Achebe's essay critiquing Conrad's attitude to Africa and Africans in *Heart of Darkness*. To demonstrate both your interpretation of the novel *and* your response to Achebe's, you could write a dialogue between the two men, and dramatise it for the presentation. (A pair presentation would work here). You would need to decide whether to give an introduction outlining your point of view first, before the dramatised debate, or clarify this afterwards.

This choice of presentational approach calls for a number of challenges: clarity of argument, close and critical reference to the works, creative writing of the dialogue, and energy and persuasiveness of the debate. PowerPoint or visuals in this case might play a lesser role or not even be helpful at all.

Comparison of tone in two poems using voice or sound recording

You could be interested in the importance of *tone* in two or three Sylvia Plath poems. As students are often unclear about what tone is and how it is produced, this could be a valuable investigation. The audience would need to *hear* the poems with the appropriate tone, which could involve your own reading or the use of recordings.

You might put the two texts on a screen and refer to those (rather than using handouts). Visual aids would help in revealing how tone is inferred from the text. Such a presentation could appeal to a drama or theatre student, but is also within anyone's capacity.

Exploration of two settings in a novel, with visual images

Suppose you want to explore the use of the two cities (New York and Lahore) at the heart of Moshin Hamid's *The Reluctant Fundamentalist*. There are many descriptions of these two settings in the novel, resulting in a complex and ambivalent view of each of them. You could research effective visual images to underline your argument about the role of these settings. The settings of many other texts lend themselves to such visual strategies.

A presentation on the *Death and the Maiden* motif using art and music

A visual arts and/or music student might explore the significance of this medieval visual motif to the play, and also demonstrate what kind of effect Schubert's music (of the same title) has in Dorfman's play.

Visual and literary (narrative) exploration of a graphic novel

A student might make a comparison of the parallel narratives (allegory and real life study) in the graphic novel *American-Born Chinese* by Gene Luen Yang

---

Reflection:

What kind of presentational approach appeals to you? Remember, content should drive the approach.

Design an approach for a work you might consider using.

1.11 Is PowerPoint an "effective strategy"?

Students sometimes think this is obligatory. The effectiveness of PowerPoint (or other presentational software like Prezi or Keynote) depends on the nature of your topic and the skill with which you use it. It would not suit all the above examples, but it can be an effective tool if you consider the function you want the slides to have, and how you and the audience will relate to them. You can use it:

(i) To *underline* your thesis and argument

Use headings on slides to underline your main ideas, and help the audience (and you) keep track of your sequence of thoughts. It helps for you to glance up at the heading and share this with the audience rather than looking down at notes that only you can see. Keep to *headings only* on your slides; *do not cram other information on them*. They should not be doing your work for you, or creating a parallel discourse.

(ii) To *illustrate* content

An illustration (picture, diagram, or map) can be an effective way to introduce unfamiliar ideas or information. Use the visual as you would use a quotation or reference in an essay, to illustrate and make clear what you are saying. Give the audience a moment or two to take it in and process it, because an audience can have difficulty focusing simultaneously on what you are saying *and* the illustration on the screen.

Introduce the slide and interpret it if necessary. Don't flash up the image and leave the audience to figure out the implications while you move on to another point. Turn to the slide to establish the connection it has with your argument, keeping yourself at the heart of your presentation.

(iii) To *reference* a piece of text you are discussing

If you are discussing a piece of text it is more effective for you and your audience to be looking at the same place (screen) rather than for your audience to be looking down at handouts. You can more effectively control the discussion, and keep yourself at the centre of it by indicating visually the words or lines to which you are referring.

1.12 Is there an advantage to writing out the presentation beforehand?

Advantages (with a caution!)

Writing your material out can be a helpful tool in the *preparation process* of clarifying for yourself what you want to say, but it should not be the final product as a memorised script. This would be missing the point of the whole exercise, and would not earn good marks in Criterion B (presentational strategies) because you would not be engaging your audience.

There can be an advantage to writing out the content in that the act of writing pushes you to *express your thoughts* more completely and precisely, as in the saying: "I know what I think when I can see what I say". Once you have assembled your evidence and organised it into sections for presentation, writing can be a helpful way to develop clear, concise and structured communication.

The process of writing can *deepen your knowledge and understanding*. Physically writing down your thoughts engages you more thoughtfully in the material. You can also construct effective headings to use from your written work.

Another possible advantage to writing out the content is that it can help you *time* your Presentation more accurately, and to gauge whether you need to add or omit material.

Disadvantage (if misused)

The *disadvantage* is that writing your content out might tempt you to try to memorise it or to bring it to the Presentation and try to read it. *This must be avoided at all costs.* Memorising or reading a script does not demonstrate oral skill, is not persuasive, and does not engage an audience. An oral should not sound like a perfectly written essay.

What engages an audience is the sense that you know your material well, have pleasure in communicating it, and the confidence to find the right language spontaneously. Know what you want to say, and the words will follow. Do not bring a script with you, or practise with one beforehand.

Section Two: Preparing for the Oral Presentation

2.1 Four ways to develop effective oral skills

Many students are initially daunted by the idea of speaking for up to fifteen minutes in front of an audience and keeping it engaged. They worry about being overcome with nervousness, and doing 'badly' (though as stated above, the majority of students normally do quite well in this task).

Some teachers help students to develop oral skills earlier in the course by setting them mini presentations on other topics. If this is not possible because of numbers of students or other reasons, there are various ways you can develop effective oral communication.

2.1.1 Practise expressing ideas orally on a regular basis

Class discussion of texts in both small and large groups develops your oral skills. It helps you overcome fears about speaking in front of others without preparation, and pushes you to find the language to express your thoughts in an informal but structured and supportive context.

Make the effort to contribute regularly to discussion from early in the course, and to take initiative in speaking when you work in small groups. Discussing texts with a small group of peers outside of class time will also help you articulate ideas, especially if class does not provide the opportunities.

2.1.2 Gain ownership of your texts so that you are confident about what you say

Presentation experts will tell you that when you have something significant to communicate, and the authority of knowing it well, you will command the attention of an audience more effectively.

Ownership of your texts will make you feel more motivated and confident to communicate what you want to say. Although you cannot know in advance exactly how your sentences will emerge in an oral, or exactly how you will express your ideas, what you *can* know, control and plan in advance is *what* you have to say, and how this is best *structured*. Chapter Two demonstrates many ways you can gain this ownership of texts. The sample plan in Section Two below (2.2.7) illustrates a confident structure.

2.1.3 Know the language and terminology you will need for discussing texts

This is an extension of (ii) above. The more you understand how to read texts in different genres, and know their different features and the terminology for these, the easier it will be for you to speak about your topic knowledgeably and effectively. Chapter Four on Paper One, Chapter Eight on Paper Two, and the Glossary will help with this. If you are discussing film or graphic novels, your understanding will benefit from some knowledge of critical terminology for these media.

2.1.4 Practise a good level of language when speaking in class

You are expected to use a reasonably formal level of language for your orals in both Parts Four and Two. 'Formal', for purposes of these orals, means that your language should be grammatically correct as well as effective in style and choice of vocabulary.

You should avoid the colloquial, slang, or abbreviations. Lady Macbeth has 'no children', not 'no kids'. Hamlet's father, not his 'dad', was murdered. Make a conscious effort to use a careful level of language and vocabulary in class, and to enlarge your vocabulary so as to be "precise" in what you say. However, your Presentation will be a little less formal than your Commentary, as it will be for a student audience.

Reflection:

Do you need to work at oral skills? If so, which of the above might make a difference?

2.2 Ten ways to develop a topic and presentation effectively

Students are generally more concerned about content than delivery. They worry about whether their ideas will be 'good' and interesting to their audience, and valid or 'correct' to the teacher who is assessing them. The following points indicate how you ensure interesting content, and do your content justice through the presentational approach.

2.2.1 Plan and manage your time

Time management is one key to success, and this is a good opportunity to develop the skill. Students often say after their Presentations that if they were to do one thing differently it would be to manage their time better and have less pressure at the last minute. Yet many students have never seen or used a model of a time plan that can make all the difference to their efficiency. Your Oral could take 5-6 hours, or more. Ask yourself:

- How much time do I have to complete this assignment? (eg. 2-3 weeks)
- How many tasks does it involve? (eg. reading, illustration research, planning)
- When will I do these, and how long will each take (realistically)?
- How many hours do I need for the whole thing?

Sample student time-management plan for an oral presentation

"The vision of America in Tennessee Williams *The Glass Menagerie*"

The stages of the task (calculated at total 7 hours):

(a) Create relevant questions as I re-read the text; re-read text (2-3 hours; 2 evenings?)

What is the 'America' Williams shows us? (Buildings? Life-style? Values? Other things?)
Is he presenting it critically, sympathetically, or both?
How is his view coming through? Through the characters and their values, the setting, or what?

(b) Locate resources on this period of US history and on Williams. (1 hour; free period; library and internet; discuss sources with teacher)

Questions to ask:

What was going on in the US around the time Williams was writing?
What was there in Williams' background and context that creates the attitudes he seems to have?

(c) Read and take notes on the historic and biographical sources. Note where this reflects my reading of *The Glass Menagerie* (as in 'a' above). (1+ hours; evening)

(d) Organise all notes into a plan for the Presentation. Decide on main section headings (2 hours weekend)

This will be my toughest task – deciding on my argument and sequence (allow time!)

(e) Decide on illustrations for each section (some slides, one clip from performance) 1+ hours

(f) Practise with partner to get the timing right (30 minutes)

Student Comment:

I took longer than I had planned, partly because I got interested, and also because I didn't really know how long each bit would take. Breaking it down into separate tasks or stages was really helpful because I could just focus on that one thing and didn't feel stressed about everything else. Also, because I planned when to do each task, I didn't feel that I was taking time from other things. The subject was a bit too big but the assignment has helped me see how I can work more effectively. Although I practised the oral aloud, in class it was a bit rushed and a bit too long. More practice would have helped.

As you see from this plan, only by breaking the main task down can you see what it really involves and how much time it will probably take.

2.2.2 Review "effective topic" suggestions in Section One (1.7)
Review what makes 'an effective topic', and the range of possibilities suggested.

2.2.3 Know your texts and their contexts
Good content can *only* come out of good knowledge and understanding of the text, so this is where you start. Re-read the whole text where possible, because with the benefit of class discussion you will have a better perspective on it and will more easily identify a topic of personal interest. Read with a fresh mind and eye; you should be moving *beyond* class discussion and your first reading.

2.2.4 Research where necessary

In general, some research using reliable sources will enhance your knowledge and understanding of text, author and context, and *sharpen your personal angle* on the text, as in the examples on *The Glass Menagerie* and *The Things They Carried* (below).

However, background knowledge should only be used to *develop your own insight into the text and its significance*, not presented for its own sake. You are assessed on *your knowledge* and understanding of the text.

2.2.5 Evidence first: the 'grid of evidence'

Students often think they must come up with an idea, and then find evidence to support that. This is rarely if ever effective. You do not begin with knowing what you want to say. You develop your content and argument out of thoughtful reflection on the 'evidence' you collect on your topic. *Your particular selection of evidence,* and how you analyse and organise this, is what makes your presentation unique and interesting.

Look at the 'grid of evidence' from Chapter Six, Section 3.6 and the discussion of the grid. This demonstrates how you start with evidence or quotes, and your reflections on these, and work towards a line of thought.

2.2.6 From evidence to organisation: using the third column of the grid

Students say that the most challenging and time-consuming aspect of the preparation is finding a way to organise and structure the content so that it will be clear to the audience. This is exactly like the challenge of essays. The grid helps you do this effectively as it gives a clear visual overview of your evidence and the ideas arising from this. This enables you to see how ideas can be grouped for presentation.

Even if you are planning a more creative presentation, you need to be sure what your main ideas are, and in what ways you aim to illuminate the text.

2.2.7 From organisation to 'headings': making a plan for the presentation

Organise the material from the third column under headings. Then arrange the headings or sections in a logical order that will reveal the spine of your argument or line of thought in the same way that you would arrange paragraphs in an essay. (Chapter Three, Section 3.8 provides a model for this). If you put the headings on index cards, you can move them around to find the most effective order. Make sure that you have whole sentences for headings, to make your argument clear.

Write your thesis or main argument out clearly at the beginning of the plan, so that your aim and direction is clear to you, and will be to the audience. An audience likes to know where the presentation is going. Alternatively you might begin with a research question, as in the plan below on *The Things They Carried*, and take your audience through your investigation of the question to the conclusion. In this case the student creates a clear 'path' through her topic, with its three main headings, by means of a visual in her introduction (see visual at end of chapter).

2.2.8 Decide on presentational strategies, using the plan of contents

Once you have the outline of your content you can see where the material calls for strategies that will clarify, illustrate or enliven your presentation. These should not distract from your line of thought and ownership of the content. "Strategies" need not only be slides. Your choice should be based on what is comfortable for *you*. Effective strategies do not necessarily mean technical wizardry. You audience is interested in *you* and what you have to *say*.

Preparing your illustrations will take time, so allow for this. If you use slides to reinforce your points, use headings only, not other information (see section 1.11). Do not have too many slides. One or two per minute is usually sufficient.

It is usually best not to use handouts. Time and attention may be lost in the process. The eyes of your audience go down to the handout, and each student engages *separately* with what you have handed out. You cease to be at the centre of your presentation. It is more effective to have information (such as a poem text) on a screen, so that the whole audience is looking at the same thing at the same time, and you can keep control of the process.

A sample student plan for _The Things They Carried_ (Timothy Winton) with Prezi

PLAN	VISUALS (17)
Introduction Title: "_Carrying Expectations_" Research question: "_How are the soldiers presented in relation to conventional expectations of soldiers?_"	• Title heading + plan of oral in form of footprints making a path from introduction; through three aspects; to conclusion • The research question
Context Conflicting expectations of US soldiers in Vietnam (influenced by memories of American World War 2 GIs). Changed circumstances.	• Heading: "Conflicting Expectations"
Aspects to be Explored: Patriotism, Honour, Courage Did the US soldiers in Vietnam show these?	• Heading: Patriotism, Honour, Courage
1. Patriotism (anti-patriotism) • Different definitions of Patriotism • "Patriotism means no questions" • Soldiers in Vietnam had questions • They were fighting because drafted • Resentment • Episode of narrator killing a Vietnamese solider	• Heading (Patriotism) + definitions +propaganda art ("no questions") • Heading (The Draft) + quotes from text re. Draft + photo of anti-war demonstrators • Heading (The Man I Killed) + quote from text illustrating his attitude to this
2. Honour (Dishonour) • The mocking of the dead man episode • Torturing the baby buffalo episode	• Heading (Honour) +definition • Heading (Mocking the dead man) + quote • Heading (Torturing the Innocent) +quote
3. Courage (redefined) Contrast cowardly courage: • "Fear of showing fear" • Standing up for one's ideals is real courage	• Heading (Courage) • Original definition of courage • Heading (Fear of Embarrassment) + quote: fear of fear
The major change (clash with society's view of courage, and redefinition) Key quote " He had been braver than he ever thought possible, but not as brave as he wanted to be. The distinction was important".	• Quote
Conclusion Soldiers are shown in relation to societal expectations of Patriotism, Honour and Courage in order to show the truth and humanity of a real war story.	• Heading
	• Bibliography

Note how, by using such a plan, you can ensure that your content is logically developed and your illustrations relate closely to your main points. In this case, slides of headings only keep the audience aware of the argument, and quotes from the text show supporting evidence for the ideas. This is just one way to plan effectively. You may find other equally clear models.

2.2.9 Get the timing right
One way to help you get the timing right is through your plan. Look at it to estimate how long you will spend on each section, and make a note of your halfway point at least (for example "Reach this point by 6+ minutes"). Gauge how long each point will take, and try to ensure it will

all fit. It is better to cut down than to try to cram too much in by rushing towards the end. You can always run through the presentation with family or friends to ensure the timing is accurate.

2.2.10 Getting the voice right

Students often say they hate the way their voice sounds, and that they are not confident speaking to an audience. First, focus on your presentation as *an act of communication* with an audience. When you have a desire to communicate, and take your audience 'on board', you will sound (and look) interesting and convincing.

You could record yourself, to help identify speech traits that you want to eliminate (such as the colloquial 'like'), to gauge whether you need to slow down your delivery a bit, and to practise timing.

> **Reflection:**
>
> *Which of the above ten suggestions do you need to pay most attention to?*

Section Three – On the Day: Giving the Presentation

This section addresses students' specific worries and questions about the Presentation.

3.1 How do I overcome nervousness?

Almost everyone is nervous before presenting, even veteran professionals. First, if you have prepared your content and presentational approach carefully, as illustrated above, you are very unlikely to do 'badly'. Your marks are spread across three criteria. Use your preparation time well, and this should give you the confidence to perform.

Second, think positively about the task. Your attitude to this will make a big difference. You will enjoy watching others' Presentations, and they will enjoy watching yours. Focus on that act of sharing and communication, and see it as an opportunity. The chance to develop such a skill at this stage will stand you in good stead for the future. Many students say at the end of the course that their oral was the task that made the biggest difference to them, and gave them most confidence and pride.

3.2 How do I best engage the audience?

Enjoy your topic
Focus on *sharing* your enjoyment and discovery of your topic with your audience. When they see and feel your interest, they will be engaged, because your eyes, face, and especially your voice, will reflect your interest and the authority of the effort you have made. They will want to hear what you have to say.

Learn from other presenters you have seen
You can also be strategic about engaging your audience. Think of presenters you have seen at your school or in public or on TV or in TED and TED-Ed talks. What did you like or not like about their manner and approach? What worked well or didn't work? How might this help you with your presentation? Review a few such talks on the Internet.

Make contact with your audience
It is a very good (and professional) idea to begin with an informal or personal remark that gives you and your audience time to 'settle in' and establish contact. This also gets you used to hearing and using your voice. For example you might say: " My topic is the role of Schubert's music in *Death and the Maiden*". I was attracted to this when we heard it in class, and I was intrigued by the title". If you plunge straight into the formality of the presentation, as if

unpacking your content is your only aim, you will not allow yourself to build that relationship, and the audience has no time to ease into attentiveness to your argument.

Before you begin speaking, take a moment or two to look around the group and make connection with them. This also 'disciplines' your audience, giving them time to begin to focus on you. Your audience is an essential part of your Presentation, and *you must establish that relationship*. Keep your mind on what you want to convey to them about your text. Remember, during your Presentation, to look at your audience, establishing brief eye contact with different members of the group.

The attention of the student audience does make a difference to your level of confidence and effectiveness. If they are looking at you and listening with interest, you are more likely to be inspired to speak effectively. Students should remember that when the time comes for their Presentation, they will appreciate attentiveness, so they should give their attention respectfully to each speaker. Further, the audience will be involved in the questions following the presentation, and so should be engaged from the beginning. The teacher may remind students of this before the presentations begin.

3.3 I'm afraid of forgetting what I want to say. Can I use notes?

Use headings, but not notes. Trying to read notes may cause you to lose focus, and risks losing the attention of the audience. You should know what you want to say by mastering your material beforehand, but not by memorising sentences or blocks of text. Glancing briefly at headings, whether on note cards or slides on the screen, maintains the flow, reminds you of your main points, and helps you keep track of the sequence of your ideas.

3.4 How do I get the volume and tone right?

Your audience is usually an intimate one, generally in a classroom, not a large space, so you do not have to project your voice too much. However, your volume should be sufficient to reach comfortably those who are furthest away. Gauge how much this should be by looking at the most distant students and focusing on reaching them. If you know you have a soft voice, take deeper breaths to help your voice carry. You may need to practise this at home or in a convenient place. *A good Presentation is one that allows everyone to hear it comfortably.*

If you focus on sharing your own interest in your topic with your audience, the appropriate tone should normally follow. It is the rare person who is interested in a topic and is eager to share it, yet speaks in a monotone. Don't 'put on' a special tone for the occasion. Be natural.

3.5 How do I deal with questions at the end?

You will have questions at the end. IB regulations for the IOP make this clear. They are not part of the timed 12-15-minute Presentation, and two to three minutes is probably appropriate. Although you are only assessed on the *Presentation*, a good performance in the subsequent questions enhances the general perception of your ability and may help the teacher affirm the marks he or she is considering. Questions give you the chance to show further knowledge and understanding of your topic and to show your skill in responding spontaneously to questions (a skill also required in the Higher Level Oral Discussion for Part Two).

It is also a satisfying way to end the Presentation as it involves you directly with your audience. Your sense of their response is important for your feeling of closure and accomplishment. The teacher may open the discussion as s/he may have questions to put to you about your content and choice of approach. As the students are also your audience, it is important that they too be given the chance to ask their own questions. You are not expected to invite the questions.

3.6 How can I know I have been marked fairly?

It is not in the interests of any teacher to be unfair or to show prejudice, quite apart from this being against the instinct and ethics of a professional teacher. When you have later completed your Part Two Oral Commentaries, these are added to your Oral Presentation marks, and samples of Commentaries will be sent away to an examiner for moderation. The examiner will check that your teacher is interpreting the criteria appropriately. Teachers want to be recognised as accurate assessors, and also want their students to receive marks that reflect their standard.

3.7 If I do badly, do I have another chance?

This is an exam. You will have had time and advice to prepare it adequately, and so should not run the risk of 'doing badly'. You can do it!

Reflection:
Which of the above suggestions are going to be most helpful to you?
What steps will you take to put them into practice?

Introductory visual (Prezi) for Oral Presentation on *The Things They Carried (see 2.2.7-8 above)* showing introduction, three main topics, and conclusion.

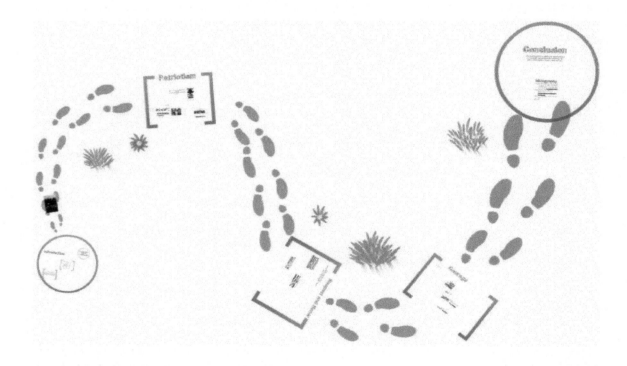

CHAPTER SIX

Part One: Works in Translation

Chapter Overview

Part One has a special place in the Literature programme and is a fascinating part of the course for both students and teachers, opening up other, often unfamiliar cultures and their perspectives. It reflects the IB commitment to intercultural understanding, through the literary study of works in translation chosen by your teacher or school from a prescribed list of titles.

The outcome of Part One, a Written Assignment or formal essay of 12-1500 words, carries a substantial 25% of the total mark for this programme (more than any other component except Paper Two). This rewards the unique challenges of this Part, but also makes it important for you to understand how to meet these.

Three features of Part One distinguish it from other Parts:

1.   There is a particular focus on the *culture and context* of the texts

2.   There is a carefully prescribed *process* for the teaching and studying of each text, designed to help you grasp your texts well, in preparation for your final Assignment

3.   Students have *significant control* over the outcome. The final 1200-1500 word Written Assignment is written *in your own time*, on the text and topic of *your choice*.

This chapter takes you through the prescribed process of Part One:

*   Section One provides an overview of what Part One involves, its assessment and challenges

*   Section Two discusses the requirements of the first three Stages of the study process, and provides samples of work for each of these Stages

*   Section Three focuses on the final Stage Four: the production of the Written Assignment, with an analysis of sample work

You should read this chapter in conjunction with Chapter Three, which focuses on the skills of the formal essay. You will need these for your Written Assignment.

Section One: What Part One involves

1.1 Texts and timing of the teaching

Higher Level students study three texts; Standard Level students study two texts. The texts may be of any genre. They must be in translation, by different authors, and selected from the IB *Prescribed List of Works in Translation.*

There is no prescribed time to teach Part One, but many schools teach it in the first year, as each text requires quite a long, intense and tightly linked sequence of study (the "Four Stages", outlined below). In addition, it involves skills and tasks that are likely to be new to you and need time and practice to master, which you have more time for in the first year. Researching and writing your own essay is probably the most notable of these skills.

Some teachers complete the Part One work in the second year, when their students' skills are more developed, though the workload is heavier then. There are advantages both ways.

The Written Assignments are sent away to an examiner in the second year, two months before the final exams, but almost all schools require them to be completed much earlier, before the pressures of the final months of the Programme. This early completion of a major (25%) assessed component of the programme is a distinct advantage.

Part One does not have to be taught as an uninterrupted sequence of texts. However, your teacher is unlikely to leave too much of a gap between the end of the study of the texts and the writing of the final Written Assignment.

1.2 An outline of the Four Stages of the Part One study

The Stages are outlined here and discussed in greater detail later. The first three Stages apply to each work. They put you in a strong position to proceed to the writing of your final Assignment (Stage Four). The work and effort that you personally put in *at each stage* is a determining factor in your success.

---

1. The "Interactive Oral"
This is the outcome of the class study of the text (though it can be done earlier or later in the study). It is a class discussion that focuses on contextual and cultural aspects of the work, led by students and facilitated by the teacher. The main areas for discussion are *specified* (as shown in Section 2.1 below)

⇓

2. The "Reflective Statement"
This is a 300-400 word reflection on how the Interactive Oral contributed to the development of your understanding of particular cultural aspects of the work (usually one or two) and their place in the whole text. You write one after *each* Interactive Oral. The Statement on the text you choose for your final essay, is sent away with the essay, and is part of the assessment. (Mark: /3)

⇓

3. The "Supervised Writing"
This is a piece of in-class writing supervised by the teacher soon after Stage 2. The teacher supplies "prompts" on literary aspects of the work to stimulate your thinking about the text. You choose **one** and write about it in continuous prose. The aim is to start you thinking about possible topics for the Written Assignment. It is not marked or sent away for assessment. It is not a formal or structured essay.

⇓

4. The "Written Assignment"
This is a 1200-1500 word formal essay on your choice of ONE of your texts, and on your choice of topic in that text. You write this final essay when you have studied *all* your Part One texts and completed the three Stages above on each. It is sent away to an examiner in the second year. (Mark: /22)

1.3 The Assessment Criteria for Part One

You will see that the criteria involve three areas of knowledge, understanding and skill:

- Cultural/contextual understanding (A: 3 marks)
- The text and its literary features (B and C: 12 marks)
- Writing and language (D and E: 10 marks)

Each of these skills is discussed in detail in subsections below.

Criterion A: The Reflective Statement (/3)
Does the student's reflection on the Interactive Oral show development of understanding of cultural and contextual elements?

Criterion B: Knowledge and Understanding of the text (/6)
Does the essay show detailed knowledge and perceptive understanding of the text?

Criterion C: Appreciation of the writer's choices (/6)
Does the student appreciate how the writer's choices of style, structure, technique and language shape the meaning of the text?

Criterion D: Organisation and Development of ideas (/5)
Does the student organise and develop ideas effectively, integrating examples (references and quotations) from the text smoothly into the essay?

Criterion E: Language (/5)
Is the language and grammar clear, careful, precise, accurate and appropriate?

1.4 The implications of Part One for your independent reading and study

Because you select your own topic for the Written Assignment, and prepare it in your own time, your independent reading and study habits play a particularly important part in your success in Part One, in the following ways.

(i) Although Part One is a *literary* study of texts (like the other Parts), it has a particular emphasis on the role that the cultures and contexts of the works play in the meaning and significance of the texts. The study process will thus need some special effort and attention on your part. (Chapter Two, Section 2.3.1 demonstrates an effective strategy). If you are attentive to cultural and contextual elements as you read independently, you are more likely to meet the requirements of the Reflective Statement (/3).

(ii) Part One texts also demand good independent reading and study habits, because your Written Assignment will be based on *your own* choice of text and topic, and *your own* angle on and interpretation of the work. 12-1500 words comprise a significant amount of knowledge and personal understanding of a topic, which you develop *in your own time*.

Close reading, note-making and note-taking skills are significant in this process. Chapter Two focuses on independent reading, modelling strategies for this, and specifically addressing the study of a text in translation. The more effective your notes, the better your understanding of the text will be. You will also have a greater range of ideas for a topic later, and be more able to develop your ideas well. Examiners have observed in the past that candidates' essays often show an insufficient understanding of the texts, and a lack of personal response. Good study habits will make a huge difference, and ensure that you avoid this weakness.

(iii) Your independent study (and that of your peers) impacts on the level of class discussion. This is relevant because there is one group activity (Stage One: The Interactive Oral) that leads to an assessed outcome (The Reflective Statement), carrying three marks. The quality of thoughts and ideas in the group plays an important role in your success in this task. Each of you contributes to this.

The implications of Part One for your *writing* are discussed in Section Three.

Reflection:

What responses do you have to any aspects of Part One, as above?

What do you feel your challenges might be in response to any of the above subsections?

1.5 What 'culture' and 'context' mean

The study of any text involves some cultural and contextual consideration. All writers reflect to some extent where they come from and what has shaped them. The model in Chapter Two (Section 1.4) emphasises how this plays a part in the 'meaning' of a text. In Part One, however, these elements are the *focus* of the Reflective Statement and Criterion A, as well as the underpinning of your literary topic in the Written Assignment.

The following definitions should provide a more concrete idea of what 'culture' and context' mean, and how to use these in the study of your texts.

'Context' embraces many possible aspects, only some of which may be relevant to any given text. It can for example relate to:

- *The personal context of the writer* – his or her background, times, values, and social and personal circumstances, and *how this impacts on the work*. (However, the writer's work is his or her 'construction' with its own meaning and purpose, and should not be read as biography, even though his/her biography may influence some aspects of the text).

- *The circumstances of production of the text* - the specific reason the writer may have embarked on the work, or the original public response to it, which can throw light on the writer's position in relation to his or her "time and place" and its values. Ibsen's *A Doll's House* is a good example of this, as shown in the sample Reflective Statement below).

- *The geography and history; the intellectual and artistic 'climate'; the sociology of the time the text was written.* For example, to understand Lorca (quoted in Chapter Two) you need to know about the geography and culture of Andalusia in Spain where he lived, as well as the political and religious spirit of the time of his writing (1930's Spain). However, writers may set their work in a different historical or cultural context from their own, in which case you might need to address several layers of context (the writer's own, and that of the time s/he uses as a setting).

- *The context of the reader.* The way you read the text is influenced by the context and culture you are in and have come from. This plays a part particularly in the Interactive Oral, where each member of the group will have a somewhat different background (see Chapter Two, Section 2.1).

'Culture' is a concept that has evolved in recent history and can mean a number of different things. For the purpose of Part One, it generally has to do with the language, history, customs or practices, values, beliefs, and laws of a particular group of people *in a particular time*. It is what gives a group its identity. This can be a group *within* a country or nation. The Andalusian culture is different from the Catalunian culture, but both are in Spain.

'Culture' tends to overlap with '**society'**, in that 'society' means the system of relationships or social interaction in a group of individuals.

Cultures generally evolve with time, and thus are entwined with 'context'. A text reflects a culture in a particular context or period of time. Lorca's (1930s) Andalusia is not exactly the same as the Andalusia of today, and in studying his work, you need to remember the difference.

1.6 How you use 'culture' and 'context' in your study for Part One

The rationale for the cultural focus
One reason for studying the texts of other cultures is to appreciate the *distinctiveness* of their perspectives, values and experiences, and their *difference* from our own. This is one of the aims of the programme, and forms part of what you do specifically for the Interactive Oral, as you will see later from the prompts you will be given for this Stage.

Although appreciating this cultural distinctiveness is interesting in itself, it is also a necessary foundation for appreciating the texts as literature. We need to understand the role that the culture and context plays in the meaning and significance of the texts. Without this understanding, we might for example inappropriately judge a character and his or her actions and values, or condemn a ritual that takes place in the text, using our own cultural perspective as a standard.

The interconnectedness of cultural/contextual/literary elements
Students have been concerned about how they balance 'culture' and 'literary' aspects in their study of the texts. In reality, both are entwined in the construction of any work. Literature arises from the context of a culture, and cultural aspects are part of what the author writes about. Both

need attention throughout the study process. The student questions on the Lorca passage in Chapter Two, Section 2.3(i), and the analysis of the kind of questions she asks, illustrate this interconnectedness.

The Interactive Oral and Reflective Statement focus on culture and context but also consider *literary* aspects (as you will see in the sample in Section 2.2.1 below). The Supervised Writing and the final Written Assignment, conversely, are on *literary* topics, but this may explicitly or implicitly embrace cultural aspects. This is also illustrated by the samples in Sections 2.3 and 3.8.

If your Assignment topic was the role of the Servant in Lorca's *Blood Wedding,* this would be a good *literary* topic, exploring how the servant's presence, actions and words create a particular impact in the work and contribute to its meaning. At the same time, you would need to understand something of the social status and nature of servants in that time and place (a *cultural and contextual* aspect) in order to write about the topic knowledgably and appropriately.

Reflection:

Which two or three statements on culture and context above make this aspect of Part One study clearest for you?

Is there any statement that remains unclear or leaves any part of the task unclear?

Identify a cultural or contextual aspect of a work you have read, not necessarily for Part One. What part does it play in the significance of the whole text?)

Section Two: The First Three Stages of Part One
The Interactive Oral; the Reflective Statement; the Supervised Writing

2.1 Stage One: The Interactive Oral

The Interactive Oral is a student-led discussion on each text, with a particular focus on *cultural and contextual* aspects of the text. The aim of it is to develop your understanding of these (often unfamiliar) aspects and what they contribute to the text and its meaning. This is what you write about in the Reflective Statement, completed soon after the Oral.

The Oral is an opportunity to explore and analyse the text more deeply, and, especially, to see it from other students' perspectives. It should allow each student to feel that s/he has a better grasp of the text. The Oral is set up strategically – including four prompts or items of discussion (listed below). The prompts help you to meet the requirements of Criterion A (which assesses the Reflective Statement). Other aspects may be included.

The rationale for an 'interactive' oral led by students is that you learn more by being responsible for it. The teacher facilitates the discussion and ensures that an appropriate focus is maintained. You, and the other students, need to prepare thoughtfully, to ensure a good result. Although you need to follow and engage in the discussion closely, you should also take notes. You will need to recall the discussion in order to write your Reflective Statement.

The discussion, following the prompts below, should relate to *specific aspects of the text* itself, not focus on cultural aspects for their own sake, however fascinating these might be. Exposition or explanation of unfamiliar cultural aspects should ideally have taken place before this, so that you can focus on discussion and interchange about the text during the oral. The discussion points to be addressed in the Interactive Oral are:

- The importance of context (time and place) to the work

- Social and cultural issues in the text that are easy to grasp and those that are difficult to understand, as viewed by different students

- Connections that individual students have found between their own lives and cultures, and issues in the text

- Literary techniques that are striking in the text

These points reflect that:

- Contextual and cultural issues are discussed but do not exclude 'literary' aspects of the text

- Each student's point of view is of importance (specifically on the second and third bulleted items), and contributes to the meaning of the text.

As Chapter Two (Section One) makes clear, readers read in different ways, according to their own experience and culture. The Interactive Oral provides a chance to hear and ponder these different perspectives, in order for you to arrive at a more considered personal viewpoint.

2.1.1 How the Interactive Oral is set up and conducted

The Interactive Oral may be set up in many different ways. Whichever way the teacher chooses to organise it, it should enable fruitful discussion of the points bulleted above, leading to Reflective Statements that show genuine development of understanding of the culture and context of the text.

The teacher may, for example, assign some students to make short presentations on aspects of the work that will stimulate relevant discussion. S/he may assign each of the four prompts to a different group, who discuss it and report back to the whole group to open up further discussion. Or the teacher may ask the students to set up the Oral and decide on how the prompts and other aspects are to be covered.

The Oral should last at least 30 minutes. More than one Oral on each text may be conducted, depending on the length and complexity of the work, the time span of your classes, or other factors, but you write a Reflective Statement on *each* Interactive Oral that takes place.

Each student is supposed to take a particular initiative in at least one of the Interactive Orals on the Part One texts. This underlines that the study is *collaborative* and that *you help each other* towards better understanding. The teacher, or even an appointed student, may ensure that you keep on track and address the prescribed points for discussion (listed above).

2.1.2 Ways to prepare individually for a good Interactive Oral

- Know your texts as well as possible – this will enhance discussion and help lead to a good Reflective Statement.

- Use the Reading Stages in Chapter Two (Stages One, Two, even Three) to generate good ideas and questions, and to identify problem areas to raise in discussion.

- Consult the Internet, teachers and members of your school and community to find answers to specifically cultural questions, or to suggest resources. There are an increasing number of scholarly books on works in translation, such as Cambridge University Press's *Landmarks of World Literature* series, and the *Cambridge Companions* to various authors and periods of literature (see the website). Translation editions of texts often have a *bibliography* indicating further good resources.

2.2 Stage Two: The Reflective Statement:

What it is

The Reflective Statement demonstrates that the Interactive Oral has taken place as prescribed, and that your *personal* understanding of cultural and contextual elements has *developed* as a result of the discussion that took place. Each of the four Stages of the Part One process is designed to develop this personal grasp, as the final Written Assignment is your own choice of topic.

The Statement should answer the question: *"How did the Interactive Oral **develop your understanding** of cultural and contextual aspects of the work?"* The key word here is "developed". Your grasp of any particular issue is not expected to be *definitive* or a matter of "getting it" completely. This is a relatively early stage in the whole process of grasping the text, but the Oral should open up your thinking and move it forward. You will be assessed (3 marks) on the extent to which you demonstrate this "development". Your work in the later Stages will take your thinking further.

How and when you do it

The Reflective Statement is not supposed to be just a description of what took place or what was said in the discussion, nor is it supposed to cover all (even many) of the aspects discussed. You should identify what particular part(s) of the discussion stimulated the development of your understanding, and what it is that you now understand differently or more fully than before. In your Reflective Statement, you trace this shift of understanding.

The Reflective Statement is usually written shortly after the Interactive Oral takes place. The discussion needs to be fresh in your mind, but you also need the time and space to process what you heard, and *think about* in what way that has developed your understanding of the text. Make sure that as you write, you are really answering that question.

There is no expected formal shape to your Statement. It is an informal reflection, not an essay. However, some organisation of your ideas is necessary to ensure that the Statement has focus and communicates effectively within the word limit of 300-400 words. Your teacher does not comment on it and it is not re-drafted. All your Reflective Statements are kept on file. When you complete your Written Assignment, the Reflective Statement relating to that text is sent away to the Examiner together with the Assignment.

If you have not practised such reflections on other works earlier in the course, it can be hard, the first time, to understand how you do it. A study of the following sample should help.

2.2.1 A sample Reflective Statement (*A Doll's House*)

How did the Interactive Oral develop your understanding of the cultural and contextual aspects of the work?

In our Interactive Oral, one group had researched the importance of time and place to *A Doll's House*. The focus of their presentation was the law in Norway at that time, how it affected women, and Ibsen's relation to it. One student explained how Ibsen been concerned about how women were judged by men's laws, and that exposing the injustice of this was his stimulus in writing the play.

This made me realise for the first time how the whole plot hinges on Nora's clash with the law because of her forgery for her loan, and the consequences of this in her relationship with Torvald. I also now saw how the men and women characters react differently to the forgery. Nora sees it in terms of love, as the 'right' thing because it saved her husband's life. Mrs Linde doesn't condemn her, even though she understands society, but urges her to tell Torvald in the interests of a good relationship. Krogstad and Torvald (Ibsen pointedly makes them both *lawyers*), see the forgery as criminal and discount the human motives. I began to see how Nora is really baffled by this, ethically, and that gave me more insight into why she had to leave, to decide for herself whether she or 'society' is right. Until now she has had no opportunity to make such judgements.

The other connected and really revealing discussion point was another student's account of a real-life situation behind the play – the young woman friend of Ibsen who had secretly borrowed money to pay for a vacation for her husband's health and like Nora, forged a note. In her case her husband committed her to a public asylum, away from her children. She begged to return and the husband agreed but imposed humiliating terms. I now appreciated how Ibsen had *reversed* this story's ending in the play, giving Nora the power of decision to leave the family, and making Torvald powerless to prevent her going. This gave me insight into what Ibsen was trying to do: his ending is about the human need in the *male* case for a relationship, in the *woman's* case for self-knowledge and an understanding of the world. I can now understand that these can only be achieved through reforming the law to give equal human rights, and through marital equality. I see how the play comes out of its social and legal context and the context of Ibsen's personal life.

(394 words)

2.2.2 Comments on the sample Reflective Statement (above): does it meet the terms of criterion A?

(How far does the student's Statement show development of understanding of cultural and contextual issues?)

This Reflective Statement meets the criterion descriptors. It clearly shows how, in two specific parts of the Interactive Oral, aspects of context – cultural and biographical – were presented that helped enlarge the student's understanding of significant elements of the text. The two items threw light upon the text for her and caused her to feel she had a clearer personal grasp of it.

The larger part of the Statement shows what she now sees that she did not see before. In this case it is the significance of the two characters' respective positions at the end of the play, which reverses a cultural norm of the time. The way the student's thinking has developed is demonstrated in this analysis, not merely stated.

2.2.3 Student comment on her Reflective Statement

The hardest things about doing the Reflective Statement were extracting what was specific and relevant from the discussion, keeping it sharply focused, and especially keeping to the word limit. I had no doubts about the two parts of the oral that really moved my thinking along, but the challenge was deciding how much to *state* what they said and how much detail to include about my thinking. As an examiner is to read the Reflective Statement I decided I had to be clear about *what* inspired me as well as *how* this enlarged my thinking.

It was quite hard to keep it focused because I had so *many* thoughts especially after the Oral when I was thinking about the play in the light of what we said. What I had not realised was that the 'development' of my thoughts would not so much happen *during* the Oral but mostly over the weekend, afterwards, when I was faced with the Reflective Statement and thinking in what way the discussion had shifted how I saw the play. I had to select and focus those thoughts, limiting myself basically to one main idea about each inspiring 'prompt'. To keep focused I kept going back to the questions: "*How* did this shift the way I see the play?" and "What do I now see about the culture and play that I didn't see before?" Although I wrote it quite quickly I had to edit it carefully to keep within the limit.

2.2.4 The significance of the student's comment on her work

This demonstrates well how the Reflective Statement is not a completely formless and free piece of personal writing but how time and thought need to be given to selection and development of material, a challenge in view of the word limit. It is a careful communication in respect of its ultimate audience or reader (examiner). Appropriately, she shapes her writing with that audience in mind.

It is also interesting in that it draws attention to the *process* of reflection that takes place *after* the Interactive Oral. She has to process what was said, to develop her *personal* understanding. The understanding does not necessarily come in a flash during the Interactive Oral discussion. The same items of presentation could have a different effect upon another student. This demonstrates that however appropriate and interesting the discussion points presented in the Oral are, it is what *you make of them* upon reflection that creates your success in this task.

It is helpful to see that this is one of *three different kinds of writing* you do in the Part One process, each representing a stage towards a polished essay. This one *articulates understanding* of an aspect of the text; Supervised Writing explores and develops a single topic, focusing on the idea; and the Written Assignment shapes the topic into a clearly presented, formal essay, with a focus on the structure of the writing.

2.3 Stage Three: the Supervised Writing

What it is and when you do it

The Supervised Writing is an in-class written response to one of several *literary* prompts or questions provided by your teacher on the text you have just studied (as demonstrated below). You do one piece of Supervised Writing on each text, and it takes place shortly after you write the Reflective Statement. It is assumed that there will be *some* link between the topic you write about in one of your pieces of Supervised Writing, and your eventual choice of topic.

The purpose of the writing

Although it takes place during one class period and is supervised by the teacher, it is not an exam or an exam essay, and is not marked or sent away. The Supervised Writing is intended as a way of *stimulating your independent thinking* on the kind of literary topic suitable for your final Written Assignment. It is not supposed to restrict you too narrowly. It should 'prompt' your ideas, rather than directing you to a particular answer to a question. You explore the prompt in your own way. You have the text to hand, but you do not use notes or the Internet.

The kind of prompts you will be given

You do not know ahead of time what prompts the teacher will give you, so your response is spontaneous. Suitable prompts might be:

"Discuss the use of one or more symbols or images in the work"

"What is the role and the effect of journeys and geography in this work?"

"What contribution does one of the minor characters play in this work?"

As stated above, some literary topics may, more or less explicitly, have cultural or contextual elements to them, such as the prompt about geography and journeys in the above list.

The benefits of the writing

The Supervised Writing has a number of benefits. Generating and exploring ideas in this way is an effective way to start the essay writing process, because you are freely focusing on exploring ideas rather than worrying about the structure of your writing. The fact that everyone in the class is writing together creates energy, and encourages you to see that you have something to write about. Students are often surprised that they actually know so much and have ideas. If you want this exercise to be really beneficial to you, it is good to re-read the text beforehand (if not too long) and read over your class discussion notes.

What happens to it afterwards

At the end of the class you hand the work in to the teacher, who keeps it on file. When the time comes for you to write the Assignment, the Supervised Writing will be handed back to you to remind you of the ideas you had, and help you select a topic.

2.3.1 A sample of Supervised Writing

Prompt: (*A Doll's House*)

How is Nora made interesting? Discuss some of the ways she is presented.

There are many ways in which Nora is interesting but I will focus on two that I find especially so. They are: how we see her in relation to other characters, and the way her 'secret life' works in the play.

Nora is on stage almost all the time, usually with one other person. This presents her in a series of different roles and relationships: as Torvald's wife, as Mrs Linde's friend and confidante, as Krogstad's client, as employer of but also 'child' to the nanny, and as old friend to Dr Rank. What I discover about these is that they all show her to some extent to disadvantage, or challenge her in some way, and so reveal her dynamically. She is patronised by Torvald, she is not an experienced working woman of the world like Mrs Linde, she is blackmailed by Krogstad, Dr Rank jeopardises their comfortable relationship with his love, and the nanny is a more competent and experienced housekeeper and child carer than she is, because of Nora's social position which in that society left her with little to do. Seeing the cumulative effect of this set of relationships helps one understand why Nora feels so strongly that she has to leave her home at the end of the play to discover who she is.

What is interesting is how Ibsen positions her in relation to these characters and how Nora negotiates the relationships, usually in such a way that her courage and dignity are shown. For example, once she knows that Rank loves her, she cannot ask him to help repay her debt, even though that seems like the only way out of her crisis. With the two other women (who have both experienced hardship and sacrifice), there are certain parallels that ultimately show Nora's particular courage. Mrs Linde in contrast to Nora 'comes home to roost' and forges a new relationship

---

with Krogstad to give her life meaning; Nora goes out into the wilderness without any idea of how she will survive but only knowing that she must do that. Anne-Marie has given up her own child for the security of work and home, first with Nora as a child, then with the Helmers and Nora's children, but Nora gives up the one thing that has defined her role – the children, and the comfort of her nanny and her protected home, to go into the unknown to become a better mother for her children. She faces the cold realism and menacing of Krogstad, which destroys all her material and mental comfort, even though it paves the way for greater fulfilment. And finally, when Torvald fails to meet her expectations of him, she makes the courageous decision to leave and educate herself.

An even more interesting aspect of Nora to me is her 'secret life', which works in different ways at specific moments in the play. Ibsen uses this to advantage, creating tension and dramatic irony but especially focusing attention on Nora. Until close to the end of the play her scenes with Torvald all have a duality because of the secrets she keeps from him, which we gradually become aware of. These help us appreciate her strength, in contrast to how Torvald perceives her. There is also a contrast between the 'honest' scenes – with Mrs Linde, Krogstad, Dr Rank and the nanny Anne-Marie – and the interspersed 'dual' scenes with Torvald. In the 'honest' scenes Nora has to confront something or work something out or expresses her real self, whereas with Torvald she has to act or pretend or conceal or conform to his image of her.

The difference between who Nora is, and what she has to pretend to be, creates strong dramatic irony and heightens our response to Torvald and Nora. When we first see Nora, alone, back from shopping, she secretly eats *two* macaroons, not just one, with obvious relish. This makes us aware of her real self, her capacity for pleasure and high spirits, and thus more sympathetic when we see Torvald's tyranny, trying to control her eating. Later, when we hear from her conversation with Mrs Linde how she has been repaying her debt over many years by working in secret, we admire her perseverance and determination, honouring her commitment by earning through tedious and low paid work. We see her sacrifice time with family and nice material things in order to work and save, and we witness her creativity in finding ways to prevent Torvald and others finding out what she is up to. Because we know all this, Torvald's words to her, and his attitude are cringe-makingly misplaced and obtuse.

The 'secret life' scene that has for me the strongest impact of all is the rehearsal scene for the tarantella dance. This is because it comes at the end of a series of scenes in which we see Nora becomingly increasingly tormented and desperate with the fear of Torvald reading Krogstad's letter and finding out about her forgery. She understands all the implications this will have, and it hardly seems possible for her to survive these, so our sympathy for her is especially acute at this moment. The last thing she needs is to dress up and perform to please Torvald, although this is a way to distract him. When we see Torvald so ignorant of what is going on with her and so oblivious to her emotional state, the contrast between her 'secret life' and his world could not be greater. This paves the way for her decisive action later in the evening.

2.3.2 Comment on the Supervised Writing sample
Note:

- How she keeps focused on the prompt in a *literary* way – exploring the 'how' or manner of character presentation and its effectiveness This is good practice for the Written Assignment

- How a good question (literary but not too prescriptive) stimulates *individual* thinking and interpretation - she is not constricted at all by the prompt

- How the depth and energy and concreteness of her writing about the text is enabled by knowing the text well (ie: this is her second or third reading)

- How many appropriate topics for a Written Assignment could come out of this writing (see the sample Written Assignment below to see what she chooses)

- How the lack of formal essay requirement at this stage promotes deeper exploration and development of ideas. She can concentrate on ideas and perceptions alone, as in 'pre-writing' for a Written Assignment, or 'free association' writing. However, the informal approach does not mean formlessness. Her thinking is clearly focused

- How much more work will be required (in the Written Assignment) to develop and shape one idea into a structured formal essay. The student's struggle with structure is made evident in her comments (below) on her Written Assignment

There is no word limit to this exercise. At 926 words, this quantity of writing was easily achievable in the 55 minute class time, especially as the student knew the play well. However, quantity is not required or *necessarily* advantageous. In this case, the advantage is that the quantity and quality of ideas she has developed take her a long way towards the Written Assignment. She is not thinking strategically about developing a topic for the eventual final essay, but simply allows the prompt to open up her thinking. This produces a range of options for her writing later.

2.3.3 Student comment on the Supervised Writing

I loved this question and had a lot to say about Nora but decided to restrict myself to two main ideas and to explore each more or less equally. I treated it a bit like an exam question and thought of two main lines of approach that I could use as starting points. We knew the play well and had done quite a few mini assignments on it, and the teacher also advised us to re-read it, so I was able to write from memory. I thought it might be distracting to start looking at the text. The Interactive Oral had really helped by going deeply into certain issues and highlighting a few of the technical literary aspects like the way the scenes are structured, which I was able to use in my own way. The tarantella dance had come up in one of the presentations as a late addition of Ibsen's, so that stuck in my mind.

The really liberating thing was knowing that the writing was not going to be examined or assessed, so I could be free to explore ideas in a flowing way and not think about paragraphs or structure or the construction of my sentences, but concentrate on responding to the prompt. I was quite surprised that while writing I found I came up with some new ideas, like the way Nora is shown to disadvantage by other characters but how this ultimately highlights her strength.

I think if I'd done this at home I would have been distracted, but everyone in the class got down to it so quickly, we all got swept up in it. There was a lot of energy in the classroom that inspired me to keep thinking and writing. There was the adrenalin rush and focus of an exam, but the freedom of knowing that the writing was for our own benefit later.

Activity on the Supervised Writing Sample:

What topic(s) could you envisage developing from the ideas in this writing? Try to come up with a specific title.

Section Three: Stage Four: The Final Written Assignment

3.1 What it is and when you do it

The final Written Assignment is a formal essay on a literary topic on your choice of **one** of the texts. You choose the topic after you have gone through the three Stages of study (as above) on each of your texts. It should relate in some way to your Supervised Writing on the chosen text. Exactly when you start the Assignment depends on your teacher or school and the programme timetable.

You teacher may give you a practice essay at the end of the study of each text, or may wait until all the texts are finished before inviting you to choose your text and topic for the final Assignment. A practice essay has advantages because you acquire experience with the formal essay structure. On the other hand this takes time, and your teacher may wish to finish all the work first and then devote the time to the 'real' essay. Each method has its advantages.

Although the IB deadline is in the second year, your teacher or school will probably set an internal deadline at a much earlier date, as stated above.

3.2 Choosing the text and topic; the link with the Supervised Writing

Your teacher will tell you when to start. At this point, he or she will give you back a copy of your Supervised Writing to help you with your choice of text (if you haven't decided that yet) and topic. Choose the text you enjoyed most and for which you can design the most interesting topic. If you choose poetry you can focus on one poem (if long and complex enough), or treat several poems of the same author, linked by the topic.

The choice of topic is very important. It should enable you to investigate an aspect of genuine interest to you, and to demonstrate your knowledge and understanding of the text. This is your opportunity to develop, at some length, your own interpretation of an aspect *of your choice*. Only in the Oral Presentation (in Part Four) do you have a similar opportunity.

The topic should be specific, concrete, play a significant role in the work, and be capable of development to the prescribed length (examples are given below). You do not have to write on exactly the same topic as the Supervised Writing prompt you chose, but it is intended that there be some link, even the germ or seed of a link. The link is not intended as a restriction, but to ensure:

- That there is personal continuity in *your* study of the texts, and that the Written Assignment is the genuine outcome of your involvement in the carefully designed process of study.

- That you have an appropriately *literary* focus for your final essay, as the Supervised Writing prompts should be literary, not cultural, and set you off in the right direction.

You can clearly see the link between the Supervised Writing sample (above) and the same student's Written Assignment (below). The student mentions the tarantella dance in the Supervised Writing, but it is not the focus of her response. There it is part of the broader 'presentation of Nora' topic, but in her Written Assignment she makes it the specific topic.

If your Supervised Writing on a particular text does not inspire you or seem helpful, but you think you want to select that text, it may be best to read the work again closely and think about topics. The likely result is that you find an interesting literary angle that does in fact have *some* relation to your Supervised Writing.

3.2.1 What is an appropriate 'literary' topic?
A literary topic is an aspect that helps reveal the purpose or point of the work, or contributes in a meaningful and effective way to the whole work. It is a choice on the writer's part to convey his or her purpose, and may be, for example, stylistic or thematic or linguistic.

The kind of topic may vary according to the genre. For example, a play will have specific dramatic elements that you may want to investigate, such as "The impact of entrances" or "The implications of laughter" in the play *Hedda Gabler.*

If your text is a novel, you may be interested in *thematic* elements such as "The use of religious references in *Chronicle of a Death Foretold*".

The sample plan in Chapter Three shows a *linguistic* topic: "An analysis of Torvald's language in his conversations with Nora, and its implications in Ibsen's *A Doll's House*". Poetry offers topics such as the use of imagery (for example sea or animal or flower imagery) but these can also apply to other genres. For ideas about the features and conventions of genres, which might help with literary topics, consult Chapter Four (Section Two) and Chapter Eight (Section Two).

Your teacher must approve your topic and ensure that it is appropriate and capable of meeting the criteria, before you begin the task. He or she will also read and comment on your first (and only) draft.

> **Reflection:**
>
> *What literary topic(s) can you think of from your reading of one or more of your texts?*

3.3 Understanding the formal essay requirements as you approach the draft

(i) The significance of the draft: the stage it represents
The draft is the preliminary written version of your final essay. It is the point at which you *organise and structure your ideas* into an argument or coherent line of thought. It should not be

the point at which you are still struggling to know and understand the text. Trying to grasp the text *and* simultaneously structure ideas is almost impossible, as Chapter Three emphasises. The two things are completely different stages of the process.

The teacher only provides feedback on this one draft. You therefore need to know how best to approach the writing of the draft. You want it to be as good as possible, so that it is easier for your teacher to make clear recommendations for improving it. The student's comments and reflection below on the process of drafting and re-writing her Final Assignment should provide an idea of the value of the draft and what it involves.

(ii) The formal essay requirements

As suggested in Chapter Three, this programme may be the first time that you are required to write a formal essay. It is a manageable task if you know what the elements of the essay are. Examiners have frequently commented that many students' Assignments for Part One lack understanding of these formal elements, so this chapter and Chapter Three specifically outline and model these aspects. Re-read the relevant section in Chapter Three when you reach the draft stage.

Examiners pay close attention to the writing aspect (Criterion D) because *you have had the time to work at it*, unlike in the exam Papers One and Two. The main elements you need to be clear about, which are all to do with 'organisation' and 'presentation' of ideas, are:

- The thesis
- Building an 'argument' or developing a clear line of thought
- What paragraphs are for and what they should contain
- How to use quotations and references to the text effectively
- What a conclusion should look like

Reflection:

How clear are you about each of these elements? Revise Chapter Three Section 3 if not.

3.4 The first step towards a draft: gather 'evidence' for your topic

Many past Assignments for Part One have lacked good 'evidence' or textual references in support of their argument. Before you even think about *writing* the essay, you should know the text well and gather good specific evidence for your topic (in that order). This serves several purposes:

- It will show you whether you have enough to say, and whether the material will yield interesting literary development; or whether the topic is too broad and needs more focus

- It serves as the *source* of your argument. As Chapter Three makes clear, your argument arises *out of* your analysis of your evidence. You should not have a pre-conceived idea for a thesis and then look for evidence to support it (though students often do this)

- The evidence (or selected examples) serves as the *support* for your argument and helps *carry the line of argument*. The references or quotations are *part* of the argument, not decoration. The *effective 'integration'* of your quotes or references into your argument has a particular mention in the assessment criteria, unique to this component (*Criterion D: Organisation and Development*)

You may want to re-read the text carefully through first, to be sure you understand it and have found the topic you want to develop, and *then* go back to collect the relevant evidence. Or, you might proceed directly to a close re-reading of the text, taking notes as you go. This should be at least your second reading and preferably your third (see Chapter Two, the Reading Stages).

You should only skim through the text picking out relevant quotes and sections if you already have a good grasp of the whole work. Whatever your topic, it will need to show how it relates to the whole text (Criterion B).

Record page references (citations)

It is very important to note down *page references* as you collect your evidence, because you should cite your references in your essay. A reader or examiner will want to see the sources for your ideas. As the Assignment is produced in your own time, there is an expectation that it will be carefully presented in formal respects such as citations and bibliography (even if the 'bibliography' is one text).

The use of secondary sources

A good Assignment will have a close focus *on the text,* and show your detailed personal knowledge and understanding of it. This should be your main concern and the focus of your efforts. The primary text is generally sufficient: the Assignment is not a research paper. However, you may need to consult secondary sources on some cultural and/or contextual issues that impact on your topic (see Section 1.6 above). It is legitimate to use them in this way, so long as you reference them.

You should not be using secondary sources for *literary* ideas about the text or using them as if they were your own. This would be plagiarism and would jeopardise your Diploma. If you *do* make reference to an idea, make sure you position yourself in relation to the idea, for example partly agreeing, or disagreeing with it and making your own standpoint clear. Any such references should be cited in your footnotes and bibliography.

3.5 The benefit of the 'grid of evidence'

One way to organise your evidence is in a grid such as 3.6 below. This helps you:

- Base your essay clearly *on the text* (column 1); ensure good and *relevant* evidence

- See the evidence visually *at a glance* and ensure it all relates to the topic (for example, all the references to party/dance/costume in column 1 below); ensure there is enough evidence

- Reflect on your evidence as you collect it (column 2) moving you towards analysis

- Think about *patterns* in this evidence and its significance to the whole (column 3))

- Start *linking ideas* and generating possibilities for organising the essay (column 3)

How to use it

The following table only shows the first part of the whole grid but demonstrates its use and purpose. As you re-read the text with a focus on your topic, you enter relevant references in column 1, generating comments on each piece of evidence in turn in column 2. Put key words in the evidence in bold (as demonstrated) to help you see relevance and patterns more clearly. If you begin to get ideas about how to group or *organise* your evidence as you go along, you can enter these tentatively in column 3. Number ideas to help you keep track of possible paragraph topics, and to make it easier to group or organise these topics.

When you have gathered all your evidence:

- Read down column 1 (the quotes) as one sequence. Patterns should emerge
- Next, read down column 2 as a sequence of thoughts. You may want to add to the comments
- Return to column 3. The patterns and points of emphasis will now be clearer, and you can proceed to develop these topics as paragraphs, moving towards an argument (as modelled in Chapter Three, Section 3.8)

How this process helps you meet the criteria

The whole process should help you avoid the typical weaknesses in Criteria B, C and D (Knowledge and Understanding; the Writer's Choices; Organisation and Development of the essay, and the integration of well-chosen examples or quotes). These three criteria represent *two thirds* of the mark on this Assignment.

3.6 A sample grid of evidence (for "The meaning of the tarantella dance")

1. Quote/reference	2. Comment/development of idea based on the quote in its context	3. Plan. Ideas (numbered) for organising evidence into paragraphs
1. Act 1 p 15: Nora to Mrs Linde: (about telling Torvald about the loan) *"When he's lost interest in watching me **dance** or get **dressed up**"*	Nora *knows* the shallowness of Torvald's love for her – (objectification) but doesn't see the implications. This is how Torvald sees her in the tarantella.	1. Torvald's **"Objectification"** of **Nora.** Her awareness and 'use' of it, but unsustainable.
2. P 30 Nora (mentally) to Torvald *"I'll do anything you want... **dance for you**"*	Nora will use his image of her to distract him about Krogstad. Her 'game' here contrasts with her strength about the loan.	Connect with (1) Nora acts as Torvald's plaything or object, but is 'using' this for her own benefit.
3. P 31: Nora to Torvald *"I'm so looking forward to the **fancy-dress ball** at the Stenborgs"*	First mention of the party, early in the play. Nora is using the idea to divert Torvald about Krogstad's visit and her lie.	2. The dance is strategic in the **structure** of the play. References to it throughout, build the tension and focus attention on the dance
4. Act 2. P 40 (while Mrs Linde is mending the costume for the dance) Torvald: *"wasn't that a good idea of mine."* (to select the **costume**) Nora. *"Wasn't it also nice of me to let you have your way"*	Really interesting and surprising challenge of Nora's, claiming equal credit. The role of pleasing can't be kept up all the time. Her independent spirit will out.	3. Signs of **Nora's assertiveness and independence** Connect/contrast with (1)
5. P 41 Nora preparing to persuade Torvald to let Krogstad keep job: *"I'll dance a moonlight **dance** for you"*	She is playing her usual game but the issue about Krogstad shows up her inability to accept Torvald's "petty" attitude and how Torvald puts his pride before love for her Foreshadows breakdown	Connect with (1)
6. P 46 Rank sees Nora as *"rascal"* Nora says she's *"full of mischief"* today	Rank enjoys her like this. Nora can be herself with him. It shows he 'knows' and likes her as she is. Contrast with Torvald who tried to make her conform to his image.	4. **Nora's real self.** Connect with (3); contrast (1). It goes against the grain to be entirely submissive. Moments of rebellion and assertiveness foreshadow decision to leave.
7. P 47: Nora to Rank *"You can pretend I'm doing (the **dance**) just for you"*	This is ambivalent. Is she preparing to ask him for the favour/money; or is she being nice out of pity him for his condition? (Or both?) I go for the second. They are open with each other.	5. **Nora's bond with Rank.** His acknowledgement of her real self. Her comfort with him. Connect w/ (4). Contrasts with Torvald.

Reflection on the grid of evidence:

How helpful does this process look to you? In what ways might you use it to improve your practice?

3.7 From evidence to paragraphs to argument: the big leap

The next step is the one that all writers find challenging, as it calls for *synthesising* your ideas, or building them into a connected sequence, with an argument or line of thought highlighted by your topic sentence in each paragraph. Refer to the model in Chapter Three (3.8).

Embedding your quotes or references

You will see from the sample Assignment below that all the quotes are 'embedded' in the student's own sentences as part of her argument. You are assessed on your skill in integrating quotes or references in Criterion D, so it is important to ensure you can do this skilfully. Chapter

Three, Section 3.11 provides extensive discussion of this skill and illustrates different ways of quoting successfully.

The thesis may need further focusing or sharpening as you progress, as the student shows in her comments (below) on the difference between her first and second versions. A good formal essay depends upon a clear thesis and a firm line of argument. Don't worry if you don't begin with one that completely satisfies you. The experience of writing the first draft should help you get it right.

Now read the following and assess it to see if it seems to meet the expectations of a formal essay, and the criteria for the Written Assignment.

3.8 A sample Written Assignment

The meaning of the tarantella dance and costume in Ibsen's *A Doll's House*

The Stenborgs' party, at which Nora dances the tarantella, takes place on the final night of the play's time, the last of three Christmas evenings for the Helmers. The party has been much anticipated and prepared for, in reference to Nora's costume and rehearsal for the dance. However, it is not the party that Ibsen makes his dramatic focus, but the rehearsal the night before, and the aftermath of the party, both of which put the spotlight on Nora and her state of mind. Both the dance and the costume have a powerful impact in these scenes, because of their visual incongruousness in their contexts. Even greater significance comes from the ironic layers of meaning these contain; the way they express the characters' different attitudes; and how they catalyse momentous change.

The dance carries two contrasting associations, contributing to the layers of its meaning. Each of these contains a striking irony. The tarantella that Nora learned in Capri the year she spent there with Torvald, which he "taught" her (p 59) and for which he had a costume made for her, was a popular southern Italian folk dance with a fast and lively beat. This was a suitable party piece for Christmas, but even more, it was a spectacle to satisfy Torvald's fantasy of Nora as a "Neopolitan fisher lass" (p 37), and to conjure romantic memories of that exotic year of their marriage. Torvald gives the impression he controls Nora's image, by commissioning the dress, teaching Nora the dance, choosing this costume for the party, deciding that Nora "should" do the dance (p 37), and rehearsing her. But this control is undercut for us by the dramatic irony of the reader knowing that the Capri holiday was only possible through Nora's secret loan, and that she "lets" him select her costume (p 40) for her own purposes, as she tries to avoid Krogstad's blackmail.

The second association of the tarantella is the wild traditional dance pre-dating the folk dance. This was believed to help cure people of the deadly poison of the tarantula spider's bite, and simultaneously to enable the dancer to enact the pain of the symptoms. The increasing wildness of Nora's rehearsal dance (p 59) and her manic behaviour (pp 58-9) is more suggestive of this version than the folk dance that she was supposed to perform. Torvald exclaims that she is "dancing as though (her) life depended on it" (p 59). Even her stunning performance at the party, described by Torvald, was "rather realistic", and as he remarks, even after the party she still seems to have the tarantella "in (her) blood" (p 70). The dramatic irony is that *we* know Nora's 'secret' story, how her confrontations with the moneylender Krogstad have driven her to suicidal thoughts. Her wildness is understandable to *us* as an expression of her mental torment, but Torvald is entirely unaware of this, and the fact he is the cause of it.

This irony deepens when we look more closely at this mental torment, as it could contain two conflicting elements: her love and fears for her family, and her need to express herself freely. Nora's torment seems caused by her love for Torvald and her certainty that "he would never hesitate for a moment to sacrifice his life for my sake" (p 48). She will prevent this "sacrifice" by accepting responsibility for her own crime through suicide. She is also tormented by Torvald's lurid vision of how "lies and deceit", especially those of the mother, spread "disease and infection to every part" of a household (p 33). Her love for her children cannot permit this. Our sense of the torment in her mind makes the spectacle of her dance not just shocking and alarming, because it is uncharacteristic, but poignant and isolating, a dance of death. This is made clear when she reveals her calculation after the rehearsal: " Thirty one hours to live" (p 61). The party will be her final hour. The irony is that she is preparing to sacrifice herself for the man who will not sacrifice himself for her, and who does not know her worth or permit her to be what she is.

Alongside this love and generosity of spirit, however, there could also be an unconscious need to break from her birdcage, to give wing to who she really is. She does not realise this, but there have been many signs throughout the play that she is not comfortable in Torvald's role for her as his "own little singing bird" (p 60) or doll. She has her own mind. This has emerged in her conversations with Torvald, Mrs Linde, and Rank. Early in the play she seems at least subconsciously aware of the shallow nature of Torvald's 'love' but does not register its implications. She airily tells Mrs Linde how she might tell Torvald about her loan: "when he's lost interest in watching me dance, or get dressed up, or recite" (p 15).

It is through the crucial scene with Rank right before the rehearsal that the unsuitability of Nora's relationship with Torvald becomes most clear. The scene is critical for both Rank and Nora, opening up a bond of understanding, which contrasts with Torvald's unawareness of who she is. Rank now knows how near death he is; and Nora has just failed to prevent Torvald sending Krogstad the fatal letter that will cause him to reveal her crime. Because of their desperate respective circumstances, they take risks in the conversation, becoming more open and intimate, making playful and sexual innuendos and leading Nora, in sympathy for Rank's condition, to tell him that he can pretend she is doing the dance at the party "just" for him (p 47). After he confesses his love for her, she confesses that she enjoys 'being' with him more than with Torvald. The implication is that with Rank she can be herself –spontaneous, a 'rascal', as he calls her (p 46), a lover of good food, rather than conforming to a fantasy or being a "doll". Watching her dance, he seems sympathetically aware that this is more than just rehearsal, even if he does not know the cause.

In contrast with Rank and Nora, whom circumstances have changed, as reflected in the dance episode, Torvald is unchanged at this moment in the play. This creates the inevitability of a breaking point. Nora has always been for him an object of fantasy, stimulating his desire and giving the satisfaction of possession: "All this loveliness that's mine and mine alone" (p 69). He revels in what he perceives as her helplessness, her need to be "taught" the dance, which bolsters his masculinity. His language, as he enthuses afterwards about her stunning performance at the party, illustrates his unchanged attitude: "My lovely little Capri girl –my capricious little Capri girl" (p 67). Her wild dance (its implications lost on him) makes her "even more desirable" to him: "As I watched you darting and swaying in the tarantella, my blood was on fire" (p 70). Knowing what we know, the dramatic irony creates almost tangible discomfort. Nora and Torvald are poles apart at this moment.

The spectacle of Nora in her fisher-girl costume after the party presents further dramatic irony: the symbolism of the dress in comparison with her nightmarish mental reality is striking. She knows that her hour has come: she cannot delay Torvald's opening of the letter. For his part, Torvald is clearly inebriated and wanting to go to bed with her, full of fantasies about her as a young virgin bride and the chance to be "quite alone with (her) young and trembling loveliness" (p 70). Incongruously in her fancy dress, she says what she imagines to be her last goodbye to her home, attempts to escape to suicide, faces Torvald's fury at the contents of the letter, experiences shattering disillusion with him, and finally, suffers his patronising response when he is 'saved' by the returned IOU. Only at the end of this scene in which Nora sees Torvald and their relationship clearly for the first time, does she go to take off "this fancy dress" and reappear in her everyday dress, intending to leave, and stating with double meaning that she has "changed" (p 79).

In conclusion we can see that everything in the play, and much of the back story of the play (the Capri holiday), has led to this moment. We see the dance with dramatic irony through the lenses of all the characters' narratives, their attitudes and differences. For Nora and Torvald, the dance is the moment between illusion and understanding, leading to radical change. In itself it does not change anything, but it illustrates the gap in their understanding of themselves and each other and how that is unsustainable. Torvald has to shift his role from imagined 'teacher' and controller of Nora, to listener and learner, and Nora has to "educate" herself for an understanding of herself and the world (p 81), and this can only be done "in full freedom on both sides" (p 85).

Word count 1497.

Bibliography

Henrick Ibsen: *Four Major Plays*. Oxford University Press 1998

Reflection on the sample:

Using the criteria, how would you assess this essay?

What do you feel are the strengths and weaknesses of this essay?

What might you learn from it that you could apply to your own work?

3.9 The student's progress from first to second draft: introduction

Having seen the finished product, it is helpful to look at some aspects of the process that led the student to this point. Compare her first draft and her final introduction and thesis.

First draft of the introduction

The tarantella dance falls two-thirds of the way through *A Doll's House* at a moment of crisis, although on the surface there appears to be harmony –three friends preparing for a Christmas party. The dance and dress create a strong dramatic impact, partly to do with their incongruousness in their contexts. The wild rehearsal at the end of Act Two seems bizarrely at odds with the usual formality of this group of people and their behaviour. The fisher girl costume Nora is wearing after the party, in Act Three, is out of tune with the seriousness of her dialogue with Torvald about the contents of the letter. An even greater impact is created through dramatic irony, the gap between what we know of the different characters' state of mind, and what they know of each other's states in those two moments. It is this gap that highlights the inevitability of change specifically in Torvald and Nora's relationship

Final version

The Stenborgs' party, at which Nora dances the tarantella, takes place on the final night of the play's time, the last of three Christmas evenings for the Helmers. The party has been much anticipated and prepared for, in reference to Nora's costume and rehearsal for the dance. However, it is not the party that Ibsen makes his dramatic focus, but the rehearsal the night before, and the aftermath of the party, both of which put the spotlight on Nora and her state of mind. Both the dance and the costume have a powerful impact in these scenes, because of their visual incongruousness in their contexts. Even greater significance comes from the ironic layers of meaning these contain; the way they express the characters' different attitudes; and how they catalyze momentous change.

Reflection:

How might you describe the difference between these two?

Student comment on how she improved the first introduction and thesis

I could see that my first introduction was not clearly focused. I knew what I wanted to say about this topic, but had too many ideas that were only loosely connected with each other. There was no clear thesis. What helped me improve it was thinking how someone else would read it. How could I help them see, from sentence to sentence, why this topic was significant? I put this first draft out of sight, imagined an outside reader, and tried to explain as clearly as I could:

Why is this moment so striking? Why is it significant? What does Ibsen tell us through this moment? What three things does it do, in my view?
By focusing on the logic of my thought, sentence-by-sentence, I was able to completely re-do it. This logic was:

The location and occasion of the party and its timing in the play (identification of moment to be considered)
Everything in the play leads up to the party (its significance in the whole structure – it's worth investigating)
The focus for Ibsen –rehearsal for dance, and aftermath of party (writer's choice is significant)
The dramatic impact of this on us (the choice has impact)
The 3 things the choice accomplishes (why this moment is so rich – my interpretation)

Because I had gone through the whole process of the first draft and trying to shape my thoughts coherently, I had grasped my material better and could more easily pare it down to what was essential.

3.10 Student reflection on the Written Assignment process: three unexpected challenges

Reflection: Three things that stand out to me about the process that I had not anticipated.

1. I thought I knew the play quite well beforehand and was very surprised how much my close reading with a focus on the topic (for the grid of evidence) enlarged my understanding further. It made me think that I hadn't known it *that* well. As I read the text through with the dance in mind I noted down so many bits of dialogue that threw light on my topic in some way. They sprang up on almost every page. The whole play came together much more – I understood the text better *because* of the focus, and knowing the whole play better made the importance of my topic clearer, so my ideas came quite easily *(The benefit of 'Reading Stage Three'-Chapter 2)).*

2. This connects with the first point. I thought that because I knew my material and was sure of my ideas, I would be able to write the essay quite easily, but almost the opposite was true. I could *express* the ideas, but *linking* them in a logical sequence was hard. There was so much relating to my topic that I couldn't easily see how to organise the

ideas into paragraphs and include everything I thought most important. My best ideas seemed like separate statements, and I couldn't always see how they could be grouped. *(The challenge of 'organisation' – Chapter 3)*

My teacher's major feedback, along with a comment on the lack of clear thesis, was that I hadn't made it clear what the dance was and how it connected with the play. Also, I hadn't been clear enough about the writer's choices. This made a big difference to the way I re-wrote the final essay.

3. My third surprise was what happened between the first and final draft –the way I basically *re-wrote* the essay making it much clearer to follow, for myself and a reader. My first draft was structured round the three main characters in the scene, and the dance from their point of view in turn. I had given each of the characters one or two paragraphs developing this idea. At the time this seemed quite a good way to organize and structure it, but looking back, each paragraph had a focus although they weren't clearly linked.

Following my teacher's feedback, I wrote extra paragraphs on the dance, and emphasised the dramatic irony more.
I re-wrote the introduction with a focus on the party – this is what links each sentence consecutively.
To get the whole thing coherent, I had to put the first draft aside to get away from how I had originally done it, and focus on *coherent development.* In re-writing, I made myself answer the question as I came to each paragraph: *How does this link with what I have just said? How does this develop my thesis statement? What is the point I am really trying to make in this paragraph? Am I illustrating writer's choices?*

It's hard to describe, but I could only see what I really wanted to say because of having gone through the process of the first draft. It wasn't the actual re-writing that took time, but the re-thinking of the logic. *(The challenge of structure that shows a clear line of thought – Chapter 3, 3.8.)*

3.11 The sample Written Assignment in relation to the criteria

(A) The marks for the Reflective Statement (Section 2.2.1-4 above) would be added to the marks for B - E

(B) The student shows very good and detailed knowledge and understanding of the text as a whole through her treatment of her specific topic. The discussion shows independent insight *(note how the grid of evidence helped to meet this criterion at a high level).*

(C) There is clear appreciation of the writer's choices: of strategic positioning of the dance in the structure of the play; of ways in which layers of 'meaning' are created around the dance; of the dance as symbol; of the use of dramatic irony; and (through the use of quotations) of the impact of language, especially Torvald's. The student also shows clear awareness of the visual and theatrical impact of costume and movement.

(D) The response is well organised and structured with frequent and well-integrated examples that support the main points. Introduction and conclusion link with each other, demonstrating that the essay has investigated what it set out to do. Each paragraph has a clear focus and develops the line of thought. Though some paragraphs are long, each shows unity of thought.

(E) The language and style is very clear and accurate. The register and style are effective and appropriate to the task.

3.12 Sending off the Written Assignment: the final stage

Before you submit your final version of your essay:

- Make sure that you have a clear straightforward **title** that provides a concrete idea of what the essay is about, as the above sample does. Resist playful or abstract titles, unless you provide a clear subtitle

- Proofread the essay carefully for **grammatical accuracy, punctuation and formatting**, including spacing and margins. When examiners see that you have taken care, they tend to be more positively disposed towards your work

- Include a **bibliography** even if it is only the edition of the text you used. Examiners need to know this: there are various translations and different pagination

- **Reference** any ideas you have included from secondary sources, to avoid any risk of plagiarism.

The last stage of the process is filling in an official IB cover sheet for this task, given to you by your teacher, who supervises the filling out of this form. You attach to it the Reflective Statement *on the same text*. If you have did more than one Reflective Statement on that text you should attach the one that most clearly relates to it.

Chapter Reflection:

What points do you especially want to remember from this chapter?

Chapter Overview

Part Two is the other half of the oral component in this programme. The marks for the Commentary are combined with those of the Oral Presentation in Part Four to form 30% of your final grade. As oral 'exams', they are very different, and complement each other. The Presentation is broad ranging and creative in topics and approach; Part Two has a traditionally *literary*, close and detailed focus.

- The Commentary is done individually with your teacher, as a formal exam, and is recorded. The Oral Presentation is designed for an *audience*, with a focus on presentational strategies.

- For the Commentary *the teacher* selects the passage for you to comment on, from the works you have studied for Part Two, and you have twenty minutes to prepare it. For the Oral Presentation *you* choose your text and topic for the Presentation, and prepare it in your own time.

- Part Two texts are selected from the *Prescribed List of Authors* and represent classic or well-established authors. Part Four texts are 'freely' chosen by the teacher.

- In Part Two, Higher and Standard Levels are clearly differentiated in the length and the demands of the exam. Higher Level students have *two* tasks (Commentary and Discussion), which take twenty minutes in total. Standard Level students have one ten minute Commentary.

  There is also a difference in the number of texts studied. Higher Level candidates study three texts; Standard Level candidates study two texts. For the Oral Presentation the number of texts and the task are identical at both Levels.

It is important, for two reasons, to remember that the two oral marks are *combined*. On the one hand, it helps put the Oral Commentary in perspective, because students often see this as an intimidating task that looms overly large as they approach it. In reality, it carries equal weight (15%) with the Presentation. On the other hand, you should aim to do as well as you can, because together the oral marks form the biggest slice of your marks in the programme (30%).

Part Two has a number of features and challenges for which other Parts of the programme specifically help. You should consult the relevant chapters to benefit from this:

- The Part Two focus on **close reading, literary analysis** and interpretation is similar to Paper One (Literary Commentary/ Analysis), as discussed in Chapter Four.

- Each text in Part Two is a **different genre**. Chapter Eight (Paper Two) provides suggestions about close reading and analysis for different genres (Section Two). Chapter Four also gives advice in close reading of different genres.

- Part Two Higher Level criteria stress **individual interpretation of texts.** Chapter Two discusses ways to build this skill.

- For Part Two at both Levels you will need to have substantial texts in your heads and at your fingertips. **Revision techniques** outlined in Chapter Eight (Section Three) are indispensable for being exam ready.

- Chapter Five (Oral Presentation) provides reminders of ways to **develop your oral skills** and confidence.

This chapter focuses on:

- What the Oral Commentary is; how it is conducted; and how it is assessed
- Suggestions as to how to prepare effectively for the Oral Commentary and Discussion
- Samples of oral work

Section One – The Oral Commentary: tasks and assessment

1.1 The timing of the Oral Commentary

The oral exams have to be completed and the samples sent to a Moderator a month or so before your final exams in the second year, but they usually take place much earlier than this. In some schools they are done towards the end of the first year, but more typically in the middle of the second year.

Individually conducted orals take considerable teacher time and planning, and also require concentrated revision for the students, so it is normally considered best to hold the exams before the rush of other exams and commitments. The Commentary is usually, though not always, done after the Oral Presentation.

1.2 The recording and assessment process of the Oral Commentary

Each oral is recorded digitally and assessed by the teacher. All the candidates' combined marks for the Oral Commentary and the Oral Presentation are sent to the IB, who then requests a *representative number* of Commentary samples. The school sends these to an external Moderator, who ensures that the marking criteria are being interpreted accurately. As with the Oral Presentation, your teacher will want to mark you fairly, as it is his or her accuracy that is being judged by the Moderator.

1.3 Standard Level: task and challenges in the Oral Commentary

Although Standard and Higher Level have the same amount of time and the same exam process for the Commentary, there is a difference in the kind of texts studied, and in the marking criteria, so each Level is discussed separately in these regards.

The texts
You study *two* texts in detail, from different genres and authors, from the IB *Prescribed List of Authors*.

The exam
You have a ten-minute Individual Oral Commentary based on a 20-30 line passage or poem from one of the two texts you have studied. You do not know in advance which text or passage you will be given. You are given twenty minutes to prepare the commentary, using the given passage only (no text). You then present your oral to the teacher for around eight minutes, followed by two minutes of questioning from the teacher. This is recorded.

The challenges the task presents

- To **know your two texts** well, to be able to comment on any passage from either, in detail
- To **identify significant literary aspects** and discuss their role and effectiveness
- To **select and structure your comments** into an eight minute framework
- To **speak lucidly and effectively** about the passage for eight minutes

Ways to meet these challenges are discussed below and in Section Two.

1.4 Standard Level Assessment Criteria: how to meet them

Note that Criteria A and B (10+10) carry twice the marks of Criteria C and D (5+5). This reflects the substantial study process involved in A and B, and *is a reminder to you to invest in this process* by way of the bulleted suggestions offered. Your study and revision strategies will be very similar to other Parts of the programme, so relevant references are provided.

Criterion A (/10) Knowledge and Understanding of the extract
How far does the candidate show good knowledge and understanding of the extract, and can interpret it with detailed reference to the passage?

Although your concentration is on the passage or poem itself, some brief 'placing' of the extract in the wider context of the whole work is necessary to focus it and to indicate its particular significance. The sounder your knowledge and understanding of the whole work, the better you will deal with the specifics of a passage.

- For a clear definition of 'knowing' and 'understanding', refer to Section 1.4 of Chapter Eight
- To revise effectively in order to remember whole texts, see Chapter Eight, Section Three
- For ideas about what to look for in genres, and for literary features, see Chapters Four and Eight

'**Placing**' in context works differently for poems, which are self-contained wholes, compared with prose passages, which are part of a larger whole. If poetry is one of your 'texts', you should have a sense for how the different poems of the author relate to one another rather than seeing them as isolated poems.

- See Section Two below, the student's comments on how he prepared for poetry.

'**Interpretation**' is a key word in Criterion A. It means describing what thoughts and feelings you think the writer is communicating, based on your close analysis of the language.

- This is where your 'ownership' of the 'meaning' of the text comes into play, through the study processes described in Chapter Two (Reading stages One and Two). Chapter Four Section 2.7.4 dealing with tone, also helps you understand this
- Look at the sample on poetry in Section Two below, and the evaluation comments following it, to see 'interpretation' in action.

Criterion B (/10) Appreciation of the writer's choices
How far does the candidate appreciate the literary choices of the writer (language and style) and how these shape meaning?

This is the specifically literary aspect of Part Two, and involves both your knowledge of what to respond to in texts, and your responsiveness to the way these stylistic choices work – to the impact or effect they have. Your work on Paper One (Guided Literary Analysis) closely correlates with this aspect of Part Two.

- Revise the generic and the genre-specific sections of Chapter Four (Paper One) for knowledge of what features to look for and for discussion of how language 'shapes' meaning.
- Consult Chapter Eight Section Two for how to read drama and the novel, specifically.
- The kind of notes you have taken throughout your study of the works (Chapter Two) and your part in class discussion will also contribute to your performance here.

Criterion C (/5) Organisation and Presentation
Does the candidate plan and structure the commentary clearly and keep it focused through the eight minutes?

The unique challenge of the eight minute presentation and how to prepare for it
Although this criterion carries fewer marks than Criteria A and B, it nonetheless involves a significant challenge in selecting, organising and synthesising your material, and in presenting this in this tight time frame of eight minutes. It is also in this eight minute frame that you meet Criteria A and B, so your selection and structuring affects 25 marks.

The focus is on the content rather than the style of your presentation
Unlike in the Oral Presentation, you are not marked on your presentational strategies. The focus is on your content. You will speak well if you are confident in your knowledge, as above. If you play an active part in class discussion through the course, this will stand you in good stead when you come to express your ideas.

Find an overview or overarching focus for your passage/poem
As with your essays (Chapters Four, Six and Eight), you should create an overview or thesis for the beginning of your presentation, based on your close reading during the preparation time as well as your previous study. The overview will show the teacher/examiner that you have grasped the whole passage coherently, and will give you a guiding principle for the rest of your commentary. Few students do this in their commentaries, but it is what makes a good one. Look at the poetry sample in Section Two below for a good example of this.

How to structure your content

You need to select what you consider most important, which will be a combination of interesting details and broader issues of theme, and find a logical way to structure them. As with Paper One (Chapter Four) the passage itself may well suggest the best way to do this. Many students favour a 'linear' approach, but a line-by-line commentary is likely to take too much time and locks you into an *unselective* approach to detail. Either find a structure within the passage (perhaps it falls into two or three sections or aspects), or create your own structure from the evidence you assemble.

- Look at the sample poem commentary and student plan in Section Two below for a way to select and plan.
- This is the only time in the programme that you perform this particular (eight minute) task, and you should practise it, preferably with a friend. This is easy to do and makes a big difference to your confidence and competence, as follows:

   Each selects a passage for the other, and creates guiding questions (following the samples in 1.7 below). Exchange your passages, and each work on your own for twenty minutes. Each presents to the other on his/her passage in turn, with questions for two minutes. Each provides feedback on the other afterwards, using the criteria. Having a sympathetic audience or listener in this way will help you articulate your ideas, and keep to the time. You will learn a lot from the experience.

Criterion D: Language (/5)
Is the candidate's language clear, appropriate and accurate in grammar, sentence construction, style and register? Is the literary terminology appropriate?

The language requirements are the same across all your assessed tasks.
- Chapter Five (Oral Presentation) gives extensive advice on developing oral skills and knowledge of terminology.

Reflection for Standard Level:

What particular implications for your study and revision do the above criteria and suggestions contain? What would you highlight?

1.5 Higher Level: tasks and challenges

The texts

- ***For the Oral Commentary*** you study 15-20 poems by *one* author from the *Prescribed List of Authors.* Your exam will be on *one* of these poems but you will not know which, before the exam.

- ***For the Discussion*** you study two further works, each of different genre (fiction, non-fiction or drama, also from the *Prescribed List*).

The exam (in two halves)

The completely different nature of the two halves of the exam is valuable, as it assesses different skills. It also provides fairer coverage of the works studied, as you are assessed on two out of your three texts, and your study of these is thus rewarded. It makes sense for a poem to be approached through detailed analysis, and a long text through broader consideration of various significant aspects.

- You have a **ten minute individual oral commentary** based on one of the poems, which should be 20-30 lines long. It may be shorter, if rich and complex, as illustrated by the sample oral on a sonnet, in Section Two. You have twenty minutes to prepare the poem you are given. You then present your detailed commentary for eight minutes, followed by two minutes of questions from your teacher.

- After the Commentary you have a **ten minute Discussion** with your teacher on one of the other texts. You will not know which text until that moment. Details of this follow below.

The challenges
- To **know (and remember) your texts well**, as you will not know which you will be examined on
- To be **comfortable discussing a poem**

- To **select and structure your material** on the poem to fit effectively into eight minutes
- To **speak in a concise, focused and effective way** during the whole oral
- To **answer the Discussion questions with focus, relevance and independence**, spontaneously

1.6 Higher Level Assessment Criteria: how to meet them

The unique aspects of the task

You will see that there are *seven* criteria, together covering your two tasks, which is more than in any other assessed component. They are each worth five marks. (This compares with the differentiation in marks at Standard Level).

Each of your two tasks (the poem Commentary and the Discussion questions) calls for competencies that are not specifically assessed elsewhere. This is the only time you are *required* to discuss a poem (though you may have done this for your Oral Presentation, or for some other aspect of your programme). You may therefore need to become more comfortable with presenting poetry analysis. Chapter Four covers this in some detail.

Answering questions on a text *for up to ten minutes* is also something you may have little or no experience with. You may feel comfortable with this if you enjoy debate and discussion, and if you tend to be one of the students who always answers in class. But many students are not so forthcoming, so developing this competence may take some special efforts. Chapter Five (Oral Presentation) has suggestions in Section Two.

Criterion A (/5) Knowledge and Understanding of the poem

How good is the candidate's knowledge and understanding of the poem? How individual is his/her interpretation, and how effectively supported by appropriate references?

- What 'knowledge and understanding' mean, and how they are different from each other, is stated in 1.4 above and Chapter Eight, 1.4
- For what 'context' means for poetry, see above, Standard Criteria (1.4)
- If you are not studying a 'body' of a poet's work elsewhere, consult the student comments on revision in Section Two below. This shows how you can relate the poems to each other and develop a sense of the author and the whole selection. This enhances your knowledge and appreciation of any individual poem.

This is the only Part in the programme where you are specifically rewarded for the *individuality* or independence of your interpretation (you are also rewarded for this in the Discussion). This means that you do not simply repeat what others have written or said about the poem but position yourself in relation to others' opinions, take 'ownership' of the text and given it some personal meaning.

- This process is discussed in Chapter Two, Section One (on 'meaning') followed by Section Two on strategies to develop this skill. Your 'interpretation' is to do with your response to the thought and feeling of the poem, to what is implied or suggested

Criterion B (/5) Appreciation of the writer's choices

How well does the candidate appreciate how the writer's choices of language and style shape meaning in the text?

To greater or lesser degree, all the assessed components in this course call for this skill, which is to do with close reading and analysis. However, it is a particular focus of the Commentary, as it is of Paper One.

- Chapter Four (Paper One) Section Two discusses extensively how you build the skill
- The poetry samples in Chapters Four, Eight, and Section Two below will help you see "appreciation" of "choices" in action, and understand what it means for language to 'shape' or create meaning

Criterion C: Organisation and Presentation (/5)

How effective is the candidate's structure, and how well is the focus sustained?

- For suggestions as to how to achieve a good structure and focus, read those for Standard Level Criterion C above (1.4), as the same principles apply, and also consult the poem sample below. The structure and delivery of an oral in eight minutes is something that needs practice

Criterion D: Knowledge and Understanding of the text used in the Discussion (/5)
How good is the candidate's knowledge and understanding of the text and its implications?

You do not have the text when you are in the Discussion, so a sound understanding calls for effective study and revision techniques.
- Use Chapter Eight Section Two for ideas about studying plays and fiction, and Section Three for revision strategies. The skills for Criteria D and E are similar to those for your Paper Two exam.

Criterion E: Response to the Discussion Questions (/5)
How informed, persuasive and independent are the responses to the questions?

Consult the subsection below on the Discussion, for what this process involves. The better you know your texts, the better prepared (informed) you are for the questions. The more carefully you have studied and taken notes, as suggested in Chapter Two, the more independent your answers will be (see Criterion A above for discussion of 'independent').
- Answering questions orally, spontaneously and independently, is something you do not specifically do elsewhere for assessment, though it relates to the skill of answering the question on exam Paper Two
- You will benefit from practice. With a friend, each devise a range of questions on your two texts (follow the Discussion subsection below for appropriate kinds of questions). Examine each other for ten minutes on each text in turn
- Look at Chapter Five Section Two, on building oral skills through discussion work in class, etc.

Criterion F: Language (/5)
How clear, appropriate, accurate and effective is the use of language (grammar, vocabulary, sentence construction, terminology, etc.)?

This covers both parts of your exam. Look over language development in Chapter Five on Oral Presentation for ideas about developing your oral skills, and Chapter Four for language skills.

Reflection on the Criteria and their implications for you (Higher Level):

What particular implications do the above criteria and suggestions have for you? What will you need to focus on to meet the criteria at a good level?

1.7 The exam process: the Commentary (Higher and Standard)

The process for the Commentary exam is the same for both Higher and Standard Levels except that Higher Level must only study poetry for this.

Notice of the exam
Your teacher gives you plenty of notice about the date and time of the exam, so that you have time to revise your texts and practise skills of structuring, speaking, etc. At both Levels, you should know *all* your works well, as you will not know which poem or text you will be given.

How your passage is selected
The teacher will have prepared a number of passages, according to the number of students, though each student does not always have a different passage. In the case of large numbers, two students may get the same passage. In the interests of fairness, it is usual for the teacher to ask you to choose from a number of envelopes or folded papers each containing a passage.

Higher Level candidates will not know, on entering the exam, which their second work will be. The preparation period is only for the poem, in their case.

You are given twenty minutes to read through the passage/poem and prepare a commentary on it. This is often in an adjacent, supervised room, as your teacher may be examining another student while you prepare. You do not have the text or notes to refer to, just the passage. The passage will be 'clean' – it will not have chapter or scene headings or notes – though titles of the poems will be supplied.

Guiding Questions and how you use them

Your teacher must provide one or two guiding questions for the passage. These are designed to help you focus on important elements, and normally cover both content and style. For example:

"What do the details in this passage suggest about Gatsby and his world?" *(Content)*

"What effects are created by the use of language?" *(Style)*

However, it is not obligatory to answer the questions if you feel that they do not fit your interpretation or response. Note that in Paper One (Guided Literary Analysis) at Standard Level you *must* answer the questions. This could be confusing, so teachers sometimes remind you on the passage you receive that you do not have to answer the questions.

On the other hand, you should not necessarily confine yourself just to 'answering' the questions the teacher has supplied, because this could limit your response.

How you use the preparation time:

Close reading and responses

As you should be very familiar with the text, you do not spend the preparation time figuring out what the poem or passage *means* (as you do on the unseen commentary in Paper One). However, you give it a close and intense reading to take ownership of it, which will give persuasiveness to your commentary.

In this process, you may find aspects of the passage or poem that you had not noticed before, or that you see in a new way. (*See the student's comments on his preparation process in Section Two below*). You bring your understanding of the text at this point to a higher level.

Establish an overview and structure

Once you have assimilated your passage and generated as many responses as you can, write down a clear overview that pulls it all together, and decide on a basic structure you will follow (perhaps following two to three main aspects or divisions in the passage).

Select your main points for discussion (related to that overview and structure)

Although you only have eight minutes to present your passage/poem, a good deal can in fact be said in this seemingly short time, and you *can* do justice to your passage or poem, as you will see from the sample poem below. At the same time, you cannot comment unselectively on every detail, so selection is important.

Do not try to write out whole sentences to *read* out in the exam. This is an *oral* exam. Make brief notes so that you know what you want to say, organise them into a clear plan or structure and trust to your powers of spontaneous expression. Focus on *what* you want to say, and on a structure for this, and the way to express this should follow.

1.7.1 The commentary and the teacher's subsequent (two minute) questions

You have an uninterrupted eight minutes to present your commentary. The teacher will be timing the presentation and will indicate when you need to conclude it. S/he will then ask you a few questions in the remaining two minutes of the time. These are compulsory. If you cannot continue for eight minutes, the teacher will begin to ask you questions.

The purpose of the questions is to prompt you to reveal more of your knowledge and understanding of the passage/poem and the writer's choices, which can affect your grade positively. The questions may have to do with the meaning or words or phrases, or the clarification of points you have made, or the addressing of aspects that you may have missed.

Your answers to the subsequent questions can help your marks in Criteria A and B (Knowledge and Understanding, and Language Choices).

1.7.2 Reminders of good practice for your commentary (Higher and Standard)

The following tips are based on what has often been lacking in candidate performance in the past, and highlight what is highly recommended for successful commentaries.

- As with Paper One Unseen Commentary, your **understanding of the content *and its significance*** (what it is about and why it is interesting, important or striking) must come first. No amount of discussion of literary techniques is very impressive if you do not show this understanding, which should be evident in your overview.

- When you have that understanding of content, make sure you express this **in a clear thesis or overview.** This is very often lacking in orals, as with Paper One commentaries. The poem sample below, and the written commentaries in Chapter Four, illustrate a thesis or focus well.

- **Your own *interpretation*** of the passage is expected. You are not asked to paraphrase the passage/poem, or put it in your own words, but to show what you think the writer's, narrator's or characters' *thoughts and feelings* are, from your close reading of the text and attention to the language. Your interpretation is your response to your close reading, and should be reflected in your opening 'focus' as well as your discussion of aspects of the passage.

- (Standard Level only). ***Brief contextualisation*** or situating of the passage will enhance your commentary, especially in the case of a long text (drama, fiction or non-fiction) where you should show understanding of the significance of this passage in the whole work from which it comes. What comes before in the plot or narrative impacts on your passage, and you need to be able to indicate this, explicitly or implicitly. The passage itself may also impact on what happens later.

- **'Context' in poetry** works differently. A poem comes from a body of work by the author, and may be similar to or different from other poems in that body, stylistically or thematically. Its relation to (one or two) of those other poems can be briefly indicated at relevant moments in the commentary (again, as shown in the poem sample in Section Two below), not necessarily in an introduction, but they should be very brief. Any contextualisation must be *specifically* related to the text. It should not be a set of random facts about the author and his or her context, learned by heart and repeated.

- (Standard Level) **Be clear about the *genre*** of your passage and the features or conventions characterise that genre. Sometimes students seem unclear about whether *Macbeth* is a play or a novel. Your presentation should reflect your knowledge of genre, in ideas and literary *terminology*. For example you might need to refer to a first person narrator or an interior monologue in a novel, or an 'aside' in drama, or the use of iambic pentameter in poetry. Refer to Chapters Four and Eight for details on these features and conventions. If you can use the terminology relevantly, your commentary will be precise as well as more impressive.

- If you **identify a *structure* in the passage or poem**, this may be a useful way to understand and focus the poem/passage. (See the poem sample commentary in Section Two below where the candidate uses the sonnet structure). Structure may have to do with the form of a poem; or the way the thought or narrative or dialogue develops; or a contrast. Your understanding of this should be reflected in your overview. The structure of the passage may also suggest a way to organise your own presentation.

- As you refer to the content, ensure that you make clear **how techniques of language *shape* or *create* meaning**, producing effects that make the passage/poem memorable and interesting, and contribute to the overall meaning. Recognising the relationship between content, effect and language is a vital part of good performance. (See poem sample and evaluation, Section Two).

- Ensure you understand **the difference between a colloquial and a formal register** or level of *language*. Chapter Five, Section Three, has some advice on this.

- A **conclusion** should arise out of what you have said. Saying 'That's about it' is disappointing.

Reflection:

Which aspects of the commentary process will you need to focus on?

What are some of the ways you might do this?

1.8 The exam process: the Discussion (Higher Level only)

For Higher Level candidates, the Discussion takes place immediately after the ten minutes of commentary and subsequent questions on a poem. There is no break. The teacher will tell you at this point which text is to be discussed. It can seem very challenging to move from one intense task to another very different one in exam conditions, with no time to reflect. However, if you understand the nature and value of the Discussion, and some effective ways to prepare for it, it will be a manageable task.

The difference between the Commentary and the Discussion
The Discussion is a very different way to talk about a text (in comparison with the close commentary). Both require solid knowledge and understanding of whole texts, but the Discussion is more holistic and wide-ranging, though with reference to specific details. You can do a long text (and your own learning) more justice by discussing it from a number of angles rather than focusing on one small part.

In the Discussion you *respond* to questions provided, rather than having to *initiate* and *organise* ideas yourself as in your Commentary preparation. In that sense the Discussion can seem less intense, a little less formal. The interchange with your teacher throughout the ten minutes takes off the constant pressure and can be stimulating and interesting for both of you.

The particular challenge of the Discussion (recalling and answering)
Some students, however, have found that it is easier and more controllable to talk about the Commentary passage than the Discussion text because for the Commentary they have the passage in front of them, providing something concrete and limited to focus on. They also have twenty minutes to prepare it.

In contrast, in the Discussion, you have to navigate the text in your head, from one angle to another, on the spot. You have to be able to zoom in mentally to access the relevant evidence. You also need to provide your own *individual* standpoint on questions, as this is a key word in the criteria descriptors. The ability to remember and select the right material, and to be able to give considered independent answers spontaneously, is achievable if you:

- Use the revision strategies (Chapter Eight, Section Three) that you also need for Paper Two
- Use the suggested revision techniques in Chapter Eight: Section Two for different genres
- Practise answering questions, as discussed in 1.6 above, under Criterion E

The Discussion process
The teacher will ask you a series of questions ranging over different aspects of the chosen text, as illustrated below. The questions should allow you to show your knowledge and understanding of the text in a detailed and specific way, as well as more broadly, and to demonstrate your independent evaluation of aspects of the work.

This is not a question and answer exercise – a 'test' to see if you can give 'correct' answers that the teacher has in mind. It is an opportunity for you to explore your own ideas and interpretations of the text, as well as showing your knowledge and understanding of the text. You may not have thought of some of the questions before. For these reasons some people have called it a "guided discussion".

Your teacher may follow up any of your responses to a particular question with a further question to enable you to explore more ideas on that aspect. In other words, the discussion itself may generate interesting questions. See the comments on the sample Discussion questions for how this can happen.

Although the exercise is called a 'Discussion', the teacher's role is not to enter into a discussion with you by exhibiting his or her knowledge, or expanding on his or her ideas. It is to draw from *you* your considered and relevant responses. You should expect around five or six questions. This is where you have an opportunity to position yourself in relation to the views of others: critics, peers or teacher, so as to demonstrate the independence of your responses. For example:

"Conrad has been criticised by Chinua Achebe as having racist or imperialistic attitudes to the Africans in <u>Heart of Darkness</u>. How do you interpret Conrad's presentation of them? Does Achebe have a point?

The kind of questions to expect: sample questions on *The Great Gatsby*
These may invite your response to a particular scene or character, your discussion of an aspect that has provoked different interpretations, your interpretation of an event or setting, and so on.

What do you think is the purpose of Fitzgerald's first description of Tom and Daisy's house? What aspects of it are especially striking to you?
This is a specific, straightforward and concrete question (and therefore a good one to start with) that allows you to access quickly some significant details you remember. It also allows you to refer to the role of Tom and Daisy in the novel (so both knowledge and understanding are involved, and there is scope for your independent comment views).

How do you feel Fitzgerald has used the Valley of Ashes setting in the novel?
Like the first question, this is capable of both detailed and broad discussion, and extends the consideration of the novel into wider aspects of symbolism, social criticism and plot.

Fitzgerald is said to have been interested in writing about 'dreams' in a general way in this novel. Do you see <u>The Great Gatsby</u> as being about this theme? Or is it about something else, for you?
This is a broad-ranging thematic question and calls for some quick synthesising of knowledge and understanding, but also asks you to position your response in relation to a purpose of the author.

Daisy has been described as a "monster of bitchery" by some critics. Is this the way you see her?
This too calls for your positioning of your views and interpretation, supported by specific references to moments in the novel.

Do you think it is justified to call Gatsby 'great'?
This is a big question and asks for a broad ranging response to the whole novel as well as specific references to parts of the work dealing with Gatsby.

What do you think is implied by the language and tone of the ending?
This involves memory of close attention to details and language effects, and an evaluation of the impact of the work.

Reflection on Discussion task and the sample questions:

What are the particular challenges of this task for you?

What is your response to this range of sample questions? What implications do they have for your study and revision?

At this point we will turn to the end product, to see what an individual oral commentary at either Level, and a Discussion at Higher Level look like. This should help you reflect on how you can best work to develop the relevant skills.

Section Two: Sample Commentaries and Discussion

2.1 A sample Oral Commentary (Higher/Standard) on a poem

The text
Read the poem in order to follow and assess the Commentary. Although the poem is only fourteen lines long, this is acceptable because of its complexity and the density of its literary

aspects. Note that the lines are numbered so that the candidate can refer to them easily during the Oral.

"Anthem for Doomed Youth" by Wilfred Owen

What passing-bells for these who die as cattle?	1
-Only the monstrous anger of the guns,	2
Only the stuttering rifles' rapid rattle	3
Can patter out their hasty orisons.	4
No mockeries now for them; no prayers nor bells;	5
Nor any voice of mourning save the choirs,-	6
The shrill, demented choirs of wailing shells;	7
And bugles calling for them from sad shires.	8
What candles may be held to speed them all?	9
Not in the hands of boys, but in their eyes	10
Shall shine the holy glimmers of goodbyes.	11
The pallor of girls' brows shall be their pall;	12
Their flowers the tenderness of patient minds,	13
And each slow dusk a drawing down of blinds.	14

Guiding Questions:
- What does the title suggest about the speaker's attitude to his subject?

- How do diction and imagery create a sense of that attitude?

The candidate's response
The transcript is paragraphed with numbers so that you can refer to it more easily when evaluating it. Read over the criteria before reading the commentary, so that you have these in mind. Make notes about what you observe in his performance, that meet the criteria and could help you.

Good Morning. My name is _____ and my candidate number is _____ I am a Higher Level candidate

1. My poem is "Anthem for Doomed Youth" by Wilfred Owen, an English poet of the First World War. He wrote it in 1917 while he was recovering from shell shock at Craiglochhart Psychiatric hospital in Scotland. This was where he met the poet Siegfried Sassoon who influenced him in his writing and also in his attitude to the war. Sassoon had turned against the war and accused the authorities of deceiving the soldiers and causing needless suffering. He had developed a new style to express this and written about war graphically and without glorifying it.

2. So this poem is interesting because it reflects this new spirit of disillusion (which Owen's own experience in war had also made him feel) but the sonnet form puts it in the classic tradition of poetry, and even of war poetry because Rupert Brooke had written patriotic sonnets earlier in the war. The sonnet suits the seriousness and formality of Owen''s subject here – the slaughter of a whole generation, the fact that religion can't dignify their deaths, and that only the families of the dead and those who love them can dignify them.

3. The title "Anthem For *Doomed* Youth" makes it clear that Owen sees the war as sacrificing large numbers of young men ("youth" as a whole), and that they are doomed before they start. An anthem is usually a celebratory hymn, it has religious associations, so the title seems shocking – celebrating young men who had died, or were doomed to die – but it's in fact Owen's personal celebration of these young men, showing his respect and compassion for them. The Church can't dignify them through its usual funeral rituals like prayers and bells, not just because the youths are dying in battle, but also because the war has caused the Church to lose its status in Owen's eyes. So the title is quite bitter and paradoxical.

4. In my presentation I am going to show how Owen's diction and imagery, especially auditory imagery, move us from the horror of the battlefield in the first section, to a softer sense of the families and their lives back home in the second section, where there is love and a real sense of the loss of lives. The diction and imagery is predominantly that of war and religion, which might seem to form an opposition, but they are interlinked here in a way that suggests that religion is condemned along with war, or perhaps has died with war, in Owen's mind.

5. Owen opens with a harsh accusing rhetorical question (*he quotes line 1*), which suggests his disgust at the fact that soldiers die pointlessly in thousands. A '"passing bell" was rung traditionally in England to announce the death of a person in a community and to invite prayers for the dead. Owen is implying that war and those who make war do not respect the individual's worth, especially suggested through the simile of "cattle" and its implication of mass slaughter. The word "cattle" stands out even more because of the harshness of the sound, (*"cattle"*), and because it breaks the rhythm of the line. We have an extra syllable, which is very dissonant, and because it falls at the end of the

line it forces us to stop and think, to take in this strong statement. Although it's framed as a question, it's really a statement. This language and attitude is similar to other poems of Owen where he refers to the dehumanising effects of war – like in "Dulce Et Decorum Est" where he refers to the dead soldier being "flung" in a wagon like an object.

6. Owen answers his own question in a bitter tone, stating that there are no passing bells, just gunfire and rifle fire and the sound of shells on the battlefield. The repetition of "only" "only" "no" "no" emphasises this absence of the traditional rituals. He creates a cacophony of the terrifying sounds of that war, by personifying the weapons, giving them a kind of huge force of their own that overwhelms the soldiers. "Monstrous anger" doesn't just give us the noise, but the idea that the weapons themselves carry the destructive force, more than the enemy using them. War has become a matter of machines rather than men.

7. "Stuttering rifles' rapid rattle" creates an onomatopoeic effect that reminds us of the sounds made by those weapons – but it is the "rapid" bit that is frightening. The "shrill, demented choirs of wailing shells" is different. It connects with the religious imagery – we associate choirs with beauty and harmony – so "demented" is quite shocking. It suggests that civilisation (where we have choirs) has lost its mind, as well as it being a very precise way to describe the sound of shells, along with "wailing" and "shrill", like the sounds of a mad house.

8. To say that the gun and rifle fire take the place of religious ceremonies or rituals to mark the death of soldiers is very shocking. Owen compares their sounds to the "patter" of "hasty orisons" like priests saying prayers quickly without meaning what they say. Owen's use of the word "mockeries" is very strong. He's denying that the Church has any meaning any longer. This could be because of its connection with those who prolong the war, or because it is impossible to believe in a God who allows such atrocities. That's something suggested in "Exposure".

9. In the last line of the first section (line 8), there is a reference to another sound, the bugle, which links war and home. It acts as a kind of transition here between the octave and sestet. The battlefield has an association with bugles, as they're played at the end of the day, but here he connects the sound with home, with the shires, the country areas that the young soldiers have come from, which might have seen them off to war with bugles, and would announce their death with bugles. "Calling for them" personifies the bugle, but in a tender way, like a parent calling for a child to come home. This auditory image emphasises the idea of the uniqueness of each death for the families who love them, and leads us into the sestet where the idea of the mourning families is the subject. Personifying the shires as "sad" reminds us of all those rural communities like the one Owen himself came from, where the impact of the war was very strong.

10. The sestet has a different tone from the octave because of the visual imagery. It also begins with a rhetorical question but the impact is softer because of the imagery of candles, which carry associations of warmth and light. They also have religious associations, for example being placed round a coffin, symbolising eternal life. Owen denounces that candles will be held by boys in Church, but suggests that real 'holiness' is found in the loving eyes of boys saying goodbye to their family, maybe when they leave for war or when they die in battle. Even if religion has lost its meaning, the individual is sacred. We could say that Owen sees it as his aim to convey that on behalf of the soldiers and their families.

11. The usual ritual objects of the pall and flowers covering the coffin won't have their place for these soldiers lost in war, but the pale faces of girls – maybe sisters or fiancées or both, and the patient suffering of families, will take the place of these things, and carry more meaning. The last line has a very strong impact because the imagery suggests closure: the end of the day, when people draw down their blinds; death; and how people close their blinds traditionally when someone in the family dies. Instead of this tradition, Owen suggests the idea of evening bringing a kind of peace and closure, contrasting with the bombardment on the battlefield.

So in conclusion I would say that Owen manages to combine honouring the dead and their families, and showing pity for them, with anger at the destructiveness and savagery of war and at those who make it or fail to prevent it.

Teacher: Excellent. Thank you. I'd just like to ask you a couple of questions. Can you say something about sound effects in the sestet, in the second part of the poem?

Candidate: (pause) Well, the effect is more musical, I think. The consonants – there are a lot of m's and l's- – are softer than in the octave where we can find a lot of harsh sounds. And there are rhyming effects, assonance – "eyes", "goodbyes", "minds', "blinds", where the sound is mournful. There's a sense of finality, but not in a negative way.

Teacher: What about the last line, specifically?

Candidate (pause) It's a heavy and slow line, with heavy sounds from the alliteration, the "d"s. It's solemn and final.

Teacher: Could you mention something about how Owen uses the sonnet form here? I mean, has anything been 'resolved'?

Reflection and evaluation of the commentary:

Which of the criteria does the candidate meet at a particularly good level?

What could you learn from this commentary? What implications does this have for your preparation?

2.2 Evaluation of the candidate's performance

The use of the criteria

Another candidate might approach the poem differently but equally well, with an exploration of at least some different effects. There is room for individual emphasis and response. The teacher and the Moderator will look for the criteria descriptors and level that *best fits* the performance. They are not measuring the performance against some idea of perfection. An 'outstanding' performance is not a 'perfect' one.

Criterion A: Knowledge and understanding

The candidate shows good knowledge (in the introduction and throughout the commentary), of forms of poetry, and of the context of the poem – the war, the poet's circumstances, the influence of Sassoon, the sonnet form and its use, the anthem form, traditional religious practices and Church rituals, and weapons of the period. We see this in his references to passing bells, rifle fire, the use of bugles, church candles, the closing of blinds. This knowledge is related to the candidate's sense of the meaning and effects of Owen's images and references, not displayed for its own sake. The two brief references to other Owen poems are relevant.

The candidate's understanding is clear in his interpretation of the title (3) and how this relates to Owen's *thought and feeling* about the soldiers, their families and war throughout the poem. He also understands the relationship between religion and the war, and how this provides an effective 'opposition' in the poem as a whole. Paragraphs 8 and 9 in particular especially show *individual* understanding and interpretation in his exploration of the word choice 'mockeries' (8), and of the auditory image of the bugle and the complex associations and connotations it has. The candidate's understanding is consistently shown to come from precise details of the text. It is "effectively supported".

Criterion B: Appreciation of the writer's choices

The candidate appreciates Owen's choice of the sonnet form (2, 4 and questions) and the title with its reference to another poetic form (the anthem). He sees the structure and pattern of the diction and imagery in the poem as a whole, and how war and religious images relate to each other (4). In (5) he discusses just the opening line from different aspects (rhetorical question, diction and sound) and shows how all these vividly express the poet's thoughts and feelings about war.

He understands and discusses the force and effects of repetition, onomatopoeia, personification (7) and notably the connotations of the image 'choirs" (8). He explores the association of the choice of the 'bugle' image (9) and especially its structural function linking the octave and sestet. He conveys the complex effect of the visual imagery in the sestet (10).

Note how in referring to 'cattle' and 'choirs', the candidate does not just *identify* the feature or make a random comment about 'effects'. He shows how this simile and metaphor express the speaker's attitude and response to war and *relate to a wider pattern* in the poem. They 'shape' meaning, or help us to see the poet's intention and the feelings he is communicating.

Note also that among the many literary aspects to comment on in this poem, the candidate has to make his own choices of the words and effects that for him carry the greatest weight or are key to his interpretation ('cattle', 'rifles', 'choirs' 'bugle', etc). You will need to *select*. Eight minutes does not allow for exhaustive exploration.

Criterion C: Organisation and presentation
The student is able to structure his commentary (3 and 4) well because he sees the:

- Structure and purpose of the poem itself clearly in terms of form (the sonnet's octave and sestet and their relationship to each other)
- Pattern of imagery in this framework (religion and war)
- Purpose of the poet as a whole (his thought and feeling about the subject)

He provides an overall focus (*3, underlined*), creates a personal structure he will follow (*4 underlined, diction and imagery*), and keeps to that focus and structure throughout the commentary. There is no single way to organise a commentary, but this one works well for this text. It is important to provide a clear overview at the outset, so that your listener sees your grasp, and in order to relate everything you say later to this. You don't have time (nor is it effective to a listener) to 'work your way into' it.

Criterion D (S Level) or F (H Level): Language
The candidate has a good knowledge of literary terms, which forms the spine of his presentation. Apart from the word 'denounce' (10) his choice of vocabulary, his grammar and sentence construction, etc. are accurate and varied. At Higher Level the use of language in the commentary and discussion is combined.

The questions
The three teacher questions pick up on aspects the candidate has not mentioned and allows him to show more detailed understanding of techniques and structure. Other questions might have been equally or more appropriate but the questions need to be manageable in the two minutes.

The use of the guiding questions
The student has addressed the questions but they are only part of what he has achieved overall. It looks as if he has approached the poem holistically and fully in his own way (which is desirable), but taken on board the significance of the first question. Had he limited his response to the questions, the commentary would obviously not have been so strong, or so clearly indicated his 'ownership' of the poem.

Reflection on the evaluation:

What can you learn from this evaluation? What were you not aware of previously?

2.3 The student's comment on his revision and performance

Study

We studied the poems in class in the first year. There was a lot of information about Owen and his life, and about the war and other war poets, and there was the analysis of the poems, what they meant, how the language worked, and so on. There was a lot to take in, in the time that we had. I made lots of notes. That was really important. There just wasn't time to do that work again. But at that point it was a bit of a jumble – no pattern.

Revision

When I revised the poems in the second year it was a different process. We didn't have time to revise in class. I read some more background material from the Internet as well as going back through my notes. Then I took each poem, more or less in chronological order, and re-read it, finding my own way of seeing it and understanding it. I put each one on a separate A5 page and organised notes around it – a combination of things I thought relevant from class notes and my own thoughts. (After that I abandoned my pages of class notes). It was at this point that I got some new ideas For example with "Anthem" I got the idea of the contrast between sound in the octave and sight in the sestet. I used some 'checklists' *(as in Chapter Four)* for more ideas about literary features, as our class work didn't deal with them all.

Then I put all the A5 pages in a pattern on a table and looked at them as a whole 'body' of work. We hadn't done that in class but it really helped to see them in relation to each other, and I did some colour coding of similarities. Everything else kind of fell into place once I'd got that. I felt much more comfortable about the exam once I had my own handle on the poems. I wrote a sentence or two for each one that expressed how I saw it. In the exam room I could pretty much remember what I had said in that.

Before the exam we were asked in class if anyone wanted to model a commentary (on another poem) and I volunteered, so I'd had some public practice, and I think everyone should definitely have this. What I learned from that was the need to be clear about your structure. I tried to cram too much in and it was a bit jumbled.

What I did in the preparation room
In the exam preparation room I read through the poem once quite slowly to bring back a sense of its fullness and impact, and then wrote two 'focus' sentences (*underlined in the sample*), one about the slaughter of a whole generation, and one about Owen's personal celebration based on his respect and compassion. Everything in the poem hinges on those things. My revision sentences had helped with getting that focus. When you only have eight minutes, you can make sure that everything you say is linked to it.

Then I went line-by-line identifying the literary features that I thought important and wrote these on the paper to remind myself of the terms, along with a few notes on how the features were working. I even got the odd new idea as I went along – things clicked for me. For example that's where I had the idea about the bugle. My cadet force experience was useful with the military references.

Finally I made a quick plan, all on the same sheet, to have it all together:

<u>**Plan/Structure**</u>

Context: war, Sassoon/influence/attitude, sonnet
Overview and focus: the *(underlined)* sentences
Structure signpost (underlined): diction, imagery (sound and sight; octave/sestet)
Body of presentation:
Octave: question, cattle, weapons,
      Failure of religion
      Bugle – war/home
Sestet: candles, holiness
     Pall, flowers, blinds, ending/nature, mood

Comment on my performance
I had a lot to say and it was sometimes hard to make quick choices like about the context – whether to say more about Rupert Brooke's sonnets. I think I went on too long about context. Also I could have said more about individual literary effects, but I felt I had to keep moving on. It helped to be on top of the poem – to feel I understood it, because I didn't have to hesitate. The plan made it easy, because it was short and mainly key words, which triggered what I wanted to say.

Reflection on student study and preparation process for poetry/commentary passage:

What is useful to you about the student's process?

What might you do differently?

2.4 Sample Discussion on *Hamlet* (Higher Level)

The questions are numbered for convenience of reference in the evaluation comments following the sample. Remember that this is a transcript of a live performance, not a written essay. Responses are spontaneous and, though written out, they do not have the level of formality of grammar and sentence construction that you might expect in an essay. The candidate is talking as he is thinking. Read back over Criteria D and E for Higher Level to remind yourself of how this will be assessed, and make notes as you go through it on what you feel is good practice.

Teacher: Now we're going to turn to something quite different. Would you like to choose one of these folded slips of paper, to see what the Discussion text will be?

Candidate: It's *Hamlet*

1. Teacher: I hope that's good. Let's start at the beginning. Would you like to say something about the opening scene, and how effective you think it is – what you think Shakespeare is doing here?

Candidate: I think the main thing it does is pull us into the situation very quickly because even by the second page the soldiers are asking whether 'this thing' has appeared and talking about how the ghost has already appeared twice to them, so there's clearly a central issue here. And as soon as we learn that, the ghost actually appears in a very dramatic way, in armour, and it's made even more dramatic because this is the first time Horatio has seen it, and we see how completely overwhelmed he is. And then just when they're sitting down and talking about the situation in the country, and the pending war, it appears again very briefly and disappears when the cock crows. The point is that we are just as taken off guard as they are, and so we experience it, as it were, with them, and have the same sense of suspense, wanting to know what is going on.

There are a couple of other things I think are effective about this scene – which you really notice when you see it live. The first is the atmosphere – the time of night and the dark and the sort of edgy mood the soldiers are in because of this mystery and the sense of war on the horizon. The sound – the clock striking twelve and then the cockcrow at the end – has a strong impact. The other thing is the way the soldiers behave with each other, which is very straightforward and harmonious. It seems normal, but you only appreciate this later like in the next two scenes at the court, when you see how devious most people are with each other, and how much is concealed. Hamlet belongs with the soldiers rather than the court, and we see an important side of him when he's with them and Horatio that we don't see at any other time.

2.Teacher: You talked about the ghost. Do you see a problem with the ghost? I mean, most people don't believe in ghosts today, and the ghost character has been seen as posing a problem in production. Does the ghost diminish the force of the play for you, or do you see it as having an important role?

Candidate: I don't think it matters whether you believe in ghosts or not. I think there are a number of ways the ghost contributes to the play and it's hard to imagine the play succeeding without it. Shakespeare makes us feel the reality of the ghost by the way the sceptical Horatio reacts to it, and then Hamlet – both of them are students and intellectuals, so it makes it more convincing. Another thing the ghost does is bring the past into the present and make the crime of Claudius and the betrayal of Gertrude very vivid. That sets up dramatic irony and how we see the next couple of Acts, and it makes us much more involved and complicit with Hamlet. The ghost – I know this seems contradictory – actually seems very human in his speeches because of the emotions he has about the past but also because of the sense of fatherly connection with Hamlet. It makes the need for justice, and Hamlet's mission, much more meaningful and intense.

3.Teacher: Let's take a broad view of the play for a moment. *Hamlet* has obviously captured people's imaginations and had a lasting influence. What is it about the play that makes it memorable and important for you?

Candidate: That's such a big question. Well, I'll start by saying that I think it's to a large extent because of the kind of person Hamlet is, and the things he says. I realise that quite a few people are alienated by certain things he does, like his cruel treatment of Ophelia in the 'nunnery 'scene and his callousness about Polonius's body, but I think there are ways of interpreting these moments less negatively, or justifying them. Hamlet is capable of feeling morally with great intensity. We not only connect with his emotions, like the grief and admiration for his father and the disgust for Claudius and Gertrude that he expresses in his first soliloquy, but feel that he has a very clear sense of right and wrong, and that these things matter. It's very striking how at the end when Hamlet is dying, what he is most concerned about is the need for the truth to be told.

I think our sympathy for him is accentuated in this because of how isolated he is at court, except for Horatio. He's not only isolated but disempowered, by Claudius who has usurped his place and is keeping a watchful eye on him, and also by Polonius, who has destroyed his relationship with Ophelia. That sense of someone who is very bright, very loving, very energetic, very noble, having everything taken away from him not by accident, but by ambition (as in the case of Claudius) and stupidity and arrogance, as in the case of Polonius, makes his situation very tragic. But he's also very funny and witty – this combination is very powerful.

4. Teacher: Can you talk a bit about some of the specific ways Shakespeare helps us see these things about Hamlet. For example, about him being noble and energetic, and so on?

Candidate: We see these sides of Hamlet in the respect the soldiers have for him, and the way Horatio doesn't want to outlive Hamlet at the end. We also see them particularly in Ophelia's speech at the end of the 'nunnery' scene, when she bursts out with "O what noble mind is here o'rethrown". We get a glimpse of the princely way Hamlet used to be, which actually makes the way he's treated in the play – and also the way he often behaves – quite shocking in comparison. The soliloquies reveal a lot about him, because some of them show how he thinks his way through things honestly, like the speech about the Player in Act Two, where he is trying to understand his own inaction, in comparison with the emotions the actor has for a 'fiction'. And the way he engages with the players and is completely caught up with their acting – that's a very interesting side of Hamlet where he suddenly seems himself and comfortable, and also knowledgeable.

5. Teacher: We haven't said anything about Gertrude. How important is she to the play?

Candidate: She's pivotal, actually. She's part of the situation that triggers the action, in that she was 'seduced' by Claudius though it's never clear if this was before or after the murder of the King, but more importantly both Hamlet and the Ghost see her as having betrayed the very deep love of the Old Hamlet. This seems to affect Hamlet more than anything else, as we see in the first soliloquy, and he keeps referring to it as if he's obsessed by it until he confronts her with her sins in the closet scene. He seems more set on getting her to realise her sins than in punishing Claudius. She then becomes part of the tragedy because she's the one who tells of Ophelia's death, and mourns her in the graveyard, and she also takes Hamlet's side and tries to protect him at the end when she realises she's poisoned. She starts off in the play by being quite ambiguous and shadowy but her change in Act Three and afterwards makes her a strong part of the moral impact of the play.

6. Teacher: One final question. One critic has seen *Hamlet* as being 'about death'. Is this a plausible view of the play, in your view?

Candidate: Well, it's true that almost all the key players are dead, at the end, but somehow the impact of the play isn't about all the needless deaths at the end as much as about what Hamlet says about life and people's behaviour (like Rosencrantz and Guildenstern) and the realisations he comes to, like his thoughts in the graveyard –'The readiness is all", and things like that. I think it's interesting that Shakespeare invented Fortinbras and had Hamlet quite specifically admire him and appoint him as his successor, because it introduces a note of stability and hope at the end. Also, Horatio's promise to tell the truth of the whole tale makes it look as if hearts and minds may be changed.

Teacher: Thank you very much. Well done. That's the end of the recording.

2.5 Evaluation of the Discussion sample

The two parts of the Higher Level Commentary involve what seem to be different relationships with the teacher. The Commentary gives you an obvious sense that you are presenting your best effort, as in an exam, because it is uninterrupted and fully prepared.

The Discussion can feel more like a pleasant conversation, going back and forth between the teacher and you, but you need to remember that this is still an exam and that your answers need to be every bit as *specific, concise and analytical* as in the close commentary. You are being asked to show your highest level of knowledge and understanding of the work, and to respond persuasively and independently. The sample Discussion is a good example of how this can be achieved.

The student is clearly on top of his material and is able to answer readily with specific evidence. He has a good broad grasp of the play as well as a memory of particular moments. It is evident that he has seen a production (live or film), which has enhanced his sense of how the play works as a whole, and how particular dramatic or theatrical effects are achieved. There is also much evidence of detailed reading of the text. The readiness of his responses reflects the Reading Stage Four revision process described in Chapters Four and Eight (Section Three), and the study suggestions for Drama in Chapter Eight (Section Two).

Question One: the opening scene of *Hamlet*
This is a good question to begin with because it leads the candidate into the play with something concrete that he is likely to remember, and because it is open-ended – he can talk about whatever he thinks relevant. It is also a personal invitation ("*Would you like to say something about...*") to give a personal view of the scene, rather than, for example: "*What does the first scene accomplish*", which might look as if certain answers are being sought.

The question also invites *personal evaluation ("How effective do you think...")* of literary effects. It calls for the candidate's recall of details but also analysis of effects, including the visual and aural. He makes a nice point for example about how the audience is surprised by the ghost simultaneously with the soldiers. He actually makes six points about the first scene, giving his answer substance.

Question Two: the Ghost

Here the teacher picks up on something the candidate has mentioned, so that the second question leads naturally on from the first, but it broadens the field of reference, as it applies more widely to the play. The question also specifically asks him to position himself in relation to a topic that has provoked much debate. In fact he contributes *five* ideas in support of his defence of the role of the Ghost. He is able to *analyse* the effects of the role because he has *good recall of specific moments or evidence*. Here you can see the correlation with the Written Assignment and the Paper Two essay, and their use of evidence.

Question Three: what makes *Hamlet* memorable

Now that the candidate has 'warmed up' well, the teacher can move to a broad ranging, challenging and elusive but very important question, much discussed. This draws again upon the candidate's personal response and his command of the whole play, but he has to quickly fasten on some specific moments that justify his answer. This is a reminder that, when studying long texts, it is easy to lose a sense of the forest (*whole*) through attention to the trees (*parts*). Revision strategies with long texts need to include gaining an impression of the whole.

Question Four: specific techniques in the presentation of Hamlet's character

As the previous answer centred on the character of Hamlet, the teacher now focuses on something specifically literary in relation to that. The candidate comes up with four examples of different ways the character is built.

Question Five: Gertrude

This question on a key character requires a clear idea of the sequence of plot and the structural movement of the play, as well as the way that specific moments involving Gertrude contribute to the impact of the play. The candidate's quick thinking embraces different ways in which she contributes. There is also evidence of his emotional responsiveness to the character.

Question Six: overall theme

This final thematic question is a good way to end the Discussion, asking for the candidate's position on the 'meaning' of the play in relation to another, critical view. It calls for rapid synthesising of knowledge and understanding, to come up with support for a view. He assembles three or four aspects of the play in relation to the theme.

The final impression is that the Discussion questions have tested the candidate's knowledge and understanding at a high level, have prompted him to recall, analyse, and synthesise, and give a clear sense of his independence of approach. His answers are persuasive because they are soundly based on evidence from the text.

Reflection on the Discussion:

What stands out to you about the Discussion?

What points in the comments above are significant to you?

CHAPTER EIGHT: Part Three (Literary Genres)

The Paper Two Examination Essay

Overview

The "Exam Essay", or "Paper Two", is the last thing you do in this programme. It is the second of the two exams at the end of your course, and carries 25% of your final grade. It is based on your texts for Part Three, which are all of one genre, and asks you to compare and contrast two or more of the works with a focus on the way the writers use that genre.

It may seem a familiar task to write an answer to a question, using texts you have studied, but Paper Two has a number of distinct features that impact on the way you study, and the way you approach the exam. This is the *only* Part of the course where:

- Your texts *must* all be of one **genre,** and where genre is one focus of the study. You will need to show knowledge and understanding of the chosen genre and its **conventions** or typical features in your essay

- You are asked to **compare and contrast** your texts in relation to the way the writers use the genre. This will need to be part of your approach both when you study and revise, and *central to your planning* in the exam room

- There are **a substantial number of texts** (Higher Level 4; Standard 3)), so the **time** for study and revision needs to be carefully **managed**, especially as this falls when you are revising for other exams

- You will have to **remember** these texts for the exam, so you need to use study and revision **strategies** that will help you do this

- You are required to **answer a question** in relation to your texts. Answering the question **relevantly** appears on three of the criteria for Paper Two, so practice in doing this is key to your success

This chapter addresses how you can build the competencies for success in the five areas above, to feel prepared for the exam.

- Section One outlines Paper Two and its challenges, with suggestions for ways to meet the criteria.

- Section Two presents some ways to approach genres (Drama and the Novel) in your study and exam preparation.

- Section Three focuses on how to revise effectively for the exam, how to plan your exam answer, and presents sample work in the different genres.

Section One: What you do for Part Three, and how to meet the criteria

1.1 The texts and the timing: implications for your success

Your teacher or school chooses the genre you study, which may be Drama, the Novel and the Short Story, Poetry, or Prose Other than Fiction. Each work is by a different author, chosen from the IB *Prescribed List of Authors*. There are no works in translation. The texts are chosen to offer interesting variations in the use of the genre by different writers. No one genre is easier than another, but whichever you do, you should be familiar with its characteristics and 'conventions'. These are discussed below and in Section Two.

Part Three is often, but not always, taught towards the end of the course, as the outcome (Paper Two) is the last assessed exam in the literature course. The advantage of this is that all your previous experience with your genre in other Parts of the course, and the skills you have built in reading throughout the course, will have raised your literary level. A drawback can be that the study of the final texts is rushed because time is running out. You need to be able to give each text good study time and good revision time, especially as the exam carries so much weight. To ensure solid preparation for the exam:

- *Read your texts ahead* as much as possible (try to avoid a *first* reading of any text close to the exam)
- Try to give *each text at least three readings*, using the suggestions for independent reading and class study in Chapter Two
- *Know what to look for in your genre* (Chapter Four and Section Two below offer guidance on this)
- *Begin the habit of comparing and contrasting* works in the same genre as you progress from one text to the next (see Study Activities in Section Two below)
- *Time manage your revision* as suggested in Chapter Two: Section 2.3, and Chapter Five: Section 2.2.1), and *use the recommended revision strategies* (Section Three below), so that you make it easier to remember what you need to

---

Reflection on managing Part Three:

Given that many students run out of time towards the exam, which impacts on their success in this paper, which of the above suggestions might you need to pay most attention to?

1.2 Exam "Paper Two": what to expect on the Paper

The Questions

Higher and Standard Levels have the same paper and questions. You answer ONE question chosen from three questions on the genre you have studied. The questions are specific to the *genre* and not to the particular texts and authors you have studied, because different schools study different authors. A generic question on the novel, for example, might be "*Compare the effectiveness of the endings of at least two of the works you have studied*".

The time frame of the exam

Higher candidates have two hours. Standard candidates have an hour and a half, as in Paper One.

1.3 The Assessment Criteria: implications for your study and marks

Your understanding of the implications of the assessment criteria determines your success on the exam. 60% of the marks are about the texts and the way you answer the question using the texts. 40% has to do with writing aspects.

- A: **Knowledge and understanding** of the texts *in relation to the question answered* (/5)

- B: Convincing response to the **specific demands of the question** and its implications, **comparing and contrasting** works effectively (/5)

- C: Identification, appreciation and discussion of **the literary conventions** used in the texts, *in relation to the question* (/5)

- D: Coherent **organisation, development and structuring** of ideas (/5)

- E: Clear, accurate and appropriate use of **language** (/5)

Ways to meet these criteria are discussed in the subsections below.

1.4 How to 'know and understand' your texts

This is your starting point. Knowing and understanding your texts underpins all the criteria for Paper Two. There is a high correlation between success in this exam and the degree to which you meet this criterion.

'Knowing' the text means knowing:
- What happens, in what order, to whom, why, how, and where (content)
- Something about the author and context of the writing
- How genre and its conventions are used in the text.

This 'knowing' – mostly factual – can be achieved by careful reading of the text and reliable secondary sources, and by note-taking and note-making, to help you remember the key elements (see revision recommendations in Section Three).

'Understanding' is to do with
- *What you personally make of* the 'knowledge' as identified above (how you interpret it, and position yourself in relation to others' views on it; your insights on it)
- Being aware of the writer's purpose; of the significance, role and pattern of characters, events and language
- Your *evaluation* of the way the genre and its conventions are being used

This should make clear that you study the texts for as full a *personal* understanding as possible. The quality of your exam essay depends upon this personal grasp. You achieve this through class discussion, reflective independent reading and note-making, and especially through the re-reading and revision process, where 'purpose' and 'significance' of texts become clearer. Simply reproducing what you have learned and read is not sufficient for a good answer.

1.5 How to ensure effective response to an exam question

Responding to the question relevantly (as shown above) occurs in three of the criteria (A, B and C), yet is often the *weakest area* in student performance on Paper Two. Examiners do not want to see how much you *remember* about a text, but *how well you can think*, on the spot, *about a specific question*, and how well you organise your thinking into a coherent response. This skill is certainly challenging, but there are ways to make it manageable, as follows:

- **Know the texts well,** in order to be able to turn your mind to an*y given question* and select the relevant material from memory.

- **Recognise and appreciate the way the author has crafted his/her work.** The phrasing of the exam questions makes it clear that your task is to discuss how *what the texts say is made significant by the way they are written, specifically the way the writer uses the genre.* If you simply narrate or identify the relevant content of the text, you are only partly addressing the question.

  You can develop competence in this through your reading, note-making, discussion and revision strategies (Chapter Two) and the study activities in Section Two. Also through the way you plan your essay and analyse your evidence in the exam (see the samples and plans in Section Three).

- **Know the kinds of questions you will be asked, and understand the 'terms' in the questions.** Questions will be about the conventions or characteristics of the genre, so you need to be familiar with these, know their terminology and be able to discuss them (for example, the meaning of 'point of view' in novels, or sound effects in poetry). Past or specimen papers will provide examples. You also need practice in tackling such questions with a *plan* such as those in Section Three, keeping your focus on the literary aspect and terms of the question, even if you do not write the whole essay.

  You acquire this familiarity with questions and terms through class work, glossaries, secondary sources, past papers, Chapter Four, and Section Two below.

- **Think what any given question is specifically asking you to do.** It can seem scary in the exam to be tackling a question you haven't precisely thought of or written about before, but it is in fact manageable. If you know your texts well (as defined above), you can think on your feet and construct an answer to any question on a text, even a question that you may not have thought about before in exactly that way. Avoid twisting the question to use material that you have revised or written about before, and feel secure about.

  Keep on target by **rephrasing the question, and breaking it down into prompts that define your task** in the question. For example: *"The significance is in the detail". Compare and contrast how two or more novels or short stories you have studied for Part Three have used detail to significant effect"* The task can be broken down for each text in turn as follows:

- *What details seem significant in (each) text? (Identify 4-5)*
- *In what way is each detail significant? How does it contribute to our understanding or awareness of the text?*
- *What does the writer seem to have intended by using each detail?*
- *Given the above, how do the different texts compare with each other in the use of detail?*

Creating your own prompts in this way from a re-phrasing of the question helps you keep a sharp focus on the question throughout the planning process, as well as pushing you to think analytically and comparatively.

You gain the confidence to address specific questions by making an effort to answer questions in class, and 'taking risks' with ideas when contributing to discussions. Nearer the exam, practise answering questions by yourself (using relevant questions and 'grids' as in Section Three). You can also this with peers, deciding together how you should answer any given question.

- **Comparing and contrasting texts effectively in answer to a question**
  This is the only time in the programme that you are specifically asked to compare and contrast, and are assessed on that (in Criterion B). The comparison/contrast forms *the basis of your response to the question and of your structure* in the essay. It also *sharpens your focus on each text* by placing it in opposition to the other(s). You may not have done much thinking or writing comparatively before. It is a valuable and interesting approach, but takes practice.

The comparative focus in relation to a particular question is something you create *during your responding and planning time* in the exam (using a grid or plan). Grids enable you to see your evidence and your analysis of your evidence visually, and compare the results across the two or three texts at a glance. This makes it easier to formulate a comparative thesis.

Practise the comparison during the course, in your note-making. Section Two below gives some Study Activities to help you do this. Return to this in your revision, to update your comparisons. To prepare for the exam, use sample questions or create your own based on 'conventions' or features, and design comparative answers with the use of grids such as in Section Three. This should help you generate examples or evidence, ideas, and formulate a comparative a thesis. Look at the sample essays in Section Three with a focus on how you construct the comparison in the essay.

Reflection on meeting the challenges of Part Three:

Which of the features of Part Three (Overview and 1.1 -1.3 above) are new to you and will particular attention?

Which advice about answering the question relevantly (as in 1.5 above) do you especially want to put into effect?

1.6 Understand and appreciate 'genre' and 'conventions'

Criterion C assesses how well you *identify* and *appreciate* the use of the literary conventions of the genre of your texts, in relation to the question. The exam question may focus on a particular feature or convention, such as 'endings', or 'setting', but your response should reflect wider understanding of the genre, and the work. Familiarity with the concepts of 'genre' and 'convention' gives you a more dynamic, concrete and interesting framework in which to approach the texts.

How genres and their conventions arise and evolve

Literary genres (or 'kinds') have come into being at very different moments in history, because of particular social or political contexts and conditions. For example, Western drama arose in 5th century BC Greece, but the Western novel did not appear until the 18th century, and poetry was composed long before drama appeared. You are not specifically assessed on your knowledge of the *history* of your genre, but some awareness of this, and of how variously writers have used the genre, deepens your appreciation of the *distinctiveness* of the genre and any individual text.

Genres only get labelled as 'the novel', and so on, when sufficient works have appeared for people to recognise them as similar in 'kind', with similar features. People find it convenient to sort and order things in this way. However, genres do not remain static. They may *subdivide*, as writers develop new forms (for example the "Gothic Novel"). They also continually evolve, thanks to the experimentation of writers, who take inspiration from past works, but also invent new ways to express what they want to say.

Conventions are distinguishing features or traditional elements of a genre that have become familiar and *accepted* over time. They may come into being as *convenient devices* to represent reality in a particular medium. For example, violence (usually killing people in inventive ways) was not directly shown on the ancient Greek stage, for obvious reasons. It took place offstage, and was reported by a 'narrator'. The narrator was a useful and effective 'convention' for representing the violence, and is still sometimes used today.

Conventions also develop as a result of changes in the social context the writer is working in. For example, elaborate, furnished stage settings developed in the 19th century with the changes in audience expectations, and in the technology of the theatre. Shakespeare and the ancient Greeks, in contrast, used a bare stage. Dramatists today have the choice to use an unfurnished stage, or a full 'set', depending on how they think their vision would best be projected.

As another example of how a convention becomes updated, Shakespeare used soliloquy as a convenient device to reflect Hamlet's mental processes and breakdown. Three hundred years later Tennessee Williams used the new technology of film and theatre (sound and lighting effects), in addition to words, to enhance Blanche's soliloquy expressing her mental breakdown in *A Streetcar Named Desire*.

'Old' conventions may be used in new and unexpected ways. The "epistolary novel" (consisting entirely of letters) was 'invented' in 18th century England, lost popularity, but was re-invented successfully in Alice Walker's *The Colour Purple* in late 20th century America. In any one work in a genre, you may find 'old' conventions, currently popular ones, or newly created features to express new ideas and vision. It is important to remember this constant state of flux.

Study and revision activity on genres and conventions:

What statements in 1.6 above particularly enlighten you about the idea of genre and conventions?

Look at a feature such as 'endings' or 'setting' and compare how they are used similarly or differently in two texts of the same genre.

1.7 Coherent organisation and development of ideas (Criterion D)

There is no substitute for practice in writing a full Paper Two essay, and ideally you should have the opportunity earlier in the programme. If your teacher does not set such an assignment, it is a good idea to plan and write a sample essay yourself, for the experience of the particular challenges it presents for you. Other ways to be prepared for the task are:

The formal essay elements
You should remind yourself of the elements of the formal essay (Chapter Three, Section Three), specifically the introduction and thesis, the paragraphs and the conclusion. Good use of these is what gives the required 'coherence' to your essay (along with the way you organise the comparison).

The introduction and thesis are particularly important in Paper Two because:
- They indicate to the examiner how relevantly and well you have addressed the question and compared the texts
- They set up what a reader is to expect in the body of the answer
- They provide you with a clear route in your essay

You should only formulate an overview *after* you have analysed your evidence (though this can work a bit differently in each case, as seen in Section Three samples below).

Using planning grids for revision practice

It is advisable to take 20 - 30 minutes (at both Levels) to organise your ideas comparing your texts on this Paper. Unlike in Paper One, where you have not seen the passages before, you (hopefully) already know your texts, so *your whole planning time is focused on creating a coherently organised comparison and structure*. A good plan is key to an effective structure. You can of course devise your own plan. There is no one single way to do it.

Using sample essays and grids as models

Look carefully at the structure of the samples in Section Three below. Discussion of their 'coherence', 'organisation' and 'development' accompanies them.

1.8 A quick reference guide for reading Paper Two texts for the exam

Paper Two is a test of your reading, study, and revision skills. You bring as many as four (or three) texts to a complex level of understanding for the same moment in time, and have to remember them. The key to this is to be consistent and conscientious in your study from the beginning, but also to be aware of different stages and levels of reading. Section 3.2 below, with its revision suggestions, is essential re-reading.

- **Before you embark on your texts**, some idea of the genre, its history and how it works will enrich your reading; also, some idea of the writer's context.

- **Read the text once, holistically, for enjoyment and a sense of its particularity** and impact as a whole. The work is unique to the writer's personality, interests, context and vision of the world. Give yourself the opportunity to catch this, and to have the chance to become immersed in it. Reading is about pleasure as well as reflection, as Chapter One points out. It will also make comparisons with other works easier and more effective.

- **Use Reading Stages One and Two (Chapter Two) to generate ideas and responses** about your texts, to profit from class discussion, and to devise a coherent system of notes – in other words to *take ownership both of your learning and of the texts*. This is the stage at which you will be thinking reflectively about the significance of content, the style and 'conventions', and the use of the genre.

- **Begin to make inter-textual comparisons** as you read more of your Part Three texts, incorporating these into your notes. Familiarise yourself with the typical conventions and compare and contrast the works in relation to these but avoid mere 'convention spotting', or narrowly focusing on this aspect of the work. Appreciate the text in all its fullness, along with the diverse ways the genre can be used.

- **Re-read the works in the month before the exam**, each more or less 'in one go', focusing on the impact of the whole text. After your weeks of work on a text, sometimes quite a time ago, this experience can be a revelation. Things suddenly become clear, and you realise how far you have come in your grasp of the work. It is a great way to feel ready for the exam, because it gives you the chance to understand and appreciate each text fully for the first time *as a whole*, and to see the relation of parts to the whole more clearly, which is essential for the essay. Pleasure and understanding come together. There is no substitute for this.

- **Organise your revision notes compactly and visually**, using Section 3.2 revision strategies (below). These help to condense the essence of your texts into a form that can manageably be scanned or skimmed shortly before the exam, to bring it all to mind. Remember that you memorise more effectively when your material is *visually organised*.

Section Two – How to read your genre: Drama and the Novel

This section focuses on the nature of different genres, and how you can think about your texts analytically as you read them, and as you revise for your exams in the Oral Commentary and Paper Two. It can only suggest *some* of the main ways to approach a text in your genre and to prepare for the exam. Writers each use their chosen genre and craft their work in very different ways to express their vision. There is no set of rules to follow in writing a work in a particular genre, though writers are inspired by their predecessors and may 'borrow' some ways of doing things.

Remember that as you study any text, you will need to be clear about the content as well as the crafting, and that it is best to gain the most complete view possible of the text. You should not approach texts narrowly in terms of how the writers use various conventions and features. Texts are far more than the sum of their parts.

Ways of approaching poetry are dealt with at some length in Chapter Four (Paper One). Each poet is highly individual in his or her approach to the genre, to a greater extent than dramatists or novelists, and need to be approached individually. Resources such as recommended in the short bibliography for Chapter Four will help with understanding different poetic techniques. In addition, recordings of poets (or others) reading their poems are invaluable, and you should make sure to work with these.

DRAMA

2.1. Why reading a play is different from reading other genres

Drama is a popular choice of genre in schools, but students often find it difficult to know how to read plays. It is not like reading novels, non-fiction or poetry, and calls for a different relationship with a reader. Unlike the other genres, plays have not been written for individual readers who will read them in their own time, but as scripts to be acted out on the stage, to be *heard and seen* by audiences in theatres. In a sense plays remain 'incomplete' until given life on the stage or in your imagination, whereas fiction, non-fiction and poetry present the complete expression of the writer's purpose.

Plays usually only become published texts once they have been performed. Your chosen play texts have become appropriate texts for study because they have succeeded on the live stage: they have a history of production and performance that influences their 'meaning'. This impacts on the way you read your plays.

Playwrights envisage the 'set' and space the actors/characters will move in, the objects they will use, how their words will sound, and the visual strategies and effects that will be needed to bring their intended meaning alive. But this meaning is only given life when interpreted by the director, actors, set, lighting and sound designers, and so on. The writer is just one part of a team of experts who bring the text into full being.

Writers also have to shape their material into the typical time frame of a play. A novel can be as long or short as the writer pleases, but the playwright must compress his or her vision into (typically) about two hours of performance, and hold the audience's attention through that time.

Although plays are written for performance they can still be enjoyed and appreciated as texts that you read and study. They have succeeded on the stage because *the text itself* has an emotional energy and vision that actors and directors respond to, and that continues to resonate after a production. *Good plays start with the text,* with the writer's vision of reality expressed through *the words* of characters, through *visual aspects*, and through the *interaction* of characters and what this leads to.

You should read and study the play with a sense of this energy and vision created by the writer. Fortunately DVDs and the Internet enable you to see productions. However, remember that any play produced is subject to the interpretation of the particular director, designer, actors and others involved in the production. In the exam, you interpret *the written text*; you don't comment on stage productions, however illuminating they might be.

2.2 What plays are typically about

There are a number of different ways in which plays come about. Writers have often re-told old or even recent stories or events – fictional or actual – because s/he sees the dramatic potential and interest of the story, and often the contemporary relevance it could have. Ancient Greek writers reworked old myths relating them to current issues; most of Shakespeare's plays are based on historic figures or old stories, and more modern plays such as Miller's *The Crucible*,

Shaffer's *Equus* or Frayn's *Copenhagen* give a new edge to real events. 'Re-tellings' may also be biographical – based on a particular character, giving it new life or a new perspective or opening up further debate, such as G.B Shaw's *St Joan*.

In contrast, many acclaimed plays have been entirely the invention of their author, often an expression of their vision of their society (present or past). Most of Arthur Miller and Tennessee Williams' plays fall into this category. Such a vision may be treated critically, to challenge us, or realistically, or in a mixture of modes including humour. The writer's vision may be expressed in many different forms, such as through *debate* (where two or more major characters may represent different viewpoints, as in some G.B Shaw plays) or *social drama*, where the *behaviour* of socially recognisable characters conveys the vision, or *symbolically*, as in *Waiting For Godot*.

Whichever the case, the writer is aware of the public impact this will have. A play is designed for a public place, a substantial live audience, and a particular society, though it may have a strong impact on and relevance for other completely different societies or groups (such as *Death of a Salesman* did on China). The context of the production of your play texts, and their impact when performed, can help you understand them more fully.

Study and revision activity on the nature of plays and their origins:

What stands out for you about the nature of drama (1.1)?

What was the starting point of your authors in writing the plays you are studying? How does that context help you understand the text more fully?

Can you define the 'dramatic interest' of your plays, or the vision of society expressed in them (as referred to in 2.2)?

2.3 Two ways you need to 'read' drama: (1) the formal; (2) the visual/ aural

Each of these requires a different way of responding, though they interlink and each contributes to a close understanding of the play and how it works.

The *formal* level is more conceptual and analytical: it involves seeing how the meaning of the play is created through the:

- Structure of the text – its scenes and act divisions
- Plot development, built through the structure
- Selection and patterning of characters and their relationships
- Language – how speeches and dialogue are written (grammar, literary features, punctuation, etc.)

The *visual* and *aural* level reflects how the writer has *visualised* and *'heard'* the play for the stage production. It expresses meaning in a more sensual and experiential way, and concerns what would impact on you if you saw and heard a production. Some of the most important aspects are:

- How the writer has designed the use of stage space throughout the play
- How characters should look, and how they are placed, grouped and move on stage
- What the setting is (there can be layers of setting or multi settings)
- What 'properties' or portable objects are used
- How lighting functions
- What action takes place (silently or with words)

These aspects are usually specified in the stage directions, which are part of the text (sometimes neglected by students). They need your attention and visual imagination, as they represent choices by the writer and are part of the play's intended meaning. The *aural* aspect involves:

- Sounds and music specified in the text, but also

- Pauses and silences (which may be specified, or may be inserted where the text implies and benefits from them)
- Volume, tone, pace, language and accent in speech and dialogue

2.4 Formal elements: Acts and Scenes

If you are aware of how plays are structured, it helps you grasp the work in a manageable way as you study it, and helps you make sense of the whole text at the revision stage. Structure is to do with how the narrative of the drama is told. Plays are written to be experienced live in the theatre and need to make sense from moment to moment (you can't turn back a page and re-read it, as with a novel). The playwright thus crafts *scenes* (the basic units of meaning in a play) and *acts* (which carry the larger units of unfolding action and idea), with economy and care.

Scenes and acts are the building blocks and architecture of the writer's meaning and purpose. When you track the focus of each scene (and each scene within a scene) and see its place in the larger structure of the act and play, you can identify both *what* happens and how (knowledge), and also *why* it is happening (understanding). This will help you later with answering the exam question with detailed reference to the play. Remember that your understanding of scenes and acts will grow with successive readings.

Plays can be structured in a variety of ways – using acts and/or scenes – depending on the effect the playwright wants to achieve and how s/he wants to tell the story. They may be composed, for example, in:

- Acts divided into scenes (as in Shakespeare)
- Acts with no formal scene divisions but falling into 'episodes', or mini-scenes
- A single, unbroken act (more common in contemporary plays)
- A series of scenes only (as in *A Streetcar Named Desire*), which may form a series of mini-scenes, each with a particular focus, and causing movement in the chain of action

---

Study and Revision activity: Looking at the overall structure:

How are your texts structured (as above, or in some other way)?
What is the focus of each Act and/or formal scene?
How much variety is there in the pace, atmosphere and time of each formal division?
What does the writer seem to want us to understand from this structure?
What is the cumulative effect of this structure?

The mini 'scene' and what it does

Whole sections of plays (such as designated scenes or acts) will often break down into a series of mini 'scenes', which can be defined as:

- Happening in one place only
- Framed by one or more characters appearing, and one or more departing. Any entrance or exit of a character means a new 'scene'
- A moment in which previous relationships or circumstances can be challenged or changed by new knowledge, events or feelings produced by the behaviour and interaction of characters
- A moment focusing on a shift or change in characters' relations or circumstances, caused by the above point

The mini scene (as defined above) is the fundamental unit of meaning in many plays. It is typically a page or two long, and has a coherence of its own within the larger structure of 'official' scene or act. It is what really helps you understand how your play works, and it is what provides interest in live performance from minute to minute on the stage.

Such 'scenes' ensure a necessary variety of pace and intensity but also have a specific focus and function, which is a change or shift in the situation, either for the characters themselves, or the way we see the characters and the situation.

These 'shifts' in each mini-scene generate momentum in the play, contributing to the trajectory of its plot development. Each 'scene' leads into the next, with something to resolve. Once you have understood the 'secret' of the existence and function of the 'scene', you can read a play with much more awareness of the richness of its craft. Its logic and significance will be more apparent, and you will have specific examples or 'evidence' for your essays. It is also a very concrete and manageable way to study, in coherent smaller units.

Not all plays work in clearly in this way, however, and you may need to find your own way to break down large units in your plays into meaningful smaller ones in a similar way.

Study and revision activity: looking at a 'scene' (as defined above):

As you begin to read a play, or to revise it, make notes on each 'scene', as defined.
Re-read the third bulleted point above. Provide each 'scene' (within a larger scene or act) with a title that describes the most significant shift or change in it, which may be to do with how we see things, or the state of the character(s). Compare how the first two or three 'scenes' work in any one play, for a sense of the variety, and of how one scene leads to the next.

2.5 Acts

Acts are larger units of time, and play an important part in the shaping and unfolding of a play's narrative and ideas. An act carries the momentum of the sequence of 'scenes' (described above) but usually has an overall focus. It is best to read it in one go, on a first reading, to gain a sense of this focus. Acts can have different 'flavours' and locations, and can be effective ways to shift from one location or moment in time to another.

The way acts are developed, and their relationship with other acts, depends upon the writer's purpose and the tradition s/he is working in. Where plot, especially a tragic plot, drives the play, as for example in *The Crucible,* the acts (and their scenes) will be tightly constructed, leading to the inexorable end, heightening the sense of impending disaster. Some plays conform to the classic 'well-made play' pattern of 'exposition', 'complication', 'climax', and 'denouement' (unravelling).

By contrast, Shakespeare's acts, as in *Hamlet,* are often diffuse and unpredictable, though each act usually has a thematic focus, and its parts contribute something to the complex vision of the whole work. Some modern plays may work in an even more challenging way, shifting perspective, place and time, and inviting the audience to make the connections between parts.

Study and Revision Activity:

How do the acts of your plays (where there are acts) relate to each other?
What is the overall focus of each act, in your view? How is each constructed (its episode or scenes, etc)?
How far does the pace and intensity, or our perspective on characters, change in different acts?
Create a visual of the acts and their scenes, with your headings for each, to help you remember them for the exam. These could be condensed on to one A4 page.

2.6 Action and plot

Action and 'inaction'
'Drama' means 'action', but action in drama can mean several things. It can for example mean something *that changes the situation* in some way. These changes may be subtle or momentous, and are one of the elements that make plays compelling, especially when seen live. The changes also contribute to the movement of the plot.

Action that changes things can take verbal or physical form, and can be equally effective onstage or offstage. Elizabeth Proctor's one-word lie: 'No' in court, uttered out of love for her husband, ironically destroys his case and helps cause his death. Stan's verbal action offstage in *A Streetcar Named Desire*, deliberately ruining his friend Mitch's interest in Blanche, leads to the destruction of the whole group, in different degrees. Hamlet's physical killing of Polonius on stage ushers in a whole set of consequences that produce a complex tragedy.

On the other hand there may be plenty of 'actions' in a play that can seem random and do not effect change, but produce other equally important effects. Lady Macbeth, guilty of complicity in murder, enacts washing her hands while she is sleepwalking. This action (with her words) doesn't change the situation, but it shifts the onlookers' and our perceptions and sympathies. Stan throws the radio out of the window in *Streetcar*, which contributes to the sense of his ugly control and the disturbing violence of the whole scene, but it does not directly change anything.

Actions that do not change things, such as most of the 'action' in *Waiting for Godot*, may enhance our understanding of character and idea, and our sense of the significance of the writer's purpose. Both kinds of action are important.

Study and revision activity on 'action':

Identify some significant actions in your plays (verbal, physical, on or offstage) that change the situation in some way.
What kind of change do they cause? What kind of effect does the moment of this action have?
Identify several actions that do not bring change but cause other effects. How would you describe these effects?

Plot

We may define plot as the writer's deliberate arrangement of events and actions in order to give them a particular focus and significance, and to suggest the connection between them – a sense of cause and effect. In that way a plot is a bit like the sequence of an essay argument. It is part of the writer's ordering and structuring of his or her material to produce a particular emotional, intellectual or aesthetic effect, or to convey a point.

The plot may be very apparent, driving the play and characters. On the other hand, it may be scarcely visible, where characters talk and carry out activities but little seems to change (though usually s*omething* has changed by the end). If 'change' is not what the play seems concerned with, we need to think what impact the play's content has had on us, through what the characters say and do. The significance of the play and the author's intentions may lie in this, rather than a more conventional plot.

A plot where justice is done in the end, or where things end happily after all, may be satisfying, and affirm one's hopes for order in the world. A play where the ending may seem undeserved or disturbing, or holds positive and negative elements in balance, may be asking us to reflect on some aspect of our world or our values, or to see the world and people in a new or more complex light. A play where there seems to be little if any cause or effect, may invite us to make connections and to find significance ourselves, as we might do with a poem.

Plots are different from 'stories', which are chronological accounts of a series of events without a meaningful pattern. Characters' 'stories' (previous events in their life) may emerge in the course of a play, through what they and others say, and these can be important for our understanding of the whole text, but this is very different from plot, as the following should make clear.

Blanche DuBois's 'story', as we learn from hints at different moments in *A Streetcar Named Desire*, begins with her girlhood on her Southern estate, continues with her early marriage and its tragic outcome, follows with her decline into prostitution, etc. The *plot* of the play, to which she is central, however, begins with her arrival at her sister's marital home *after* all the above events have taken place, and deals with the *consequences* of her arrival, as well as revealing her character. Each scene focuses on a particular episode in her time at the apartment, forges the chain of cause and effect, and deepens our sense of the complexity and tragedy of the situation and characters.

Plays, notably those of Shakespeare, may contain subplots or present parallel situations, which can provide a comment on the main plot, or intensify the effect of the main plot. For example, *Death of a Salesman* contains two fathers with sons. The play is deepened by the contrast in the relationships between them, and their values. Hamlet contains two 'revenge' plots, driven by Hamlet and Laertes whose fathers are killed, and who are linked by love for Ophelia. These plots are intertwined and create a much richer sense of final tragedy.

Study and revision activity on plot:

Trace the plot of your plays, for a clear sense of the actions that move the plot along. What is the effect of the way the plot develops, and of the outcome? What does the writer seem to intend by this pattern and outcome?
If plot is not easily visible, does anything of consequence happen? If not, what effect do the various episodes have? Is there a pattern or significance that emerges from them?
Are there any subplots or parallel plots? What do they contribute to the main plot?

2.7 Character: function and presentation

The genius of the playwright is in the characters that s/he creates. Great stage characters resonate in the imagination and become larger than the plays they are part of – Othello, Hamlet, Willy Loman, John Proctor, etc. Unlike characters in the novel, however, they do not come fully formed, with a fixed identity, because they exist only in their words and their interactions with other characters. Novel characters, in contrast, are formed through many strategies of the writer and the consciousness of the narrator, who influence our vision by describing them from the outside and the inside, alone and in company.

This fluid identity is a strength rather than a limitation of drama. It is why great actors can give different meaning to the same words and actions, and suggest new dimensions of a character that contribute to its greatness (whereas the fullness of identity of a novel character can rarely be translated to stage or film with complete success). It means that you need to imagine the text, hear and see it in your imagination, if you cannot see a performance.

Because of the necessary economy of the play's duration and the circumstances of production, characters in plays tend to be limited in number, and serve a clear *function*:

- They generally contribute in some measure to the plot
- They may embody ideas, significant qualities or values in which the writer has a particular interest
- They may represent social types, attitudes or issues of the writer's context
- They may give voice to those with little status or influence in their time
- They may embody some fundamental human drive or flaw, or psychological motivation
- They may express something of the writer's soul, or express depths of mind and spirit
- They may act as a 'foil' or contrast to another character, or reflect them in some way; or fill the role of 'confidant (e)', enabling another character to reveal him or herself
- They may connect with another character or characters in a significant, interesting, sometimes unusual way

Those characters we tend to remember most vividly are placed in a situation or predicament or conflict (often unexpected and unfamiliar) that tests them and impacts on others. They may rise to levels beyond their imagined capacity, and grow or develop, or they may 'fail', with varying effects on us and other characters. They often invite understanding, even empathy, rather than judgment. To be memorable, they must reflect some human quality that speaks to audiences and connects with them.
There are many ways of revealing and presenting character:

- Through what the say, and the language they use, with others or in soliloquy
- Through what they do: verbal and physical action, gestures
- Through their interaction with other characters, which may be different in each case
- Through objects associated with them
- Through dress and physical appearance – which may change
- Through what others reveal about them

Study and revision activity on character:

Take any one of your plays and look at each main character from the point of view of 'function', using the bulleted points above on functions. What seems to be the writer's purpose in selecting these characters?

2.8 The visual and aural dimension of drama

What affects you in performance, and resonates after you have seen a play, is what you see, hear and feel. You are unlikely to recall the shape of a scene, or the function of a character, but you will remember the physical position of a character, the dimming of lights, or the emotion expressed through the sound of words and pauses and the way a character looks.

Because a play takes place in a confined space, your vision is funnelled into this, and what you *see* (what the writer puts in that space physically) is greatly intensified. An object, or movement, or sound can take on symbolic force. The challenge of *reading* a play is to try to capture some of the meaning that is communicated in this way, indicated in stage directions and through the language of the dialogue. Some kinds of visual and aural language are:

Visual moments (images or tableaux)

These occur when the position of characters or a particular character creates a lasting image or picture: the aged King Lear cradling his dead daughter; Hamlet addressing the skull of his old friend in the churchyard, Stan bellowing for Stella at the foot of the apartment stairs. The power of these images is that they express visually something *integral to the whole play* and its meaning: the power of forgiveness and reconciliation in *Lear;* the mystery of time and death in *Hamlet*; the deeply-rooted interdependency of Stan and Stella, which Blanche cannot shift. These 'pictures' or groupings may be implied in speeches, or indicated in stage directions.

Stage space and setting

This may be organised into different areas that express dramatic meaning. The *Streetcar* stage set takes in the bustling street, the apartment with its 3 rooms, and the stairs to the apartment above. All of these areas play a significant part in the action and the meaning of the play.

A sense of an offstage area can create a powerful effect, for example inviting escape or harbouring menace. The stage can represent a single room, where the door or doors will have an intense effect as someone enters or leaves; or it may present an empty space, as often in Shakespeare, where it is the words of characters that embed descriptions or indications of place and time, as in: *How sweet the moonlight sleeps upon this bank".*

Objects or 'properties'

Because of the intense focus on one small space (the stage) in a play, objects used by characters often take on great force, for example, the broken glass unicorn in Williams' *The Glass Menagerie,* or the feather Lear uses to see if his daughter Cordelia is still breathing.

The aural aspect: language, speech and dialogue

'Language' is the *method* of communication, using words (which may include poetry and song as well as dialogue), gesture, facial or body language, and 'visual action'. Speech is the act of speaking. Different characters in a play may use language in very different ways. Sentence length and complexity, the kind of grammar and diction used, the field of reference or allusion, figures of speech, tone and manner, pauses, silences or fragments of speech, can all play a part in characterisation and produce particular effects.

THE NOVEL

2.9 How to study novels for exams

The novel continues to be a hugely productive, vital genre that compels great interest in society and can endlessly be adapted to suit different writers' needs and visions. Each one offers a unique world and vision. In terms of studying for exams in this programme (For Part Two and Part Three), the novel presents the challenge of length, requiring particular study strategies.

You will probably read most of your novels *by yourself,* only discussing parts of them in class. To ensure that you have grasped each part as you study it, use Reading Stages One and Two in Chapter Two, which are intended specifically for reading novels and longer texts effectively. Follow these Stages *in conjunction* with the suggestions below, which cover a few of the broadest features and conventions of the genre.

In addition there are some excellent audio books of classic novels, which may include ones that you are studying. *Hearing* a novel read expertly has much value in terms of helping you appreciate narrative 'voice', point of view, shifts of tone, and some of the subtler aspects of the reading experience, though it is not a substitute for reading the text.

For the Part Two Oral Commentary and Discussion, and for Paper Two, the challenge is to have a good overall grasp of what may be a long and complex work, with a sense of how the parts of the work fit into the whole. It is very difficult to have good grasp of a novel without at least a second and preferably a third reading. Use the subsections below to think about your novel and follow Section 3.2 of this chapter for ideas about how to organise your revision in the final stages.

For Paper Two, your focus will be *comparative*, exploring how different writers use this very diverse genre. The Study Activities in the following subsections should help you pull your texts together comparatively, as well as helping you read each text with more awareness.

2.10 Origins and definitions of the novel

Although the English novel came into being millennia later than poetry and drama (in 18th century England), it is by far the most prolific and popular genre in English now (and in many other languages). To understand what distinguishes the novel as a genre, why it is so popular with writers, and how we should understand it, it helps to look briefly at the context in which it originated, and to consider to what extent the contemporary novel resembles its ancestors.

'Fiction' existed for centuries before the novel, in various forms in England and elsewhere (exotic tales, re-workings of old stories, and short realistic tales, for example), but this new form of fiction was more focused on *character*, had a more developed and unified *plot*, and deliberately created the illusion of *reality*.

It emerged at a time of increasing social stability, when people had more leisure for reading, and were fascinated by their own society and the characters in it – prostitutes, servants, priests, upper class ladies, and so on. Biography, autobiography, diaries, books about character types, and other forms of non-fiction were already hugely popular, reflecting this curiosity about other people's lives, especially their inner lives and thoughts. The early novel owes more to these forms of *non*-fiction than to earlier fictional 'tales'.

Early novelists often made their writing look and sound like real biography or autobiography, titled with the main character's name (Robinson Crusoe, Moll Flanders, Tom Jones, etc.). But the new fiction tended to have an angle on society, satirical or ironic or moral, in addition to the central interest of character. Also, in contrast to both earlier fiction and the contemporary non-fiction, novels created *unique* stories, with unique characters, in a distinct world of the writer's imagination but recognisably reflecting society. Another feature was the narrator's presence in his or her work, addressing the individual readers, as if in a personal relationship. Jane Eyre happily (and famously) says: " Reader, I married him", at the end of the novel of that name, as if the reader were a sympathetic friend.

Reflection on the origins of the novel:

Given the context in which the novel evolved, and these characteristics, in what ways do novels you have read resemble or not resemble earlier novels?

2.11 Novel openings

If novels do not make the reader want to read on, they will not survive, so writers labour to make titles 'right' and significant, and their openings memorable, as well as creating narratives that make the reader want to 'turn the page'. Titles can indicate the writer's *purpose*, or the *subject*, but can also be provocative or mysterious, reflecting an ambiguity in the narrative or theme. Thomas Hardy purposefully subtitled his famous *Tess of the D'Urbervilles* "A Pure Woman". This indicates how *he* saw (and would wish *us* to see) his subject, the young woman who had an illegitimate baby and later murdered her seducer.

Scott Fitzgerald's title *The **Great** Gatsby* is ambiguous (given the way the title character is deserted by almost everyone at the end), and makes us examine the whole novel in the light of this adjective. How is Gatsby 'great'? Some titles quote other works, such as Hemingway's *For Whom the Bell Tolls* or Rhys's *Wide Sargasso Sea*. If you explore critically the significance of the quotation and the work from which it is taken, this can enhance your perspective on the work.

Some writers include an epigraph or quotation at the beginning of their work, either taken from another work, or one the author has made up (as in the case of *The Great Gatsby)*. Quotations are very personal to the writer, and can provide an interesting insight into something that inspired him or her, or that is significant to the core of the work. It often works best to return to them after reading the work, to gauge their relevance.

The openings of novels, as well as titles, can suggest how we should approach the work, for example, critically, with curiosity, with humour, or some other way. Jane Austen's opens *Pride and Prejudice,* with the statement that: *"It is truth universally acknowledged, that a single man in possession of a good fortune must be in want of a wife"*. This is clearly exaggeration and mockery, and leads us to anticipate her ironic (but also serious) treatment of societal behaviour in relation to marriage.

Other works take us immediately into the *action*, and make us want to find out what is happening and why. Or they tell us what is going to happen and arouse our interest us in how and why this will happen. In contrast, a novel like *Heart of Darkness* begins not with the core narrative, but a 'frame' narration, guiding us to the main *character* and his narration, creating an illusion of its reality. It also carefully evokes a *setting* (London's river Thames) that will play an important thematic and symbolic role in the story.

Other novels begin 'at the beginning', with the earliest memory of the narrator, such as James Joyce's *A Portrait of the Artist as a Young Man,* or Dickens' *Great Expectations,* and then take us on a journey of the narrator's development. Or they begin with the introduction of a character or place. They may even 'begin' at the end of the story, and then go back in time.

Study activity on titles and openings:

Look at titles and openings of two of your novels. Why might the author have chosen this title? How does it influence us or guide us to a way of reading the work?

2.12 Narrators and point of view

The narrator role is the distinguishing characteristic of the novel genre (rarely used in drama or poetry). It is a great opportunity for the writer's creativity, and shapes the way we read and receive a work. All fiction is narrated by *someone*, whether that presence seems almost invisible (as sometimes in third person narration) or is highly visible, with a distinct voice, language and personality (as often in first person narration).

Ways to approach 'first person' narration

Early novels were first person narrations (see 2.2 above), and this convention is increasingly popular today. There may be a single first person narrator, or several first person narrators, or an omniscient narrator, entering into the minds of different characters. You need to consider the purpose these serve, and the effect they have.

Does the single narrator come across as an unusual or provocative character, whose point of view we are invited to share or react to, such as the paedophile narrator of *Lolita,* or the exuberant, subversive young narrator of *Catcher in the Rye*? Are we drawn into a relationship of unsettling fascination with the narrator, sympathising with him/her, perhaps in spite of ourselves?

Alternatively, is the narrator exploring his or her own experience and development, as in *Great Expectations*, where the narrator captures his past vividly, but also gives us a sense of his present, reflecting older self. How important is the narrator in relation to the events described? Is s/he a significant part of events, or an outsider? Imagine what would be lost if the story were told omnisciently? What kind of consciousness and character does the narrator, bring to the story, influencing the way we see it?

Has the writer deliberately made the narrator's point of view a limited one, inviting *us* to see what s/he does not see or understand, as in Ishiguro's *The Remains of the Day*, or the 13-year old Huck in *Huckleberry Finn,* who describes appalling events without realising their significance? Look at the effect *produced* by these limitations of narrator perspective. Do events strike us more forcibly because the narrator doesn't understand them as we do (as in Huck's case)? Is the limitation a way of making us aware of the singularity of the *character* (as with Ishiguro's character)?

If there are two first person narrators, as in *Wide Sargasso Sea,* alternating in their narratives of the same sequence of events, how are we being invited to position ourselves in relation to each narrator? How do we see them in relation to each other and the events they describe? If there are multiple narrators describing the same event, is the interest in the *event,* seen or partly seen from different viewpoints, or in the way the different *characters* perceive?

Ways to approach 'omniscient' or 'third person' narration

An 'omniscient' (all-knowing) or 'third person' narrator can theoretically enter the consciousness of any character, and know his or her motives, but in fact is usually selective, so that our attention is focused on the characters who are most interesting and important to the plot. Elizabeth Bennet is one of *five* sisters in Jane Austen's *Pride and Prejudice,* but it is her consciousness that we follow through the novel, not her sisters.

However, Austen's use of the third person viewpoint allows us to see Elizabeth from the outside as well as the inside, both critically and sympathetically, and to see more broadly the society in which she has to make her way, the stumbling blocks she has to manoeuvre. It allows Austen to *control* more carefully how we see characters and events. Consider why any omniscient narrator in your novels might have chosen to enter some minds rather than others.

An omniscient narrator can use the freedom to shift from the mind or point of view of one character to another, involving our sympathies and understanding across a spectrum of characters, sometimes unexpectedly. Omniscience plays a different role in a work like McEwan's *Atonement.* Here we enter the minds and points of view of different characters who live at close quarters but have no access to each other's minds, causing misunderstanding and tragedy, while the reader experiences the discomfort – the dramatic irony – of knowing them all.

Revision Activity on narrator and point of view:

Who narrates your novels? Are there single,' first person' or multiple narrators? What does each writer gain from his/her choice?
What kind of person do the narrators seem to be? What does this choice of narrator seem to invite us to be aware of? Find a few points in the novels where the sense of narrator is strong or effective in some way.
In what way are the first person narrators limited?
How omniscient are the third person narrators – do they hold information back? How selective are they in their scrutiny of characters?
How do any of the examples in 2.4.4 illuminate the novels you have studied?

2.13 Character

The English novel developed out of a fascination with real characters and was presented to look like real autobiography or biography. This illusion of reality, and this power to create distinctive characters, is at the heart of the art and success of the novel. If we are not made to believe in the characters, they tend to have little interest for us.

The novel has also typically made interesting and memorable characters out of 'ordinary' people (victims, the disadvantaged, the alienated, the weak). It gives them a voice and creates sympathy for them, through first person narration, or through third person narration, which can take us into their minds, and/or present them from the outside. There is a huge variety of ways in which character is presented, and of roles they play for the reader. Thinking of one or more of your works, decide:

- What the writer seems to want to convey through different characters: a moral standpoint, unacceptable values or behaviour, someone typical of his/her time or place, an evolution of the character's understanding, or something else
- What kind of response any particular character seems to be inviting (understanding, despite his/her weaknesses or villainy, or antisocial behaviour), or admiration, sympathy or amusement for some quality of character or response s/he shows to a situation
- How the writer has made particular characters memorable: through speech traits, physical characteristics, attitudes, actions
- Whether any character seems to embody any of the attitudes, values or vision of the writer?
- How characters are presented: through what they say and how they say it; through what they think and how they see the world; through appearance and behaviour; through what the narrator tells us; through what they do
- Whether they are revealed early and completely, or gradually
- How far they have changed by the end. What the trajectory of their development or their fate in the course of the novel may tell us, or how we are invited to interpret this pattern of plot
- Whether the writer's interest in them is psychological, exploring their motivation, or social, exploring how they function in social relationships
- In what way the circumstances they are placed in reveal or test them, and affect the way we see them
- If third person narration, how many characters' minds the narrator enters, and what this contributes; and why we are not taken into others' minds

2.14 Setting

Setting has to do with both *location* (*where* a narrative takes place) and *time* (*when* it takes place). It has come to be regarded as one of the most important features of the novel, even dominating certain novels, though it was not a feature of early novels, where character and plot predominated.

The power to create memorable and atmospheric landscapes and settings is a mark of the novelist's genius, but it is closely intertwined with character, narrative and the meaning of a work. Try to take the characters and plot out of the setting of one of your novels, and put them in a different one, and the essence of the work is probably lost. Characters are of their time and place, and place gives life to narrative.

Setting may be established through extended passages of vivid description, or through details and rapid 'brushstrokes' woven through the narrative, or implicit, as in Jane Austen's small rural communities and households, which are rarely described. It may be a landscape, a city, a culture. There may be one dominant setting, or multiple settings beyond or within a dominant setting. (See the essay on setting in Section Three below). Some of the things setting can do are:

- Shape and reflect characters and their values (as the moors setting shapes the wild and passionate Cathy in *Wuthering Heights*, or the Caribbean landscapes in *Wide Sargasso Sea*)
- Embody cultural values (as in aspects of Achebe's *Things Fall Apart*)
- Provide the material for social comment or criticism, and for encounters with many characters 'typical' of that time and place (like large sections of *Huckleberry Finn*, or *The Great Gatsby*)
- Create a challenge for a character or group who encounter a new and unfamiliar setting or settings (*The Grapes of Wrath, A Passage to India, Lord of the Flies*). This may lead to tragedy, negotiation and deeper understanding, or personal triumph
- Provide a measure for a character's change over time, as when Pip in *Great Expectations* returns to his home village periodically over several years, and registers his own, or others' changes
- Reflect how the place itself has changed, providing a comment on the surrounding culture or the circumstances that have produced this change
- Create tension, and dramatic interest, as in Dickens' use of the marshes and the escape down the Thames
- Embody the vision of the writer (Fitzgerald in *The Great Gatsby* – see the sample essay in Section Three)

Weather is related to setting, and can play a significant role. It can be used strategically in the plot, causing challenges to the characters (storms or heat can do this, for example). It can foreshadow or mirror important action, build suspense or echo mood, like the rain at the desolate end of *A Farewell to Arms*.

Study Activity on Setting:

Identify some of the settings in your novels.
How does the writer create these settings (through vivid language effects, through specific details, through suggestion, or other means)?
What role do the settings have? Do they resemble any of the bulleted items above, or play some other role?
Are there any significant effects of weather in your novels?

2.15 Endings

Endings have often been problematic for novelists, as the 47 versions of Hemingway's ending of *A Farewell to Arms* illustrate. At the same time, this suggests the writer's need to 'get it right', to make the ending consistent with the development of the novel, the logical outcome of its vision or purpose, and a memorable conclusion to the 'journey' that has taken place. This need can be so strong that writers have sometimes written the ending first.

One problem with endings is that writers are aware that readers often want a sense of satisfactory closure, or at least, nothing too negative. Dickens famously re-wrote his ending to *Great Expectations* at a friend's insistence, creating one that left things more open and positive. Another problem is that whereas novels mirror realities of life, neat endings do not, and some novelists want to 'end' with the kind of open-endedness, untidiness and ambiguity that is more typical of real life and the life they have represented in their narratives.

In earlier novels, where plot is strong, the convention is to 'wind things up', solve the mysteries, and in many cases create happy or satisfactory endings, which can have a mechanical feel. In 'great' hands, however, like those of Emily Bronte in *Wuthering Heights*, 'closure' does not mean artificiality. With the tormented lovers dead and in their tomb, she paints a tranquil scene in the graveyard with wild flowers and soft wind, where the narrator imagines the lovers finally at peace, in the landscape that united them.

Endings may, among many possibilities:
- Be inconclusive, leaving a sense of life going on, with nothing 'resolved'
- Shift the perspective suddenly (as in *Things Fall Apart*) shocking us into another way of looking at the narrative
- Provide what seems to be a conclusion, followed by another, discombobulating one (as in Atwood's *The Handmaid's Tale*)
- Introduce an unexpected twist, that throws new meaning on the work
- Create an atmosphere or mood that induces reflection on the narrative and its development
- Produce a sense of inevitable ending to what has preceded
- Mirror a vision or point the writer wishes to make
- Suggest new possibilities (Huck Finn's disclosure that he will run off again)
- Have a double ending, for example where there is a 'frame narration', and the core story impacts on the frame narrator

Study activity on endings:

The real ending sometimes takes place before the last page. Which is the true ending to your narratives? How satisfactory and memorable are the endings? In what ways? Looking at the paragraphs and the bulleted points above, how far do your endings fit these descriptions? What else do they achieve?

2.16 Time in the novel

Time is a human obsession and we live in constant awareness of it. It is reflected in all genres, but novels particularly play with the notion of time, often moving backwards and forwards in time and distorting the chronology of the narrative, for particular effects. A narrator can move around in time, connecting things or remembering, in a way hard to achieve on stage except with special effects. Consider how time is used in your novels. What part does time play and how does the writer manipulate time?

For many more insights into the features and styles of novels, look at David Lodge's *The Art of Fiction,* which discusses fifty different terms and techniques, each illustrated by an extract. Refer also to Chapter Four, Section Two, the discussion of prose style and the 'checklist' of prose features.

Section Three: Paper Two – Revising, Planning and Writing the exam

3.1 What being 'exam-ready' means: twelve suggestions (in approximate order)

Remember, this is an exam over which you have a significant amount of control. You will be writing about texts you know (and it is up to you how well you know them), and a genre you have studied. Attention to all the following points in the weeks before the exam should give you the confidence to feel that you are well prepared. You will be surprised how much of what you have done flows into your mind in the exam room.

- Make sure you know **which your Part Three texts are**, their correct titles and authors, and **the genre** you are studying. It is not unknown for students to take a question from a different genre section to the one they have studied. This carries a penalty.

- Read Section One of this chapter to remind yourself of **the assessment criteria**, how to meet these and especially how to avoid the 'typical weaknesses' candidates have shown in the past (notably not **answering the question appropriately** or relevantly).

- As far as possible, re-read your works as outlined in 3.2 below. Have a clear sense of the **sequence and content of your texts** (chapters, acts and scenes, poems)) and record this concisely to help you **remember** this **'knowledge'**.

- Record, along with the suggestion above, what you consider **some significant lines or passages**. The ability to *refer closely* to the texts and to discuss specific aspects in detail distinguishes the best essays, as all the samples below illustrate clearly. Don't be tempted to incorporate in your essay quotations that you have learned, just because you know them. If they are not relevant, they won't impress. You don't *have* to learn quotes (for the prose genres), though the ability to incorporate some relevant quoted phrases enhances your essay. Students doing poetry *will* need to be able to quote.

- In your final revision, to **deepen your understanding**, formulate 'Level Three' questions (3.2 below and Chapter Two, Section Two) to test your understanding of the content, especially 'difficult' or ambiguous aspects or passages.

- Know the distinctiveness of your **genre, and its characteristic aspects or conventions** (Section Two above and Chapter Four, Section Two).

- Know **the kind of questions** you will be asked, but don't anticipate or prepare for specific questions. Be prepared to answer *any* question, by practising the skill of answering.

- Refresh your understanding of **the elements of the formal essay** and what these look like in a good essay (Chapters Three and the samples below) Pay attention especially to the **thesis**.

- **Study sample essays and plans** (as below) to understand what to aim for.

- Be aware of **effective ways to structure** your essay comparatively. It should not be two or three mini essays on separate texts, strung together (see the sample essays and the comments on these below).

- Practice making an effective **plan or grid** in a timed period of about 30 minutes, using past questions (see the grids below or create your own).

- **Write a practice essay** from a plan, without texts, to see what the challenges are. It is two hours (HL) or one and a half (SL) well spent.

- **Make a time management plan** (Chapter Two Section 3.2 and Chapter Five Section 2.2.1) to prioritise your revision tasks and ensure you can cover everything you need to do.

3.2 Seven steps for revising a text for Paper Two

This subsection is adapted from Chapter Two, Section 3.3 ("Reading Stage Four") as it is vital for this exam. Paper Two requires you to have a good grasp of *several* whole texts at once. You will not know what questions you are going to be asked, and must be ready to turn your mind to any aspect of those works without the texts to hand. There are strategies to make this a manageable process, but as the comments on the samples below reveal, your strategies may vary according to the work and the genre.

The most important thing you do is reread your texts. Prioritise this over going through old notes or reading secondary sources. *Nothing* substitutes for this third or fourth reading of the text.

(i) Re-read each whole text and write an overarching 'thesis'
Where the text is of manageable length, re-read it carefully for a sense of the whole. A good answer to a Paper Two question involves a sense of how the question topic fits into the whole text. You have probably read and discussed the text in *parts,* bit by bit. It makes a very different impact when you read the entire text again more or less at a sitting. Everything comes together.

Things that you laboured to understand when the text was new to you should now be absorbed into your reading and make more sense. Conversely, certain things may stand out to you with new force. Jot those things down. Finally, *write down one or two sentences that for you encapsulate the significance of the whole work or individual poem.* This 'thesis' should pull your response to the whole work together and show your awareness of the writer's purpose. As you will see from all the samples, this will help with any question you answer.

In the case of poetry, read your poems (author by author) as a sequence. Whatever their qualities as individual poems, each takes on more significance in relation to the others when read in sequence.

(ii) Identify significant aspects of the *parts* of your text

Your exam essay will explore a particular aspect of the work (like setting), so in addition to having a sense of the whole, you need to remember in some detail what happens in the parts. You also want to remember what is most significant. The way you prepare this is a matter of preference. One helpful strategy is as follows. While you are re-reading the work or poems:

- Prepare a sheet of card or paper (not too large) for each poem, or each part of a bigger text (act, scene, chapter or part, depending on the genre)
- **Create a title** for that section (not poems) that brings its essence and action together. (For example: *Blanche's arrival at the New Orleans apartment and her impact on Stella and Stan*)
- **Bullet the main features** of the scene, chapter, etc., as you see them – perhaps 6-8 points (as in Chapter Two, Section 2.3.4, "Headings of significant elements" – the Dickens sample)
- **Write down a quote or two** from that section that carries particular meaning for you
- For poems, make sure you see how each one works individually and what particular features it has (use Chapter Four Section Two)

(iii) Use your past notes efficiently

Read back or skim quickly through your past notes to highlight anything you especially want to remember, and *incorporate this into your new compact plan* of cards or pages as above. You will not want to be wading back through sheaves of notes more than once, but these earlier notes may clarify some points or remind you of some important ideas.

(iv) Formulate "Level Three" questions to develop greater insight into the work

Reading and noting (as in ii above) to remember the contents is a basic revision strategy. A way to gain *more* understanding and insight into the texts (for the highest levels of mark) is to create 'Level Three' questions. These will centre on passages that are ambiguous in implication, or that involve stylistic techniques. Incorporate these into the cards or sheets on each part as discussed in (ii). For example (on *Death of a Salesman*):

"How far does Linda believe in Willy's dreams at the start of Act Two?

"Does Miller invite us to have any sympathy for Howard?"

"How should we respond to the Dave Singleton story?"

Why does Miller have both Biff and Willy experience disasters on the same day and try to tell them at the same time?"

Creating such questions involves thinking about the text in a more analytical way from (ii) above. It helps to do this in a pair or group where more minds are involved. Exploring responses to these questions can transform your power and confidence to think about the text, and prepares you better for answering any question on the exam paper.

(v) Create a visual sequence of the text's contents to find patterns and connections

Arrange the cards or sheets you have prepared as above in a sequence on a table or wall, so that you see clearly both the parts and the whole of an individual text and how these relate. Connect parts where you have not seen connections before, by linking with symbols, lines or colour coding. This "God's Eye" view allows you to see the design of the author much more clearly.

For example, you might see how often a particular setting occurs, or a particular kind of encounter between characters. You might also see the patterning of the plot in a new way. Instead of the text seeming to be a 'story', you see it as a carefully designed and created whole, with 'choices' the writer has made.

When you see the sequence of parts visually, with a bulleted order to the contents of each part, it will imprint itself better on your memory and provide a quick way to remind yourself of the contents of the texts shortly before the exams.

(vi) Compare the visual sequences of your texts

When you have the above on each text, look at them visually in relation to each other. The planning models below for the samples show how a visual pulls texts together. It can also be a way to see comparisons between texts. Enter these as you look at the sequence on one text in relation to the other texts

(vii) Use secondary sources where necessary, with discretion

Read a good introduction to the author and his/her context (texts often have useful introductions). It is an advantage to have a perspective on the context of the writer and the text. Reading other secondary sources should be done with discretion and only when you have revised your primary texts well. The primary texts and your personal grasp of them is your priority. As you will know from Chapter Two, Section One, you should not be expecting secondary sources to provide you with 'meaning', but they may have some interesting observations that help you establish *your own position* more clearly.

Reflection and activity on revision strategies:

Looking at 3.1 and 3.2 above, which revision tasks do you especially need to spend time on? Using the time-management plans referred to, enter the tasks you select, the time you plan to do these, and cross them off when you have done them.

3.3 In the exam room: what you do in the planning time

Although these suggestions are for the exam room, it is highly desirable for you to try them out on at least one practice essay beforehand.

Write down the titles, authors and genre of your works, as soon as you can on going into the exam. In the heat of the moment, the mind can go blank and forget one or more of the text titles. Seeing the titles can be a comforting reminder of the content of the texts.

Once you are allowed to read the exam paper, go straight to your genre section, and do not read the questions in the other sections. Sometimes the questions in the Prose Other Than Fiction section resemble those for the Novel, or appeal even more, but you must stick with your studied genre.

Allow 20-30 minutes planning time at either Level. As with Paper One, this is a very concentrated time of various mental activities, though what you do here is different from what you do for Paper One. Your main task is *identifying and comparing 'evidence'* from your texts, and *structuring* this into a good response. During the planning you:

- **Decide which question is best suited to your knowledge and your texts**. You may need to jot down some examples from different texts to see which yield the best material for an answer to the question you have selected. You often can't tell which texts will serve you best until you have generated a few ideas.

  It is sufficient to use two texts, especially at Standard Level where there is less time, because you can go into greater depth. If your genre is poetry, you can select two poems if they are sufficiently complex, or, more usually, three or four poems (see the poetry sample below).

  It *is* possible to write a good essay using three prose or drama texts, but it is more of challenge to pull three together comparatively in the time available, and there is the risk of not exploring any of them in enough detail. Much depends on the nature of the question and the number of examples each text would yield. If the question leads to one or two good examples in each text, it could work to use three texts.

- **Consider carefully what the question is asking**; define any terms used; highlight key words that you will need to address; *re-phrase* the question in your own way if it makes it easier to understand it (as in Section 1.5 above and the drama sample below) but don't *change* the question.

- **Identify and select *the best evidence* for the question (with comments) from each text, using a grid or plan as below or of your own devising**
One way to do this is to identify a piece of evidence from the first text, think carefully about it, and develop some ideas about it, before moving on to identify another example from the *same* text. Depending on the nature of the question, you may want to deal with all the best evidence in one text, before moving on to the second text and then comparing the two.

  Or you may generate ideas about a major feature in one text, and then a similar feature in the second and compare them, before moving on to another example. In the samples below, the drama and poetry samples followed the first method, and the novel the second method. Any method that works for you and produces a perceptive comparison is a good one.

- **Identify patterns or *points of focus in the evidence* for each text.** This will help you create a thesis clearly addressing the question.

- **Establish the similarities and differences between the texts**
This is done by examining the evidence as in the two bulleted points above. It is especially clear in the drama sample plan. The conclusions you draw will become your thesis and argument, and help you structure the essay.

- **Formulate a thesis for your introduction that compares and contrasts the texts in relation to the question**
The drama sample plan makes this process particularly clear.

- **The conclusion** will arise out of what you have written, so you don't need to formulate one at the planning stage.

The planning time is concentrated thinking time. If you do all the above tasks it is obvious that you need a good 20-30 minutes. Once you have your examples, ideas and your focus or thesis, you have the material to write. Move from examples to pattern to thesis, not the reverse, as students sometimes do. Never start writing until you know clearly where you are going. The introduction to your essay should make this direction clear, to you and the examiner.

Many students feel they may run out of time if they do not start writing early in the process, and try to think out their essay as they go along. This does not lead to a good essay. Planning needs to come first. You need the brain-space for thinking it out before you begin writing. It is more important to have a shorter essay with a clear, relevant thesis and relevant examples, than a longer essay without these things. However, your ideas can become clearer as you write, and the conclusion may sharpen the comparison, as seen in the poetry sample below.

The importance of the plan of evidence for *discoveries* in comparing and contrasting
However carefully you have studied and revised your texts, you will not know how they compare and contrast on every possible question until you start examining the evidence in your planning time. The planning time is a process of discovery, when you realise things you may not have known, discussed or thought before. Don't be afraid to use these discoveries. They can be as good as anything you have thought before.

3.4 A sample Paper Two (Novel) Higher Level

The Novel and the Short Story: *Setting is usually more than a backdrop for events. Compare and contrast how settings function in at least two of the works of fiction you have studied.*

There are multiple settings in *Heart of Darkness* and *The Great Gatsby*, many of these described in detail to reveal character and human behaviour, but in both novels there is also one overarching setting that relates to the purpose of the writer. In *Heart of Darkness* the tropical forests of the African setting that pervade most of the narrative allow Conrad to explore the capacities of man's mind and heart, through Marlow's journey. In *The Great Gatsby* the Long Island setting gives Fitzgerald the possibility of exploring time, relating the materialistic and amoral society of East Coast America in the 1920's to earlier, more ideal moments in American history, and showing the impact of time on human efforts.

In *The Heart of Darkness* the African setting is far more than a backdrop for events because it provides a vivid comment on what humans can do to their settings, as well as what settings can do to humans. Conrad uses a recurrent motif of perspective to suggest humans' folly in imagining they could conquer the African continent. The setting is represented as "immense" and "inscrutable", and against this, man is diminutive and his efforts futile. For example, Marlow describes a French warship firing "six-inch" guns that go "pop" and give off a "feeble" screech into a massive continent. But he also shows the destruction humans can cause pitilessly in a setting. Conrad has Marlow describe the first sight that he comes across on landing in Africa – a mining site littered with bits of machinery, some deliberately smashed up, and even worse, with African workers in a terrible state of starvation and debilitation, dying on the hillside. This hellish scene is immediately juxtaposed with a description of the Outer Station and its Accountant, the Colonial representative, in his elegant and pristine Western clothes, keeping meticulous accounts, indifferent to the suffering around him.

Fitzgerald also suggests the impact of humans on their setting in his portrayal of the wasteland or valley of ashes that lies between New York and Long Island and is the dark underside of the rich and careless societies of those places. He makes it significant by placing it so that everyone from the rich city and suburbs must go through it, by train or car, and by making it eventually confront and symbolically take revenge on that society, through the Wilsons. The point about the careless destruction and degradation is made explicit through the imagery of ashes that resemble the wheat fields and farms of a more wholesome rural and traditional America.

Whereas Conrad makes the point about human futility through distorted images of minute size in a vast setting, Fitzgerald makes a similar point by drawing attention to the way time mocks human effort. The strange image of the advertisement for spectacles in the valley of ashes, once there to "fatten" an oculist's practice but now abandoned in this wasteland, makes that point, and the whole image of ashes is reminiscent of a funeral and its ritual "ashes to ashes". This frightening sense of time s also conveyed by contrasting images of Gatsby's house, before and after his murder. Similarly the image of New York skyscrapers across the Queensboro Bridge rising "in white heaps and sugar lumps" suggests the insubstantiality of the human dream that gave rise to the city. A sense of layers of historic and human time pervades the novel, emphasising transience.

Conrad is fascinated by what setting does to humans, specifically, what Africa does to his characters. He emphasises this by contrasting the characters of Marlow and Kurtz, and by personifying the setting. For example, Marlow emphasises the idea that the agent Kurtz was corrupted by the wilderness, that it "found him out" as someone with a moral deficiency, and had taken revenge for his invasion of that territory. It had "patted him on the head" and "taken him" like a lover. This does not remove Kurtz's responsibility for his actions but is a comment on Marlow's perception of the power of the setting. Marlow himself is "tempted" by the exotic and alien wilderness and curious about his "remote kinship" with the Africans but explains to his listeners that one must meet that "truth" with one's inborn strength. Dedication to tangible practical work (like mending the "rivets" of his boat) is one of the things that keep him sane, and contrasts with Kurtz's wordy and hollow ideals.

Whereas river and 'wilderness' and how people interact with them dominate as setting in HOD, houses and their occupants are a prominent feature of *The Great Gatsby*. The main characters are all seen in detailed domestic settings that tell us something about their status and state of mind. Although Tom and Daisy's "Colonial' style house and garden is first seen in vivid red and gold colours, the white interior seems static and sterile, with Daisy and Jordan immobile on the couch. When Nick first attends one of Gatsby's parties, the listing of Gatsby's possessions and the details of his food suggest a fabulous extravagance, and an enchanting atmosphere that builds a sense of mystery. However, when we see Gatsby in the middle of this setting, on the steps of his house, he stands apart from everyone else, a solitary and enigmatic figure. When Daisy finally visits his house in Chapter Five, the incredible luxury of his rooms and his possessions are described as only having the meaning for him that Daisy gives them. This is materialism in a romantic cause, not for its own sake. Daisy seems to understand that when she weeps at the beauty of the hundreds of shirts that Gatsby pulls out to show her. They are like a statement of his devotion. He has acquired all this to be worthy of her.

The frame setting of nightfall in each novel reflects the perspective of the narrator as well as something of the purpose of the novelist. At the beginning of *The Heart of Darkness* the frame narrator, sitting on a yacht with Marlow and other friends, describes the coming of night over London, and patriotically recalls the glorious history of the Thames. Marlow's first words, that this has also been one "of the dark places of the earth", undercut this vision. Profoundly affected by his experience in Africa, and what it has told him of the darkness of the human heart, anywhere, he sees that even their present 'civilisation' is only a precarious "flicker" of light. The emphasis on the Thames as linking all the waterways of the earth makes it clear that Conrad's viewpoint embraces a global perspective and a long view of human history.

Nick's final vision of Long Island Sound, by comparison, is specifically American. Like Marlow, profoundly affected by his recent experience, and the brutal murder of Gatsby, he looks across the darkening Sound on his last night and imagines the enchantment of the first Dutch sailors arriving on this 'fresh green breast of the new world', before this dream was corrupted by human greed and materialism, and lost in the 'dark fields of the Republic' beyond the city. All the hopes and dreams and efforts of this nation and its people seem to him "boats against the current". The profound sadness of this ending, and Nick's solitude in the setting, contrasts with the ending of HOD where Marlow has been to the heart of darkness but also come back with a 'glimpsed truth'. The image of darkness over the Thames reflects Marlow's new understanding, but compared with Nick's vision this does not seem quite so despairing.

Thus we see that while events are played out in and against settings, settings play an integral part in the significance of novels, expressing a fundamental vision of the writer as well as creating a memorable visual image that carries that vision.

3.4.1 Student comment on the revision and (mock) exam planning experience

The Great Gatsby – a visual sequence of chapters

I revised the two novels in completely different ways, because the texts were so different. Gatsby was much easier, because it was organised in chapters, and each had a particular focus. I went through, chapter-by-chapter (which was the way we'd studied it) using the 'significant headings' technique, and put these on cards, one for each chapter. My class notes and some close commentary writing we'd done on certain passages were useful at this point.

I then laid the cards out in a sequence, which helped me see patterns more clearly, for example how much Gatsby's house featured in many of the chapters. Our text also had a long introduction, which I read for the first time, and this helped me appreciate Fitzgerald's feelings about time, which hadn't been clear to me before.

Heart of Darkness – a final reading in one sitting

This was a harder text. It didn't fall so neatly into episodes like *The Great Gatsby*, and when we studied it, it didn't hang together for me. I re-read it more or less at one stretch a few weeks before the exam. This was hugely helpful to me because it all holds together as one dense experience and it makes sense to do it this way as Marlow is telling his experience in one unbroken narrative. Many things became much clearer to me on this unbroken reading, like the sense of Marlow speaking, his voice, and his sense of his audience on the boat, and also his feelings about Kurtz, which I had never really understood.

I focused on just reading (without taking notes) so that I could take in the text as one whole, but I sometimes scribbled a note in the margin where I had a new thought. I also underlined some words and phrases that I could see were important and interesting like the wilderness patting Kurtz on the head. I went back to these later, and put them on my revision sheets. I also scribbled some headings for some of the sections at the top of the relevant pages (for example: 'Harlequin character', 'cannibals'). This reading at one stretch gave me a much better feel for what Conrad seemed to be doing in the book.

Right after this reading, I wanted to get all the main episodes as headings on to one or two A4 sheets so that I could see the whole sequence at once and remind myself of the different details and ideas in those episodes (for example "The Thames", "Brussels", and so on). This was easy to do right after the reading because the events were fresh in my mind, and I had scribbled episode headings on some of the pages.

Planning in the exam

The question was great, but I had to think carefully about what the different settings did. I had lots of examples so the hardest things were (i) to select the most important and (ii) to find a way to incorporate them into an argument. I had to avoid getting carried away with too much detail, as there was so much to say about the big settings. None of my ideas for comparing and contrasting the two works had occurred to me before, but they occurred to me quite easily during the planning time on the basis of my memory of the examples.

I began with one major example from each text – Africa in *Heart of Darkness* and Gatsby's house in *The Great Gatsby*. I sketched out some ideas about what the settings did in each case and realised they were very different, so I looked for one in Gatsby (valley of the ashes) that compared with Conrad. While thinking about this example I came up with the idea of time, which was to be my major contrast idea. Gatsby's house kind of fitted into that.

I then moved on to a second major setting in Conrad – the Thames – and while I was jotting down ideas about that setting and what it did I realised there was a parallel setting in Gatsby and that would be a good comparison. I thought about starting with that but decided to use the main contrast (above) first. This worked for me because those night settings actually come from the end of the narratives in each case. When I explored them I found similarities and differences, which was a good way to end.

3.4.2 Evaluation of the student sample essay and comments

The student's comments highlight how his revision mainly consisted of a personal re-reading of the whole text. The benefit of this holistic approach is clear from the essay, where examples of settings show a perceptive relation to the significance of the whole work. The comments also show how detail stands out at this 'Reading Stage Four", and sharpens the discussion of

157

examples (either as close references or quoted phrases/ words), for example the reference to the Queensboro Bridge in *Gatsby*, and the wilderness patting Kurtz on the head in *Heart of Darkness*.

The student pulls the texts together with a clear overarching contrast in the introduction that encapsulates a basic purpose in each novel (man in the African setting, and time in the Gatsby settings) and illustrates a major difference in the role of the settings. This thesis is developed clearly through the essay, focusing on contrast but keeping comparison in view throughout. He alternates between texts but links one to the other with comparison or contrast as he moves from paragraph to paragraph. He consistently relates his evidence to the question. Notice (from his comments) how the thesis emerges from his exploration of his examples during the planning.

The student shows perceptive knowledge and understanding of the works, responds to the implications of the question relevantly, and shows some evaluation of the texts. He identifies aspects of setting and appreciates the way these are used. Paragraphs show clear organisation and underline the developing thesis. The language is effective.

3.4.1 A comparison of planning and structure in the novel and drama samples

The following drama sample compares interestingly with the previous one (novel) as well as the poetry sample below, in terms of the planning method and essay structure. It demonstrates how different questions, texts and genres may inspire a somewhat different approach, while remaining consistently comparative.

The novel plan (as described by the student) moves *horizontally*, comparing one major setting in one text with a major setting in the second text. This enables him to see a major difference in the role of the settings that is stated in the introduction.

The drama sample moves *vertically*, examining all the selected evidence on one text and finding a pattern, before moving on to the second text and repeating the process. This enables the student to formulate a clear thesis (as on the bottom of the planning grid) that both compares and contrasts, and goes into the introduction. The personal prompts that the drama student creates to help her focus on the question and its implications provide clear guidelines for her exploration of each speech.

In each case the student moves between the texts in the paragraphs of the essay, comparing and contrasting throughout.

3.5 The table or plan of comparative evidence for a sample essay on drama

Question: *Long speeches have always been a convention of drama. Compare the function and effects of such speeches in two or three of the works you have studied for Part Three.*

Student's personal prompts for creating the plan:

- What are some key long speeches in both plays?

- What purpose do they serve in context and what effects do they create?

- What wider purpose do they serve or what connection do they have with the work as a whole?

- Is there a pattern to these speeches in each play?

- What similarities or differences are there in the role and effect of these speeches across the two plays?

Text 1 **Death of a Salesman:** References/examples	Text 1: *Analysis* Role, significance, effects, connections, purpose	Text 2 **A Streetcar Named Desire** References/examples	Text 2: *Analysis* Role, significance, effects, connections, purpose
1. Act 1. Willy's description of his car trip 'windshield'	-Narrates offstage event -Musing to himself: reveals state of mind and character --- Unconscious work/life division windshield error provokes anxiety in Linda -Connection with Biff	Scene 1.Blanche's outburst to Stella about loss of Belle Reve	-Narrates aspect of her past -reveals character (strong?) - contrasts 'moth' -Contains hidden strong feelings (Stella, sexuality, death) Psychology Mystery
2.Act 1. Biff and Happy: work/life speeches	-Conscious description and analysis of situation -Strong emotions Both dissatisfied: (creates plot) --Biff knows what he loves but is trying to conform to Dream -Happy has Dream but unhappy Effect/ negative about Dream/link w/Willy	2.Scene 4. Blanche's speech to Stella about Stan (ape)	-Has agenda/manipulative -Creates negative response/unfair/snobbish -Has outcome- Stan's revenge Drives plot
3. Act 1. Linda: defending Willy to Biff/Happy	-Strong emotion -reveals love/value Contrasts with society Spokesperson for the individual (theme)	3. Scene 6. Blanche's speech about death of Alan	-Key aspect of past and clue to the way B is. -honest - creates sympathy -has positive outcome on Mitch Changes our feelings Tragic effect later
4. Act 2. Willy's 'Salesman' speech	-Narration of key episode in his career -motive to influence Howard. No effect ion him -effect: tragic/ironic -(Willy unconscious of this)		
	⇩ **PATTERN/FOCUS** Speeches all 'honest'. All relate to work/life and the relation of individual to society. Tension between personal fulfilment and pressure to succeed		⇩ **PATTERN/FOCUS** Speeches reveal initially some unsympathetic character traits (jealousy/manipulation/snobbi shness) but key speech (Scene 6) develops our understanding
COMPARISON/ CONTRAST FOR THESIS ⇩			
	Similarities between texts: -Reveals past events -Reveals hidden /denied feelings -strong emotion -Links with wider themes	**Differences** Streetcar focuses on Blanche's psychological state Lomans all reflect 'Dream'theme: family focus	

3.6 Sample essay on drama (Higher Level)

Long speeches have always been a convention of drama. Compare the function and effects of such speeches in two or three of the works you have studied for Part Three.

Long speeches have always been a convention of drama. Compare the function and effects of such speeches in two or three of the works you have studied for Part Three

In earlier drama, long speeches as in Greek plays or Shakespeare's plays establish a character's point of view or mental state, or narrate events that have occurred. In modern plays where most of the dialogue consists of brief, pithy exchanges, such as in *Death of a Salesman* and *A Streetcar Named Desire,* long speeches or monologues stand out in contrast, and have a variety of functions and effects. They allow us to focus on the thoughts and emotions of the character and to enter into his or her state of mind, creating greater understanding. Additionally they often reveal significant aspects of the character's past. But they also have a function particular to each play. In *Death of a Salesman* long speeches are made by all four members of the Loman family, and all relate to a perception of success in society. In *Streetcar* all the extended speeches are Blanche's, and reveal the complexity of her psychological state.

Willy's first extended speech, describing to Linda why he has had to abandon his salesman's driving trip, has several functions, but primarily reveals aspects of his character and situation that he seems unaware of or is in denial about. One of these is that he seemed to have forgotten which car he was driving and talks of the windshield on the car he had twenty years ago when his sons were teenagers. This alerts us to a mystery about this period of his life that he will only confront (and we will understand) much later in the play, and engages our attention. The fact that he lost consciousness of what he was doing and drove off the road also alerts us to the dangers of his state of mind and makes us wonder what is going on with him. So the speech, which is honest, musing and wondering, almost as if to himself, opens up character and plot, but also an important theme that connects with the other members of his family. He describes *with surprise* how he was enjoying the beautiful scenery as he was driving, as if this was unusual. A little later in the dialogue he nostalgically describes the beautiful spring flowers that used to grow in the neighbourhood but have been massacred by urban development. This love of nature emerges progressively in the play. It will gradually become clear that Willy has tried to pursue success in a job and environment that are actually alien to his character and real interests, like his son Biff, driven by what society seems to feel is the route to success. Part of the tragedy of the play is that Willy never does understand and accept his real needs, or those of Biff, and this sense of the tragedy is heightened by speeches like this where Willy expresses his true self, even if ironically he doesn't understand this.

Blanche's first long speech to her sister Stella about nursing her dying family at Belle Reve also tells us something important about her past and her character, and similarly reveals something disturbing about her psychological state, but the manner of the speech has a more shocking impact in context than Willy's and makes her unsympathetic at this point. She suddenly launches into an assault on Stella, though we have just seen her excited and emotional about meeting up with her sister, so this change is initially mystifying. The vehemence of her language, with many exclamations, seems out of proportion to what she is telling Stella, so we must look for a hidden emotion. The whole speech expresses resentment that Stella was not there with her at a difficult time, but at the end, this explodes into jealousy that Stella was 'in bed with (your) Polack!' We have heard Stella describe previously how much she is in love with Stan and this seems to have triggered Blanche's reaction. As with Willy, we only understand later the cause of her emotion when we hear about the death of her husband and realise her isolation and need for protection. Similarly, just as Willy's speech connects with a key theme in the play, so Blanche's repetition of the horror of dying and death is a clue to her state of mind and a major theme in the play. She has been trying to suppress that horror with 'desire', which only leads her to eventual destruction. The context of the speech – the conflict that Blanche creates with her sister, makes us wonder how this ménage a trois is going to work, and so causes suspense. In both plays, the first long speech by the main character thus has several important effects, revealing character and anticipating plot.

Biff and Happy's speeches a little way into Act One build on the theme emerging in Willy's first speech, of the difficulty of finding contentment and fulfilment in their success-obsessed society. These speeches have an important expository function, as they are telling each other – and us – what their work and lives and values are and how they feel about them. In context this seems natural because they are seeing each other after an absence, and because Biff has returned home to try to make a successful future in society's and his father's terms. But the speeches are also emotional and dramatic, because both young men are at a point of crisis, and this will fuel the plot. Biff's real love - herding cattle – is at odds with his learned perception of 'success', and this makes him desperate. Happy has all the outward signs of 'success' – job, money, apartment, women – but is discontented and 'lonely'. The length of the speeches allows their emotions to build as they speak, and to take us (as well as each other) into the lives they live outside of this moment. Their dilemmas echo Willy's unconscious dilemma and contribute to a major theme of the play, about the meaning of success and happiness. In none of these speeches is there an agenda, but simply a need to express their state of mind and being, which sets up something to be resolved in the course of the play.

In contrast, Blanche's long manipulative speech in Scene Four when she tries to persuade Stella to leave Stan <u>does</u> have an agenda, and the whole impact of the speech is heightened because unbeknown to her, Stan is overhearing it. The sheer length of the speech and the vividness of Blanche's extended metaphor about Stan as a 'Stone Age ape', create particular discomfort because we have seen Stan's tenderness for Stella and her love for him, and because we are aware he is overhearing this. The accusation seems unfair, even if we have also witnessed Stan's ugly violence with Stella at the poker night. Although Blanche has been trying to lure Stella away from her marriage, Stella has made it clear she intends to stay. In this speech Blanche uses another tack – that of class. Stanley does not match up to their background. This does not persuade Stella but it does impact on Stan, who then seeks his revenge. Unlike the speeches in *Salesman*, which mainly express character, state of mind and values, and relate to a central theme, this speech actually provokes plot development. It is a turning point from which Stan will not look back in regard to Blanche.

Linda's sudden long outburst to her sons near the end of Act One is one of the most moving and memorable in the play, and works differently from the speeches of Willy and his sons discussed earlier, as well as from those of Blanche. It is partly a heartfelt response to the immediate context. Linda is worried because of Willy's state of mind and health, and is frustrated that her sons, especially Biff, exacerbate the situation through their neglect of Willy, and seem to have no feelings for their father. But it is also an outcry based on the pent-up emotions from years of knowing and loving Willy, his faults as well as his achievements. "The man who never worked a day but for your benefit? When does he get the medal for that?" The many rhetorical questions in this speech emphasise her bitterness at the lack of reward in her husband's life, but also her understanding of Willy's state. It is the strength of her convictions and her compassion that stand out here, establishing a major value in the play, the importance of love and acceptance in the family, in opposition to society's callous disregard for the individual. Linda, who has not had much of a voice in the play, is suddenly the spokesperson for humanity. "He's not the finest character that ever lived. But he's a human being, and a terrible thing is happening to him. So attention must be paid". The use of the passive tense here makes this statement the more universal. Thus Linda's speech presents both a way of seeing and understanding Willy, and any such ordinary individual. It allows us to view Willy more sympathetically and tragically in Act Two, but also increases Linda's status as a sympathetic character who represents a moral view of things.

Extended speeches can tell important stories about the speaker's past that can influence the way we see that character and interpret their behaviour. When Blanche describes to Mitch in Scene 6 how she loved but indirectly caused the death of her husband Alan in a terrible way, we see how that has left her with consuming guilt. She seems to be honestly lost in her memory at this point, facing her actions and their consequences, rather than manipulating Mitch's sympathy. The way she tells her story, which is key to our understanding of Blanche and her state of mind, takes us into that experience, and makes us see her more sympathetically and so more tragically in the rest of the play. The way she emphasises their youthfulness, her sense of betrayal and disgust on finding her husband in bed with a man, and the horror of his suicide, is vividly told. The atmosphere of the moment, late at night on a date that is important to both of these lonely characters, makes the story more moving and leads Mitch to suggest marriage. This speech shifts our understanding of Blanche and our sympathy with her for the rest of the play, and creates a greater sense of tragedy.

Willy's long anecdote to his employer Howard in Act Two about being inspired to be a salesman by his meeting Dave Singleman also derives its effect from the context, in this case the office of the man who wants to fire him. Willy is telling the story, as Blanche does, to explain something about his past that is key to his life, because his meeting with Singleton changed the direction of his life. He seems to want to impress on Howard that his work has deserved gratitude, but the effect of the story is both ironic and tragic, not only because Howard remains unmoved and indifferent, but because Willy is unaware that he took the wrong road. He describes his vision of selling as 'the greatest career a man could want', but we have seen how Willy has never been a success nor really happy in his job except in his fantasies. He falls far short of Singleton in 'success', though how admirable it is to die at 84 in a hotel room on the job? The speech has a sad impact because the firing emphasises his failure in a job that in one way meant so much to him, but in another way, was never right for him.

In both plays the long speeches have a cumulative effect, enabling us to understand what is central to the main character and to the writer's vision. In both cases they take us into the main character's psychological depths and relate to significant themes in the play. In *Death of a Salesman* the vision is thematic and tragic, as we see the Loman family unaware of the way they are unhappily shaped by society's expectations, which are in conflict with theirs. In *Streetcar*, Blanche's colourful and dramatic speeches are compelling but also enable us to see into her heart and mind and come to understand how she is both victim and cause of her situation.

3.7 Evaluation of the drama sample

Comments comparing the planning methods for the novel and drama samples are made in 3.4.1 above. The nature of the respective questions calls for a somewhat different approach. "Setting" is more broad-ranging, whereas "speeches" call for a close examination and comparison of very specific passages, in one text relating to four different characters. In both samples the student needs to relate the selected examples to the wider text.

In the drama sample the student contextualises each speech, showing its function and dramatic impact at that moment in the play (on us as well as the characters involved). She explores how it reveals character and how it connects with wider thematic connections in the play. She pays attention to the place of speeches in the structure of the play, for example how they may only partially reveal character, or how they impact on later developments. The ability to do this reflects both class work, commenting in detail in each scene, and revision strategies such as suggested in Section Two and 3.2 above.

The student connects each paragraph with the preceding one as she moves through the essay, comparing or contrasting the speeches in the different texts and in the same texts in relation to the question. Sometimes, as in the second paragraph, the texts are pulled together at the end of the paragraph.

The essay meets the criteria at a high level. Detailed and broad knowledge is evident. The prompts help ensure that the implications of the question are relevantly explored, and the grid facilitates clear comparison and contrast. A brief reference at the outset indicates knowledge of the convention, and the essay shows detailed understanding of how richly the convention can be used. Good planning leads to clear organisation and development of ideas, and language is consistently very good.

3.8 A student's comparative plan for a poetry question

The question: *"Sound is one of the most noticeable elements in poetry. How have two or three of the poets you have studied used sound for particular effects?"*

Quotes: "Stopping by Woods" (Frost)	Quotes: "Ode to A Nightingale" (Keats)	Quotes: "Death of a Naturalist" (Heaney)
"The only other sound's the sweep/ Of easy wind and downy flake"	"My heart aches and a drowsy numbness pains/My sense"	"Bubbles gargled delicately"
		"Some hopped/ The slap and plop were obscene threats".
"The woods are lovely, dark and deep/ But I have promises to keep"	"Already with thee! Tender is the night"	
	"Through verdurous glooms and winding mossy ways"	"Blunt heads farting"
	"The coming musk rose, full of dewy wine/ The murmurous haunt of flies on summer eves"	
Analysis	**Analysis**	**Analysis**
-Creates the sound of the experience -predominant metre and rhyme (terza rima) restraint	Doesn't create the sound of the song (contrast Frost) Song creates emotional effect (pain to joy)	Creates sounds of the experience (like Frost) But content more than rhythm
enjambment assonance long vowels and 'y'	Packed line, heavy emphasis Long vowels Punctuation shows emotional movement	Diction/onomatopoeia/ vowels and consonants Diction suggests fear and disgust (consonants/ use of short vowels)
yielding and restraint	Onomatopoeia (m and n) Sound of sentence creates pictures and atmosphere	

3.9 A sample poetry essay (Standard Level)

POETRY: *Sound is one of the most noticeable elements in poetry. How have two or three of the poets you have studied used sound for particular effects?*

The association of poetry with sound is hardly surprising, considering its roots in song and performance. Sound in poetry can take many forms, for example – metre and rhyme, assonance and consonance, and the combinations of vowels and consonants in diction. In the following poems by Frost, Keats and Heaney I will show how these techniques can bring alive an experience of sound in a physical setting, and catch the tone and movement of the speaker's thoughts and emotions. However, the way sound is used by the three poets produces very different effects.

In Frost's "Stopping By Woods on a Snowy Evening" the sound of the regular iambic tetrameter and the rhyme scheme suggest the speaker's control of his situation and emotions. Whatever the temptations the "lovely, dark and deep woods" may hold, his acceptance of the "promises" he has to keep and the "miles" he has to go before he sleeps seems implicit in the discipline of the metre, and in the firmly repeated line at the end: "And miles to go before I sleep".

But the metre and rhyme can also be seen to work in another way, building the hypnotic effect of the experience of dark and snow, with the repetition of the last lines suggesting a drifting off into sleep rather than a reminder of the need to move on. This enchanted effect is also created by the sound patterns of the terza rima scheme with its three rhyming vowels in each stanza. These dense repetitions of sound – just four rhymes of long vowel sounds in the whole poem – have a sonorous effect that can lull you into the mood of the experience.

Frost creates other striking effects through sound in this poem. Through enjambment, alliteration and assonance in the middle of the poem he transports the reader into the lure of the moment, showing how powerful that is.
"The only other sound's the sweep
Of easy wind and downy flake".
In a poem where all the other lines are end-stopped or can support a pause, the enjambment here carries you away into the silence of the night and snow, only broken by the very soft sound of wind and snow. This sound is created by the sibilance of "sound's"-"sweep" – "easy" (four repetitions of 's'). The lure of the scene is suggested by the rhyming of the long vowels ("sound's" and "sweeps") echoed in reverse in the second line ("easy" "downy"). The "y" in "easy" and "downy" also softens the atmosphere, emphasising the hypnotic moment of mystery and attraction, which is then counteracted by the 'But' of the last stanza. The tension between almost yielding to the moment, and then pulling back is part of the fascination of the poem, and the sound plays a large part in that.

Keats speaker in "Ode to a Nightingale" is also enchanted by sound. However, although the poem is <u>about</u> sound – the song of the bird – he does not verbally suggest the sound itself, as Frost does of the wind and snow. Instead he brings alive the emotional effect it has on him through the long movement of sentences through the long ode stanzas, and through the sound of his diction. In the opening lines, the combination of heavy consonants and long vowels suggests the wretched physical and mental state he is in, as he contrasts the joy of the bird with the pain of his own world.
"My heart aches, and a drowsy numbness pains
My sense, "
Here, what he is saying is more dominant than the metre, in contrast with Frost's poem where metre is always in evidence. The emphasis falls heavily and equally on the vowels and on each word ("heart aches" "drowsy numbness pains"). The long "a" sound of "aches" and "pains" seems to suggest the pain itself.

In contrast, when he later escapes into his imagined beautiful forest world where the bird sings, he indicates the speed of thought, and his energy and excitement, through the change in rhythm, breaking the iambic metre with an exclamation:
"Already with thee! Tender is the night,"
The caesura here allows him to put the trochaic stress on "Tender" which ushers us into his enchanted world and suggests the physical atmosphere. He further creates the enchantment of this world through the sound and movement of his sentences and the sound of the diction.
"But here there is no light,
Save what from heaven is with the breezes blown
Through verdurous glooms and winding mossy ways".
The sound of the two and three-syllable adjectives ("verdurous"), the long vowel sounds ("save", "glooms") and the vague nouns – "glooms", "ways" – in the last line in particular. create an impression of mystery and secret enclosure. Keats also develops the sensuous richness of this world through the sounds with which he creates specific images like:
"The coming musk-rose, full of dewy wine,
The murmurous haunt of flies on summer eves".
Here, the repeated "m" and "n" sounds suggest onomatopoeically the lulling chorus of insects, but also the eternal atmosphere of a summer evening.

Like Keats, Seamus Heaney in "Death of a Naturalist" also represents the intensity of a physical scene and its sounds through the sound of words themselves. As with Keats' Ode, content is more obvious than metre, and the descriptive lines are densely packed. Heaney is less impressionistic and emotional than Keats and more precise, bringing alive through sight and sound not an imagined world but the very specific one of the rural Ireland he knew as a child. In "Death" he represents the sounds of the countryside through the diction, but also suggests the effect of the angry, ugly and threatening croaking of the frogs on the child as well as the way they looked.

In the early part of the poem he describes onomatopoeically the "festering" atmosphere of the flax dam where "bubbles gargled delicately". The clusters of explosive and heavy consonants ('d', 'b' and 'g') in the two and three syllable words slow down the pace so that the atmosphere of peaceful heavy summer is evoked. They also convey the precise sound itself, paradoxically delicate and vulgar. The speaker recalls how later in the summer the natural world has taken over his safe world, and his shock, disgust and fear are evoked in the diction. The assonance in "frogs were cocked/On sods" – with it sharp short 'o' sound – suggests the aggression and readiness of the frogs to attack, in his childish imagination. Heaney creates the ugliness of the frogs' sound as well as his fear of their anger through onomatopoeia: "Some hopped/ The slap and plop were obscene threats". Three short curt vowels also make the actions ominous, and the "blunt heads farting" creates the ugliness of the sound as well as suggesting its contempt. Through these sounds Heaney brings alive the incident itself but also the emotions of the boy, fearful of what the innocent and manageable frogspawn has become, and what this army of "great slime kings" might do in revenge.

Each of these poems creates a physical atmosphere with the speaker at the heart of it, and in each case the speaker has a particular emotional experience with sound. Yet each poet uses sound devices to an ultimately very different effect. Keats takes us on an intense emotional journey with him from heartache to ecstasy to loss, created by the sound and punctuation of sentences as well as the sound of words. Frost creates a haunting little narrative with his iambic metre and the tone of his sentences. And Heaney recreates an intensely physical experience through combinations of sounds in diction.

3.8.1 The student's plan and comments

Student Comment: the way we prepared for the exam, and the exam experience

When studying the poems, we listened a lot to recordings without looking at the text, and discussed the impact of the sound, so I had a good idea of the whole effect of individual poems. We also each had to learn one poem of our choice off by heart and present it to the other students without using text or screen. My choice was Frost's "Stopping by Woods", so I had a sense of the whole thing as well as being able to talk about bits of it in detail.

"Ode to a Nightingale" I knew from the film "Bright Star" where the whole poem is recited at the end. However it was the most challenging to write about because we had talked a lot about visual imagery but not sound, and I wasn't sure how valid my ideas were.

With Heaney we had done a lot of work about his imagery and its appeal to all the senses especially touch. I had not thought before in any detail about some of the particular lines I quoted but was able to figure out how sound worked in them, from having them down in front of me. I didn't need that many quotes as the basis for the essay and in fact could have said more about the lines I did quote.

My planning process

1. I began by thinking of poems that focused on sound or had strong sound effects and these three came to mind, starting with Frost because I knew that one best.

2. I quickly wrote down some of the quotes I remembered from each poem so that I could work with them and find patterns. Just by looking at the quotes I could begin to see how differently they worked. I could keep those in front of me as I developed the analysis.

3. I jotted down various sound techniques used in poetry to remind myself of the kind of thing I was looking for (rhyme, metre, assonance, etc.)

4. I then made specific notes on each set of lines in their contexts, to see what was common as well as different, which gave me a thesis. However it wasn't until I was in the process of writing the essay that I could see more clearly how each poem worked in terms of sound, and how they contrasted, which is in the conclusion.

What was challenging about the exam was trying to focus on each poem in turn very intensively and in detail, and paying attention to comparison. Also, as I worked out a lot of the detail in the writing process, the comparison and contrast became clearer to me as I went along, so I was able to link each poem to the previous one with a comparison. That makes the conclusion more specific than the introduction.

3.8.2 Comments on the plan and the sample essay

The way the student works here is a little different from the two previous samples, because of the nature of the poems and the question. As they are short, intense texts (compared with novels and plays) it is appropriate to deal in close detail with each one in turn, to compare and contrast them through linking sentences at the beginning of each new section, and to consolidate this at the end.

The student shows awareness of the nature of poetry as a genre in the opening sentence, and identifies different poetic techniques that create sound effects, which will all be demonstrated in the essay. The three texts are pulled together by the broad similarity of having sound *as a subject* as well as employing techniques that create sound effects. She states that techniques are used to different effects but does not define these differences at this point. She promises to explore them.

Examining the use of language effects in detail in the body of the essay leads her, as she says, to establish a full thesis in the conclusion. This essay thus works inductively. A sense of comparison and contrast is developed as each poem is more fully explored. Note that she is working from a limited number of quotes for each poem, which forms the core of her exploration, but that she is able to contextualise the quotes and refer to other parts of each poem because is each case she has a good sense of the whole.

Reflection on samples and planning:

What could you learn from the samples and the student's planning process relating to your genre?

What action might you take to ensure you write a good exam paper?

GLOSSARY

This glossary contains a number of the commonly used terms in literary analysis. Try to become familiar with as many as you can, so as to achieve the awareness in your reading, and the precision in speaking and writing, on which this course hinges. The most important thing is to recognise and appreciate how the techniques 'shape meaning' in texts. Chapters Four, Eight and the samples in those chapters contain further discussion of terms.

Allegory: A literary or visual form in which characters, events or images represent or symbolise ideas. It can be a story of some complexity corresponding to another situation on a deeper level. *Animal Farm* is about a community of animals, but reflects the Russian Revolution and satirises Communism.

Alliteration: Repetition of an identical consonant sound at the beginning of stressed words, usually close together ("The stuttering <u>r</u>ifles' <u>r</u>apid <u>r</u>attle", Chapter Seven, 2.1:) Alliteration can create different effects. Here, it suggests meaning through the onomatopoeic sound effect it creates. Used in poetry and prose.

Allusion: An indirect reference to an event, person, place, another work of literature, etc. that gives additional layers of meaning to a text or enlarges its frame of reference. Robert Frost's poem "Out, Out", about a boy's accidental death, alludes to Macbeth's line about life: "Out, out, brief candle".

Ambiguity: Where language, action, tone, character etc. are (sometimes deliberately), unclear and may yield two or more interpretations or meanings. Gertrude's actions and character are ambiguous in the early Acts of *Hamlet*.

Ambivalence: Simultaneous and contradictory attitudes or feelings towards something or someone. A writer's attitude to a character or event may not be clear-cut, but may seem to hold at least two responses at the same time. Distinguish this from 'ambiguity'.

Anagnoris: (a Greek term associated with tragedy but also used with fiction). A moment of recognition or discovery usually late in the plot where the protagonist discovers something about his or her true nature or behaviour or situation. Elizabeth Bennet, late in *Pride and Prejudice* dramatically realises her prejudice.

Antithesis: Expressing contrasting ideas by balancing words of opposite meaning and idea in a line or sentence, for rhetorical impact: "They promised opportunity and provided slavery".

Apostrophe: An exclamatory passage where the speaker or writer breaks off in the flow of a narrative or poem to address a dead or absent person, a particular audience, or object.

Assonance: Repetition of similar vowel sounds close to one another ("The sw<u>ee</u>p /of <u>ea</u>sy wind": Frost, see Chapter Eight, 3.8). Can create atmosphere in descriptive poetry. Sound this aloud to hear the effect.

Atmosphere: it refers specifically to place - a setting, or surroundings. (See Chapter Eight 3.8-9. Keats creates the *atmosphere* of a summer evening through the sounds of words).

Bathos: A sudden descent from the serious, to the ridiculous or trivial, for rhetorical effect: "His pride and his bicycle tyre were punctured in the first hour".

Bildungsroman: German term for a novel focusing on the development of a character from youth to maturity. (Joyce: *Portrait of the Artist as a Young Man* is a famous example for a male; *Jane Eyre* for a female.)

Blank verse: *Unrhymed* poetry, not broken into stanzas, keeping to a strict pattern in each line, usually in iambic pentameter. Used by Shakespeare.

Caesura: A break or pause *within a line of poetry*, created by a comma or full stop or unmarked pause needed by the sense. Used effectively for emphasis, or to change direction or pace. (See "The Black Lace Fan" in Chapter Four Section 3.8: "He was always late. That evening he was later".)

Caricature: An exaggerated representation of a character, often emphasising physical or vocal features, usually for comic and satiric purposes. Jane Austen and Dickens frequently use this.

Colloquial: Everyday speech and language, as opposed to a literary or formal register. The inclusion of the odd colloquial word or phrase in an otherwise formal work can be striking.

Conceit: A witty thought or idea or image, a fanciful or deliberately far-fetched comparison, as found in Shakespeare and other 16th and 17th century English poetry. A famous example is John Donne's comparison of two lovers to the points of a mathematical compass.

Concrete: (As in 'concrete imagery'). Refers to objects or aspects that may be perceived by one or more of the five senses, through the language used. (See Chapter Eight 3.9: "frogs were cocked/ on sods").

Connotation: An association suggested by a word, useful when discussing diction. (See Chapter Seven 2.1: "choirs' in "Anthem for Doomed Youth" connote harmony and civilisation)

Consonance: Where the final consonants are the same in two or more words close together, as in Macbeth's "Poor player/That struts and frets his hour upon the stage".

Context: (i) The circumstances, background or environment in which an event (or text) takes place, or an idea is set, and in terms of which it can be understood. Chapter Six, 1.5 discusses this at length; also Chapter Two Section One. (ii) The part of a text that surrounds a word or passage and determines or clarifies its meaning.

Contradiction: (Distinguish from 'paradox'). Stating or implying the opposite of what has been said or suggested.

Couplet (rhyming couplet): Two consecutive rhyming lines of *verse*. May clinch or emphasise an idea
(Nature's first green is gold,
Her hardest hue to hold': Frost)

Defamiliarisation: The technique of making the familiar seem new and strange, of making us see more vividly, of awakening the mind. Although a specific term of literary theory, it is generally the aim of art and all good writing. It may be achieved, for example, through point of view, or perspective, as in *Gulliver's Travels*, or unusual chronology, or diction and imagery.

Denouement: From the French, literally 'unknotting'. How the ending of a novel or play turns out, how the plot is unravelled or revealed.

Diction: The writer's choice and arrangement of words or distinctive vocabulary (its effectiveness and precision).

Didactic: Describes text where there is an intention to preach a (usually) moral, political or religious point. It usually has a negative connotation.

Dramatic irony: Where a character (or characters) is/are unaware of something of which the audience/reader and often other characters on stage *are* aware. A powerful tool especially in drama, used for tragic or comic purposes (see Chapter Six, Section 3.8 for a discussion of dramatic irony in *A Doll's House*).

Elegy: A mournful lament for times past or the dead. It is a specific poetic *form*, but the term can be used more generally. "Elegiac" describes a meditative mood in prose or verse, reflecting on the past.

End-stopped line: A line of poetry where the meaning pauses or stops at the end of the line (See the poem line in Chapter Four, Section 3.8: "The past is an empty terrace".) The full stop allows a statement or idea to stand out clearly, and provides a pause for the reader's reflection.

Enjambement: The opposite of the above. The sense flows over from one line to another, or through a series of lines, or to the next stanza. This can reflect a build-up of emotion or some other effect (see "The Black Lace Fan", as above). From the French for "leg".

Epigram: A concise, pointed, witty statement. 'Epigrammatic' *style* means those qualities in prose or poetry. Oscar Wilde is a master of epigram:" The truth is rarely pure and never simple".

Epiphany: From the Greek: "manifestation", it means a sudden realisation or moment of awakening in which something is seen in a new light, or its essential nature is perceived – which could be a moment of radiance or devastation. Used to effect in some short stories, as well as other fiction and poetry.

Form: The physical structure or shape of a work, the arrangement of its parts, the patterns, divisions and structures used. In poetry there are specific traditional, metrical and rhyming 'forms' (ode, ballad, sonnet, etc.}, and modern, non-metrical forms. (See Chapter Four, 2.11.)

Free indirect discourse or speech: is where the third person or omniscient narrator takes on (for a short while) the voice, speech characteristics of a character, taking us into the mind and thoughts of the character without indicating this directly. It can be used sympathetically or ironically. Jane Austen uses it to great effect.

Free verse: Verse written without any fixed or traditional structure in metre or rhyme. Commonly used since the early 20th century. It is very flexible because it follows the speech rhythms of the language.

Genre: A specific type or kind of literature. (See Chapter Eight, Section 1.6).

Hyperbole: A deliberate exaggeration for various effects - comic, tragic, etc. When Frost writes that the beauty of Spring "is only so an hour", he emphasises how very brief the life of precious things seems.

Iambic: The 'iamb' is a metrical measure, or foot, in which an unstressed syllable is followed by a stressed syllable ("To <u>be</u>, or <u>not</u> to <u>be</u>"). Iambic *pentameter* (five iambs in a line) is the commonest metrical pattern in English poetry, and notably Shakespeare. (Macbeth: "<u>Up</u>on my <u>head</u> they <u>placed</u> a <u>fruit</u>less <u>crown</u>". Sound it out to find those five stresses. There are other kinds of iambic line such as the four-iamb line, called *tetra*meter (see Chapter Eight, 3.8 Robert Frost: "The <u>woods</u> are <u>love</u>ly, <u>dark</u> and <u>deep</u>").

Idyll/idyllic: Refers to the innocent simple life in an idealised rural setting. It is a specific form of poetry, but the adjective is generally used to denote an experience that has those untroubled, and simple qualities, for example a childhood or a time in a rural setting.

Imagery: The mental pictures created by language (both metaphorical and literal) that appeal to the senses.

Interior monologue: Where the narrator depicts the thoughts pouring randomly from a character's mind, so that the reader experiences these as if overhearing them, unfiltered by comments from the narrator or adjusted grammatically.

Internal rhyme: Rhymes *within* a line of poetry.

Intertextuality: The shaping of some part of a text's meaning by another text, which can take the form, for example, of quotation, allusion, parody or re-working of an idea or story (see the discussion on novel titles and epigraphs in Chapter Eight, Section Two).

Irony: a gap or mismatch between what is said and what is intended. For example, between what a character or group might see or think, and what the author wishes us to see or think. A powerful tool for a writer to expose hypocrisies and lack of awareness.

Lyric: A song-like poem expressing personal feeling. Originally a song performed to a *lyre* or early harp.

Metafiction: fiction that draws attention to the fact that it is fiction or construct of the author, and to the writing process itself. The author may break the reader out of the fictional frame and comment on what s/he is doing or concerned about in the act of writing, or offer the reader a choice of endings, etc.

Metaphor: A comparison between two unlike things that are seen as alike in some aspect, without the use of 'like' or 'as'. It can facilitate understanding of an abstract concept (for example, life as a journey) or open up the imagination by creating a striking visual and sensual link between things not normally associated (for example in Chapter Seven, Section 2.1, in "Anthem for Doomed Youth" Owen compares the "shells" (weapons) of battlefield to "choirs", implicitly church choirs. The only point of likeness is that different items or people make sounds together in each case. (See also the discussion of 'dance' and "stitch" in the Standard Level sample on "Two Hands" in Chapter Four, Section 3.10). It is what the comparison *opens up* that enriches the meaning.

Metre: The organisation of lines of verse into regular patterns of stressed and unstressed syllables, to achieve a rhythmic effect. "Iambic" and "trochaic" metres are useful to know.

Mood: Describes an emotional state of *mind*. It can also describe the emotional response created in the mind of the reader or audience by elements in literature. Distinguish from 'atmosphere', which is to do with *place*.

Monologue: A speech of some length that expresses a character's thoughts out loud, sometimes addressing other characters. Distinguish from "apostrophe", "aside", and "soliloquy". (See the drama sample in Chapter Eight, Section 3.5-6).

Motif: Recurrent element in a narrative or drama (such as an image or spoken phrase) that has symbolic significance and can contribute, through cumulative effect, to a theme. For example the covered lamp in Williams' *Streetcar*, or the flute music in Miller's *Death of a Salesman*.

Omniscient ("third person" narrator: An "all-knowing" narrator who can see into the minds of any character and see any event, place, time, from the 'outside'. It is the most common and flexible narrative method. A variation on the third person narrator, the "omniscient/limited" narrator, knows everything about one character and is limited to that character. Omniscient and first person modes can be mixed in a work.

Onomatopoeia: the use of words that imitate or suggest the sounds associated with them, such as "murmur", or "buzz".

Oxymoron: Where *two words*, seemingly contradictory or incongruous, are joined, often suggesting something complex, as in *Romeo and Juliet* when Juliet says that: "parting is such sweet sorrow".

Paradox: An apparently contradictory *statement*, which on investigation is found to contain a truth. (For example Frost's title "Nothing gold can stay"). Distinguish from the compressed paradox of 'oxymoron'.

Parody: a comic imitation of another work, for deliberately comic, ridiculous or satiric effect. It is actively critical or attacking.

Pastiche: Imitation of the style of another work (content and manner) sometimes mildly ridiculing, but often in homage to the original (distinguish from 'parody') and creating a new work.

Persona: The identity or character assumed by the writer in a work (for example, T.S Eliot and Sylvia Plath assume another character in some of their poetry, as in "Prufrock" and "Lady Lazarus").

Personification: Where human feelings or sensations are attributed to an inanimate object. (See Chapter Seven, Section 2.1, the discussion of war weapons personified).

Plot: the events of a narrative in the order the writer has chosen to arrange them in, to show cause and effect or pattern, for artistic and emotional effect. Distinguish from 'story'.

Point of view: The *angle* from which a narrative is told, reflecting who is seeing and speaking. Point of view may shift within a work or even a paragraph (see "free indirect speech or discourse).

Protagonist: Main character in a work

Quatrain: Stanza or group of *four* lines in a poem. They can have different rhyme schemes. Shakespeare's sonnets often contain three quatrains and a couplet.

Refrain: Repetition of a phrase or lines in a work of literature, often at the end of a stanza.

Rhythm: The succession of strong and weak (or stressed and unstressed) syllables to create a *patterned recurrence of sound*. Distinguish this from metre, which has to do with the *technical, identifiable* organisation of lines into units of stressed and unstressed syllables

Satire: Exposing and ridiculing of human follies in a society, sometimes with the aim to reform, sometimes predominantly to deflate. May be gentle, comic, biting or bitter, or a combination. Chaucer, Swift, Jane Austen and Dickens use this tool memorably.

Setting: Context and location in which a work of literature takes place: it involves the physical place, time, and social environment

Simile: Where a comparison is made explicit with 'as' or 'like' (distinguish from metaphor). Can make descriptions vivid and unusual. Dickens is a master of the simile.

Skaz: (From the Russian). A technique of narration that mirrors oral narration with its hesitations, corrections, grammatical mistakes, interactions, etc. *Catcher in the Rye* uses this, but also *Huckleberry Finn*, amongst others.

Soliloquy: A speech by a character alone on stage, thinking aloud, revealing thoughts and emotions, or communicating directly with the audience. Powerful tool for revealing psychological complexity, used often by Shakespeare. (Distinguish from monologue).

Sonnet: A fourteen-line rhyming poem usually in iambic pentameter. Rhyme schemes and organisation of lines vary, depending on the type of sonnet (for example, Shakespearian), but often set out as a block of 8 lines (octave) and six lines (sestet).

Stanza: The blocks of lines into which a poem is organized. In traditional forms of poetry each stanza follows a scheme governing metre, lines and rhymes.

Story: (Distinguish this from plot). The events of a narrative in the chronological order in which they actually happened, not deliberately patterned and arranged as in plot.

Stream of consciousness: The representation of a character's (or first person narrator's) thought processes —feelings, sensations, memories, etc. as a random stream of thoughts

Style: The distinctive linguistic traits in an author's work, but also involves the writer's quality of vision and subject matter. It concerns theme, diction (emotional, abstract, poetic), sentence construction, imagery, sound, etc.

Subtext: Ideas, feelings, thoughts, not dealt with directly in the text (drama especially), but existing underneath. Characters don't always express their real thoughts.

Symbol: Objects that represent or evoke an idea or concept of wider, abstract significance, as roses represent love, walls divisions.

Syntax: The grammatical structure of words in a sentence. The normal order of words or grammatical structures can be slightly displaced to create a particular effect, without losing the sense. (See the discussion of "Lullaby" in Chapter Four, 2.7.2: "Lay your sleeping head, my love/ Human on my faithless arm"). A powerful tool in poetry, especially.

Theme: Central ideas or issues in a work, often abstract (for example racial injustice). Can also refer to an argument raised or pursued in a text, like a thesis.

Tone: Created where the writing conveys the attitude and emotions of the writer towards his/her subjects, through aspects of language like diction, syntax, and rhythm. (See discussion on Wilfred Owen in Chapter Four, Section 2.7.4).

Trochee/ trochaic: a metrical foot in poetry that has a stressed syllable followed by an unstressed syllable (the opposite of iambic, and much less common). For example, in Blake's "Tyger, tyger, burning bright". Often there is a mixture of trochaic and iambic metre in a poem, where the sense invites the switch.

IBDP REVISION COURSES

Summary

Who are they for?

Students about to take their final IBDP exams (May or November)

Locations include:

Oxford, UK
Rome, Italy
Brussels, Belgium
Dubai, UAE
Adelaide, Sydney & Melbourne, AUS
Munich, Germany

Duration

2.5 days per subject
Students can take multiple subjects

The most successful IB revision courses worldwide

Highly-experienced IB teachers and examiners

Every class is tailored to the needs of that particular group of students

Features

- Classes grouped by grade (UK)
- Exam skills and techniques – typical traps identified
- Exam practice
- Pre-course online questionnaire to identify problem areas
- Small groups of 8–10 students
- 24-hour pastoral care.

Revising for the final IB exams without expert guidance is tough. Students attending OSC Revision Courses get more work done in a shorter time than they could possibly have imagined.

With a different teacher, who is confident in their subject and uses their experience and expertise to explain new approaches and exam techniques, students rapidly improve their understanding. OSC's teaching team consists of examiners and teachers with years of experience – they have the knowledge and skills students need to get top grades.

The size of our Oxford course gives some particular advantages to students. With over 1,000 students and 300 classes, we can group students by grade – enabling them to go at a pace that suits them.

Students work hard, make friends and leave OSC feeling invigorated and confident about their final exams.

We understand the needs of IBDP students – our decades of experience, hand-picked teachers and intense atmosphere can improve your grades.

> " I got 40 points overall, two points up from my prediction of 38, and up 7 points from what I had been scoring in my mocks over the years, before coming to OSC. Thank you so much for all your help! "
>
> OSC Student

Please note that locations and course features are subject to change - please check our website for up-to-date details.

Find out more: 🏠 osc-ib.com/revision 📱 +44 (0)1865 512802

MID IBDP SUMMER PROGRAMMES

Summary

Who is it for?
For students entering their final year of the IB Diploma Programme

Locations include:
Harvard and MIT, USA
Cambridge, UK

Duration
Min. 1 week, max. 6 weeks
1 or 2 IB subjects per week

Improve confidence and grades

Highly-experienced IB teachers and examiners

Tailored classes to meet students' needs

Wide range of available subjects

Safe accommodation and 24-hour pastoral care

Features

- Morning teaching in chosen IB subject
- 2nd IB subject afternoon classes
- IB Skills afternoon classes
- One-to-one Extended Essay Advice, Private Tuition and University Guidance options
- Small classes
- Daily homework
- Unique IB university fair
- Class reports for parents
- Full social programme.

By the end of their first year, students understand the stimulating and challenging nature of the IB Diploma.

They also know that the second year is crucial in securing the required grades to get into their dream college or university.

This course helps students to avoid a 'summer dip' by using their time effectively. With highly-experienced IB teachers, we consolidate a student's year one

learning, close knowledge gaps, and introduce some year two material.

In a relaxed environment, students develop academically through practice revision and review. They are taught new skills, techniques, and perspectives – giving a real boost to their grades. This gives students an enormous amount of confidence and drive for their second year.

The whole experience was incredible. The university setting was inspiring, the friends I made, and the teaching was first-class. I feel so much more confident in myself and in my subject.

OSC Student

Please note that locations and course features are subject to change - please check our website for up-to-date details.

Find out more: osc-ib.com/mid +44 (0)1865 512802